501 TV-free Activities for Kids

317   56   59
63 64 62

Di Hodges

66
09
274
70   103

HB

HINKLER
BOOKS

Editors: Gillian Banham & Allison McDonald
Cover Design: Sam Grimmer
Cover Photography: Ned Meldrum Digital
Illustration and Design: Peter Tovey Studio
Typesetting: Midland Typesetters, Maryborough, Victoria, Australia

501 TV-free Activities for Kids
Published in 2005 by Hinkler Books Pty Ltd
17–23 Redwood Drive
Dingley VIC 3172 Australia
www.hinklerbooks.com

10 9 8 7 6 5
10 09 08 07

ISBN: 1 7415 7028 X
Printed and bound in China

HOW TO USE THIS BOOK

'501 TV-Free Activities for Kids' is full of ideas that you can enjoy trying with your children. Each page contains a short list of materials you will need to collect before you begin the activity. More often than not these are everyday household items you will already have. Save junk, as many activities in the book use recycled household junk. Other requirements may need to be purchased inexpensively from Newsagents, Craft Shops or your local Dollar Saver-type stores.

The book contains two indexes - an alphabetical one at the end of the book, and a Subject Index at the front. The book is divided into categories -

BRAIN POWER
COOKING & GARDENING
DEVELOPING SKILLS FOR SPORTS
FOOD FUN
HOME-MADE MUSIC
INDOOR PLAY
LANGUAGE & LITERACY
LET'S CREATE
MATHS IS FUN
OUR ENVIRONMENT
OUTDOOR PLAY
PARTY, FAMILY & GROUP GAMES
SPECIAL OCCASIONS

Each category in the book has activities for children of all ages - from two year olds to older primary children. There will be something that is exactly right for your child. The suggested age on each activity is a guide only - remember that all kids are different and you'll soon know if an activity is too easy or too difficult for your child.

Start with easy ones, give lots of praise and then move onto harder activities.

This book will help you find those areas of learning that your child needs extra time and help with. Don't forget that to succeed at school and in life our children need a healthy self-concept and we parents can foster this with lots of praise, encouragement, time and love. Have fun together!

GUIDE TO SYMBOLS

This simple legend of symbols gives a quick visual reference to the basic elements present in each activity.

Outdoor Activity:
This symbol indicates an outdoor activity.

Indoor Activity:
This symbol indicates an indoor activity.
Note: If both symbols are ticked, the activity can be enjoyed both outdoors and indoors.

Adult Participation: This activity requires some degree of adult supervision. Read the 'What to do' closely to see the degree of monitoring required. This symbol can also indicate participation with an adult is important for learning or sharing.

Pencils, Paints and Paper: This activity requires the basic drawing or painting tools. It can be as simple as a pencil and paper for keeping score in a game or more art materials for decorating etc.

Tools Required: This activity requires tools of some type. This could be anything from a simple bowl and vegetable peeler to balloons and craft materials. All these activities have been designed with the basic everyday items found in the home such as cereal boxes etc. Some activities may require items to be purchased from a shop but should be inexpensive or alternatives can be found. Read the 'What you need' for specific items. Adult supervision is required.

Learning and Imagination: Just about all of the activities in this book encourage imaginative play. There are activities that require some adult participation and may contain important learning skills designed for fun. If the activity is simply a game to occupy a bored child this symbol will not be ticked.

The symbols indicated in this book are a guide only. It is the responsibility of all adults to determine the appropriate activities for each child and the skills they possess. The use of tools requires adult supervision.

FOREWORD

Do you think your children watch too much TV?

Would you like to spend more quality family time together?

Would you like a year's worth of fantastic, entertaining, learning ideas to share with your children every day?

Then this book is for you!

Like many parents, you probably consider that your children watch too much television. For most families today, television and video-viewing have become an integral part of daily lives, in many cases becoming the only shared activity of the day.

While we all know that television can be a great educational tool, we also know, from countless studies of how children learn, that this is best achieved by 'doing'. The second-hand experiences they gain from watching TV will never replace what children learn through their play and through 'hands on' situations.

Recent research has shown that watching TV has become the most popular recreational activity for children outside school hours. This has contributed to major concerns in our community regarding the high levels of obesity in our children, directly related to sitting down watching TV rather than kicking a ball around or being involved in other active play. Research also suggests that children who watch the most television are the lowest school achievers.

If you would like to replace some of your children's TV viewing time with exciting, creative activities, this book is for you. Most activities are very easily organised from items you will have at home, and they will help develop your children's imaginations and creativity, as well as mental and physical skills.

While some of the activities require adult participation, others only need parents to help the children get started. Don't forget that you are trying to encourage independence, self-confidence and creativity, and it is important to be flexible and let the children decide how things will go. Safety is of the utmost importance though, and supervision with items such as scissors or knives should be closely supervised.

Turn off the TV for an hour a day and spend time with your children. This will help build good communication and understanding, which will stand them in good stead in the years ahead.

ABOUT THE AUTHOR

Di Hodges has been an early childhood teacher for over twenty years. She has taught in a variety of settings, including preschools, Years 1 and 2. She also spent many years helping geographically isolated parents teach their preschoolers at home through the excellent Distance Education facilities offered by Education Queensland. She is currently an Education Adviser (Preschool) with Education Queensland.

Di has a Diploma of Teaching for Early Childhood and Primary, and a Bachelor of Education. She lives on the Gold Coast in Queensland with her husband and preschool son Andrew, and strongly believes that parents are the first and most important teachers of their young children.

Unfortunately, economic pressures on families today often means that parents have to put careers and financial concerns ahead of spending time with their children, and Di hopes this book helps parents and children enjoy playing and learning together again.

Dedication
For my parents, Joan and Stew who have always been there for me, for my husband Geoff for his support, encouragement and ideas and suggestions and, most of all, for my young son Andrew, who has reminded me of the importance of parents in their children's lives.

SUBJECT INDEX

BRAIN POWER

GREEN DAY

2+

A great way to teach colours to young children.

What You Need

• *Green items — clothing, food, drinks, toys, paint, etc.*

What To Do

Tell your children in the morning that you are going to have a 'Green Day' or whatever colour takes your fancy. Use your imagination to make it as exciting as you can.
Some possibilities are:

• a small amount of green food colour in their milk: 'green milk' for their cereal
• a selection of green foods to try:
  honeydew melon
  kiwi fruit
  avocado
  green apple
  snow peas
  celery pieces filled with cream cheese
• select green clothes for you all to wear that day
• do some green cooking:
  avocado dip
  green jelly with chocolate frogs
  green cordial ice blocks
  apple pie
  patty cakes with green icing
• green playdough - make a batch and colour half yellow and half blue so they can see it change to green as they play
• add some yellow and blue food colour to their bath water and watch it turn green
• be 'greenies' and do lots of gardening - plant some new plants or seeds
• go to a park and collect lots of different leaves for leaf rubbings at home with green crayons and pencils
• make some green paint for painting outside
• read 'Green Eggs and Ham' for a bedtime story

activity

1

MAGAZINE PICTURE PUZZLES 2+

Create your own simple jigsaw puzzles with your
children from large magazine pictures.

 ✓

 ✓

 ✓

What You Need

 ✓

- *Large magazine pictures*
- *Glue* • *Scissors*
- *Thick cardboard*

 ✓

What To Do

Look through magazines with your children and let them choose some
pictures from which they would like to make puzzles. Help them cut out the
pictures and use a strong glue to stick onto thick cardboard.

When it is dry, cut it into puzzle shapes. With younger children begin
with four or five pieces. As they master the skill, cut the pictures into
more pieces.

Store and label the puzzles in plastic lunch bags in a shoe box.

activity

2

BOTTLES AND LIDS

4+

 ✓

 ✓
✓

This activity will help develop your children's powers of prediction as they guess which lid fits which bottle. A good way to develop the muscles in their hands and fingers also.

What You Need

• *Bottles of different shapes and sizes with screw-top lids.*

What To Do

Put out a selection of jars (at least ten) with lids with different circumferences. See if your children can find all the correct lids for the jars and screw them on.

Later, they might like to time themselves with an egg-timer to see how fast they can do it.

They could also put the jars in order from the smallest lid to the largest.

(Have your children do this activity on a mat or carpet rather than a hard floor. Remind them to take great care with glass bottles).

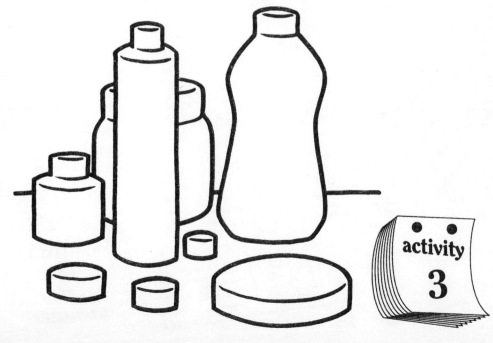

activity

3

BROCHURE MATCHING

4+

A matching activity using junk mail.

What You Need

- *Two matching advertising brochures, magazines or catalogues*
- *Scrap book* • *Scissors* • *Glue*

What To Do

When you next receive some advertising brochures in your mail box ask you neighbours if you can have theirs also when they have finished reading them. (Toy catalogues are great for this activity).

Cut out lots of pictures from one catalogue and past a picture to each page leaving the opposite page blank.

Give your children the other catalogue to look through. When they find a matching picture, they cut it out and past it opposite its pair.

activity

4

HOUSEHOLD NOISES

4+

An excellent listening activity that all the family will enjoy.

What You Need.

- *Tape recorder*
- *Blank tape*

What To Do

When you have some time on your own, go around the house taping different noises. You might include the bath emptying, the dog chewing a bone, the dishwasher or washing machine, the iron hissing, the postman's bike, the door bell, the vacuum cleaner, the 'phone, the computer and any others you can think of.

Play it back to your children and see how many sounds they can identify. Try out the rest of the family and see how well they listen. You can be sure that, unfortunately, they are not as familiar with the vacuum cleaner noise as Mum!

activity

5

I WENT SHOPPING

4+

A memory game to play with the rest of the family or some of your children's friends. A good game to play in the car on long trips too!

WHAT YOU NEED

• *A few players*

What To Do

Sit all the players in a circle. The first person says - 'I went shopping and I bought "........" The next player says 'I went shopping and I bought "........" ' and then says what the first player bought.

Keep going around to see who has the best memory. Vary it by choosing specific shops - 'I went to the toy shop and I bought "........" ' or 'I went to the fruit shop or newsagents'.

activity

6

MEMORY

A fun way to develop your children's memories.

4+

 ✓

 ✓

What You Need

 ✓

- *Assortment of small items such as a pencil, rubber, scissors, pen, small toys, hair brush, cutlery etc., tea towel.*
- *Paper and pencil (for older children who are writers)*

✓

✓

What To Do

✓

For younger children select a few items, place on the tray and let your children look at them for a minute. Have your children turn their backs while you remove a couple of items from the tray and cover them with the tea towel. See if your children can tell you what's missing.

For older children place up to 20 items on the tray and cover them up. Uncover them in front of your children and give them a minute to try and memorise, then cover them up again. Your children then write down as many items as possible.

Have a turn yourself and see if your memory is better than your children's. You may be unpleasantly surprised!

activity

7

MISMATCH

A family game to see how observant everyone is.

What You Need

• *Two or more players*

What To Do

If the whole family plays, divide into two teams. If just a few play, one person at a time can have a turn.

The first player or team leaves the room. The other team or players mismatch five things around the room - perhaps just some cushions on the floor instead of the couch, turn an ornament upside down, put someone's shoes on their hands instead of feet, or a t-shirt on inside out. I am sure you will think of heaps to do.

When the player or team returns, they have to spot the five mismatches, For any they do not notice, the other player or team score a point.

The next player or team then has a turn. The player or team with the most points is the winner.

activity
8

NUTS AND BOLTS

4+

Another thinking ahead and predicting activity. This game will also help your children learn how to screw and unscrew bolts - great for developing the hand and finger muscles needed for writing.

 ✓

✓

 ✓

 ✓

What You Need

• *A selection of different sized screws with nuts they will screw into.*

What To Do

Give your children at least a dozen different sized bolts and matching nuts. See if they can find the ones that go together and screw and nuts into the bolts.

To increase the challenge they might like to:
• beat the clock - time them and see if they can beat their PB (personal best)
• beat an egg-timer
• do it blind-folded
• time each other or another family member and see who is the fastest

activity

9

ODD ONE OUT

4+

Help your younger children begin to understand the meaning of same and different.

 ✓

 ✓

What You Need

 ✓

 ✓

- *Sets of objects that have two exactly the same, e.g.*
- *Pair of socks*
- *Pair of shoes*
- *2 matching mugs*
- *2 matching forks*

What To Do

Mix up the items and have your children find the two that are exactly the same. Then they cover their eyes. Put a pair of objects together with one that is different. They have to find the odd one out and tell you why it doesn't belong.

Make this game more and more difficult by making the differences more and more subtle.

activity

10

QUERIES

4+ ✓

  ✓

Pose some simple 'queries' for your children to solve! Activities like this increase their reasoning capacity and make them better at problem solving.

 ✓

What You Need

• *time together*

What To Do

Pose questions to your children like - 'I'm thinking of something that jingles and jangles and we need them to open the door?' ~ Keys
'I'm thinking of something you can pedal that has three wheels'
~ A tricycle
'I'm thinking of something that's pretty to look at, smells sweet and grows in a garden.' ~ Flowers
'I'm thinking of something we can make out of detergent, that sails in the air, and then goes pop' ~ Bubbles
'I'm thinking of something you like to lick that's cold and sweet.'
~ An ice-cream or ice-block
'I'm thinking of someone who loves you lots and who you love to visit.'
~ Nana
'I'm thinking of something you put up in the rain to stay dry.'
~ An umbrella
'I'm thinking of something that's colourful and soft and you like to throw and catch it.' ~ A ball

As your children gain mastery at 'queries', make the questions harder and harder. Perhaps they would like to pose some for you.

activity
11

WHO'S MISSING?

A game to develop thinking skills.

4+ ✓

 ✓

 ✓

What You Need

• *A group of children*

What To Do

A great game to play with a group of children at a birthday party or any sort of gathering. The children sit in a circle and one child is sent away where they cannot see or hear what is happening.

Another child is chosen from the group to go and hide out of sight. Make sure that all the remaining children are certain who is hiding. Then, the first child is allowed to return, and looks around the circle to try to remember who is missing. If they cannot remember, the other children can offer clues! Perhaps something the hidden child is wearing or perhaps the first letter of their name. Allow three clues only. If the first child has not guessed, the hidden child comes out of hiding and the game starts all over again with two more children.

activity

12

DOTS AND DASHES

A game of skill to play with your children.

6+

 ✓

 ✓

 ✓

 ✓

What You Need

• *Two players* • *Pencils* • *Paper*

What To Do

Draw lots of rows of dots on the paper first. The number of dots you draw will determine how long the game will last.

The players now take it in turns to draw a line connecting one dot to another. You can draw the lines any direction but diagonally. The aim of the game is to form squares between four of the dots.

The person who draws the last line which forms a square 'owns' that square and writes their initial in it. They then have another turn.

If a single line makes two squares, that player 'owns' both squares but only gets one more turn. Help your children with the strategies of the game so they understand not to make it too easy for their opponent.

At the end, tally up the squares to see who is the winner.

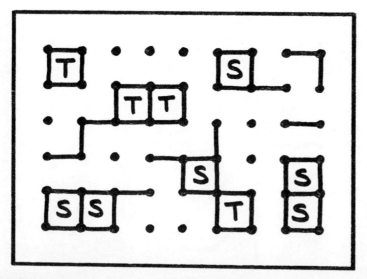

activity

13

Os and Xs (sometimes called Tic-Tac-Toe) 6+

A simple game of strategy.

What You Need

- *Two players*
- *Paper*
- *2 pencils*

What To Do

Show your children how to draw two horizontal parallel lines
crossed by two vertical parallel lines to make nine spaces in three rows.

One player draws the Xs and the other the Os. The first player to get three Xs
or three Os in a row in any direction is the winner.

activity

14

SLAP JACK

6+

 ✓
 ✓

 ✓
 ✓

A great card game to play with your children and a way to introduce the four suits in a pack of cards.

What You Need

- *A pack of playing cards*
- *2 or more players*

What To Do

The aim of this game is to collect the whole fifty-two cards in the pack.

Deal out the whole pack one at a time to the players. The cards are dealt face down and the players don't look at their cards.

Take it in turns to put a card on a pile in the middle. If a Jack is turned up the first player to slap the Jack takes all the cards in the middle.

Players must place the cards in the middle without looking at them first and turning the card and slapping must be done with the same hand.

If a player slaps a card that is not a Jack, they must pay a penalty and give a card from the bottom of their pack to all the other players.

For a variation you can play 'Slap Fiver' or 'Slap Acer'.

activity
15

COOKING AND GARDENING

BIRTHDAY GARDENS

2+ ✓

Celebrate your children's birthdays by adding a special plant each year to their very own 'birthday garden'.

 ✓

 ✓

 ✓

What You Need

• *A place for each child's 'birthday garden'*
• *A plant for each birthday*

What To Do

 ✓

When your children are born, designate a special place in your garden for each child's 'birthday garden'. Celebrate each birthday by putting in a special plant in their garden. As your children grow older they will look forward to this special event and enjoy going with you to the nursery to choose their special birthday plant.

Make a specific sign to go in their garden and encourage them to help you care for their special place.

This becomes a lovely family tradition and a great way to introduce children to the pleasures of gardening.

activity

16

PICNIC SANDWICHES

2+ ✓

 ✓

As a preschool teacher, and now as a mother, I have discovered something about children and food. If you can involve them in the preparation they are more likely to eat it. It is not always possible or practical in our busy lives, but try it and see if I am right!

 ✓

 ✓

 ✓

What You Need

* Sandwich fillings such as
  * sliced ham
  * chopped chicken
  * sliced tomato
  * mashed avocado
  * beetroot
  * chopped egg
  * lettuce
  * sprouts
  * and so on

What To Do

Next time you go on a family picnic take along the sandwich fillings, a couple of types of yummy bread and the butter. Put them all on the table with a big board, plates and spreading knives, and let the children concoct their own delicious sandwiches. They will taste better because they are nice and fresh, and the children will not complain about the fillings when they have made them!! In addition, you are developing their independence by showing them they are old enough to do some things for themselves!

activity

17

WATERING CANS

2+

Buy a watering can so your small children can help in the garden too.

What You Need

• *A watering can*

What To Do

Young children love to be involved in our activities but sometimes we have to be creative about how to do this. Our son was given a gardening set as a Christmas gift by my sister Julie when he was two and it was one of the best presents he has ever had.

He still follows me around with the wheelbarrow when I'm weeding and loves to help pick up the weeds. The small rake has broken, but I've cut down the handle of an adult sized one and he enjoys helping with the raking, but the most popular item has always been the watering can.

Children of all ages love playing with water, and letting them water the garden is encouraging a water activity that has a useful purpose. They will enjoy helping and, by encouraging them, you are building their self esteem and independence skills.

activity

18

COMPOSTING

4+ ✓

Teach your children about environmental care in your own garden by starting to make compost together.

 ✓

What You Need

• *Kitchen scrap bin* • *Compost bin* • *Soil* • *Animal manure*

✓

What to Do

 ✓

The soil in your garden is like every other living thing and needs nourishment. Take your children for a walk through a bush area or a rain forest and look at the amount of leaf and other litter on the forest floor. Talk to the children about the value of recycling by nature and about how we can replicate this important process in our own gardens.

We have a small plastic bucket beside our sink in the kitchen, in which we store our compostible materials. Your children can learn to add their apple cores, fruit peelings, and so on; to the compost bucket and be responsibile for emptying it every couple of days.

We have a large black compost bin and this works very well. Some councils sell these at a discount because they are trying to encourage rate payers to recycle garbage as much as possible. If not, and you can't afford a compost bin, make an area for a compost heap in your garden. Buy some heavy duty plastic to cover the heap as this will warm it and help to break it down more quickly. Keep the plastic in place with bricks.

Every few weeks add a layer of garden soil, together with horse, cow, chicken or sheep manure to your compost bin and keep it moist. In time the compost will have rotted down and you will have wonderful rich fertiliser to feed your plants.

Why throw out materials that can be easily composted and used in your own garden. This is a very practical way to teach children about care for their environment!

activity

19

GROWING STRAWBERRIES

4+

Strawberries are popular with kids of all ages (and their parents) and your children will love growing and eating their own strawberries.

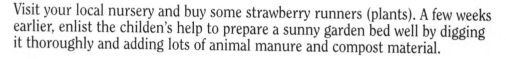

What You Need

• *Strawberry runners*
• *Bale of hay*

What To Do

Visit your local nursery and buy some strawberry runners (plants). A few weeks earlier, enlist the childen's help to prepare a sunny garden bed well by digging it thoroughly and adding lots of animal manure and compost material.

The soil should be nice and loose and really well-drained.

Help the children plant the strawberry plants in rows about 40 cm (15½ inches) apart.

Carefully put the straw around the plants so the berries will stay clean. The straw also helps keep the moisture in the ground.

Encourage the children to help look after their strawberry plants by watering and weeding, and they will be rewarded with delicious, juicy berries.

HINT!

If you live in a unit or space is restricted, buy a strawberry pot with holes in the side and plant your runners in this. You can still have a lovely crop of strawberries to enjoy with the kids.

activity

20

GROWING BULBS

4+

Nothing heralds Spring as much as a pot of beautiful flowering bulbs.

What You Need

- *Pretty pots*
- *Bulb potting mix*
- *Bulbs*

What To Do

If you have never planted bulbs with your children it is an experience they really shouldn't miss. Bulbs are self-contained seeds and little energy houses. As the temperature warms up the hard, dried-up looking bulbs they planted begin growing and burst out with lovely new green shoots and eventually beautiful flowers.

Go to a nursery with the children in early autumn and choose the bulbs they would like to grow in their own pots by looking at the pictures on the bags in which the bulbs are packed. Choose nice firm round bulbs that have been properly dried out. Buy some special bulb-raising potting mix or bulb fibre there also.

Most bulbs are planted in fairly shallow bowls so help the children add about 2.5 cm (1 inch) of potting mix or fibre and then add 4-6 bulbs depending on the size of the container. Pack the rest of the bowl with more potting mix or bulb fibre until the tops are covered.

The bulbs should be allowed to start growing in the dark and then moved out to a shaded window ledge or a spot in the garden as soon as they begin to grow. Water sparingly, bulbs are likely to rot if the conditions are too damp.

Everyone has their own favourite bulbs, but I always think daffodils and jonquils say Spring to me with their beautiful flowers and wonderful perfumes. But then hyacinths are so beautiful too! And freesias smell so divine! The hardest part about growing bulbs with the children is choosing which ones to grow.

activity

21

GROWING SWEET PEAS

4+

Sweet peas are everyone's favourite flowers, and few look and smell so beautiful when picked. Grow some with your children and they will love them too.

What You Need

- *Plastic pipes and connectors for a trellis*
- *Chicken wire*
- *Instant concrete*
- *Sweet pea seeds or seedlings*
- *Compost*

What To Do

Sweet peas are climbing plants and, for this reason, require a good-sized trellis. Make an easy trells by joining lengths of plastic piping with corner curves to make a large U-shaped section. Concrete this into the ground with instant concrete and, when it is dry, attach the chicken wire. Another more simple idea is to buy some plastic mesh and attach to two strong garden stakes for the sweet peas to climb on.

Dig the garden bed well below the trellis and add lots of compost and organic fertiliser. Make sure it is in a sunny position as sweet peas need full sun and protection from wind. Leave for a few weeks.

If you are planting seeds rather than seedlings with the children, soak the seeds in water for 24 hours before planting to hasten germination.

Plant the seedlings or seeds when ready; water and feed regularly, and in late winter and spring you will have beautiful climbing sweet peas with lots of pretty flowers.

HINT!

The trellis can be used for other climbing plants such as climbing beans, chokos, or a passionfruit vine.

activity

22

THE DINGLE DANGLE SCARECROW

4+

Sing this funny song with your children (they will know it from kindergarten) as you help them make a scarecrow for the garden.

What You Need

- *Tights*
- *Rags or more old tights or stockings for stuffing*
- *Old clothes*
- *A strong garden stake or broom handle*
- *Permanent pens*
- *Hay*
- *Old hat*
- *Wood glue*

What To Do

Begin by stuffing the top of a pair of tights with rags or more stockings for the head. Using strong thread sew up the top. The children will enjoy drawing on the scarecrow's facial features with permanent pens. Use the glue to attach some straw to his hat and place on his head.

Next fill the legs and tie together to form the body. Tie on two more legs for arms. Sew on another pair of tights for the bottom and legs and stuff it all well. Dress the scarecrow in some old clothes - an old shirt and pair of pants of Dad's are ideal. Stuff some straw into the arms of the shirt and legs of the pants for his hands and feet.

Find a spot in the garden for your scarecrow - beside the vegetable garden if you have one is perfect - and attach to a well-buried stake or broom handle.

Take some photos of your own special 'Dingle Dangle Scarecrow' for the children to take to preschool or school for Show and Tell.

activity

23

BARBECUED FRUIT KEBABS

6+   ✓

 ✓

 ✓

 ✓

Kids who love food on skewers will really enjoy these delicious fruit kebabs and they will be eager to help prepare them also.

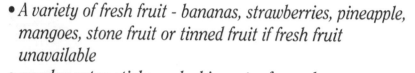

What You Need

- *A variety of fresh fruit - bananas, strawberries, pineapple, mangoes, stone fruit or tinned fruit if fresh fruit unavailable*
- *wooden satay sticks soaked in water for an hour*
- *2 tablespoons of melted butter*
- *2 tablespoons of orange juice*
- *2 tablespoons of brown sugar*
- *Basting brush*

What To Do

The children will enjoy threading equal sized pieces of fresh or tinned fruit onto the satay sticks.

Combine the butter, sugar, and orange juice to form a basting sauce.

Cook the fruit kebabs on a barbecue plate (low heat) for 5-10 minutes brushing frequently with the basting sauce.

These Fruit Kebabs are delicious served with icecream, cream or yoghurt.

activity
24

GRASS WORDS

6+

Children of this age, learning to read, are fascinated with words.

What You Need

- *Sunny patch of garden*
- *Grass seed*
- *Small stick*

What To Do

Your children will enjoy helping you dig the soil in the garden bed well for the funny writing.

They then write in the soil with the stick. They might like to write their name, a short sentence or even draw a simple picture.

Next, they carefully sprinkle the seed in the indentations, cover it with a fine layer of soil and water it with a very fine spray.

Keep it watered and in a couple of weeks the children will be able to see their writing as grass.

activity

25

MINIATURE GARDENS

8+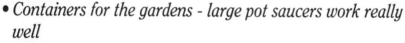

My sister Julie and I loved making miniature gardens when we were children. It is an excellent way to begin gardening. Introduce your kids to these and they, too, may be as enchanted by them as we were.

What You Need

- *Containers for the gardens - large pot saucers work really well*
- *Potting mix*
- *Tiny plants*
- *Small toys or figurines*
- *Pebbles or small stones*
- *Mirrors*

What To Do

Help your children fill their saucers with potting mix (it is best that an adult helps with this as there have been some cases of health problems using potting mix).

Next, they will enjoy planting small plants from the garden in their miniature gardens - mosses are terrific for the 'grass'.

Then they add the interesting bits - the pebbles, mirrors for ponds and some of their small toys to create a fascinating small world.

They will enjoy watering and looking after their own tiny gardens and, like all gardeners, will enjoy changing aspects of their own little 'patches'.

Perhaps they could take their miniature garden to school as a special project or for a class talk.

activity

26

WORLD'S GREATEST MEATBALLS

Meatballs are always popular for barbecues, and this recipe is so easy the children will be able to prepare them easily.

8+

What You Need

- *500 g (1lb) mince*
- *1 onion finely diced*
- *1 clove of garlic*
- *½ cup grated carrot*
- *½ cup rolled oats*

- *1 egg*
- *2 tablespoons tomato sauce*
- *1 tablespoon of Worcestershire sauce*
- *Plain flour*

What To Do

Mix all the above ingredients in a large bowl, except for the flour. (Wet hands are great to mix the meatball ingredients really well!)

Shape the mixture into meatballs or patties and roll in plain flour and then cook on a well oiled barbecue plate.

HINT!

Many other ingredients can be added to these meatballs such as chopped capsicum, corn kernels or herbs, depending on your family's likes and dislikes.

activity
27

BARBECUED VEGIE PARCELS 10+

Older children will love preparing these for your next family barbecue. Best of all, they can tailor them to each family member's personal taste.

What You Need

- *A variety of vegetables such as carrots, beans, eggplant, peas, pumpkin, onion, corn, capsicum, etc.*
- *Melted butter*
- *Garlic*
- *Seasoned salt if desired*
- *Alfoil*

What To Do

Chop or slice the vegetables. Arrange a variety in meal sized proportions on large squares of alfoil. Dot with knobs of butter and add garlic or seasoned salt if desired.

Sprinkle lightly with water and fold up the parcels so they are well wrapped in the alfoil.

Cook on the barbecue for 10-15 minutes.

HINT!

Unwrap carefully to avoid steam burns.

activity
28

BUILD A POND

10+

One of the preschools I visit made a wonderful pond in their grounds last year with the help of the children. They had raised frogs from tadpoles and, when the tadpoles were nearly ready to turn into frogs, they were released into their pond. Every time I visited, the children proudly took me to see their pond.

What You Need

- *The garden hose*
- *Spade*
- *Pond liner (available from nurseries, hardware stores, and garden shops)*
- *Sand*
- *Rocks for edging*
- *Waterplants*

What To Do

Garden ponds are best made out in the open as they will become polluted with too many falling leaves. Choose a spot in the garden with the children and mark out the diameter with the garden hose. Cut the turf carefully with a spade to use elsewhere and then the children can help dig out the hole for the pond. Make the bottom in a few levels; line it with the sand and smooth out carefully. Next, cover with the liner and carefully mould it to fit the shape of the pond. Be very careful not to make any holes in the liner as you work.

Cover the edges of the liner with the soil and then add rocks around the edge of the pool to make it look as natural as possible. Place the water plants in pots and position them just below the surface of the water.

Finally, fill the pond with water and allow it to stand for a few weeks before adding any fish or other pond creatures. It is a good idea to place a garden seat beside the pond so you can sit and enjoy it with the children.

activity

29

DESERT GARDENS

10+ ✓

Most botanical Gardens have sections where you can take the children to view arid gardens.

 ✓

 ✓

What You Need

- *Large shallow clay pot with a saucer • Small stones or gravel*
- *Cacti potting mix or regular potting mix with sand or grit added • Rocks • Cacti and succulent plants • Thick gardening gloves*

 ✓

 ✓

What To Do

Cacti gardens need little water and look best in a wide but shallow planter.

Help the children fill the container with the special potting mix or add some sand and shell grit to regular potting mix so it is not too heavy. Remind the children that these plants survive in very dry conditions and need well drained soil.

They will enjoy adding some stones to the pot for decoration and then add their selection of small cacti and other succulent plants. Nurseries will have a selection to choose from, or perhaps you have friends or family with cacti or succulent gardens who will be happy to let the children have some small cuttings or plants.

When the plants are arranged to their liking, they can sprinkle on the small stones or gravel for ground cover. During the summer the cacti garden will still need regular watering - but don't over water. Show the children how to feel the soil with the tip of a finger to see if it is moist enough. In winter, however, remind them to water sparingly, probably only once a month or the plants will rot away.

They will really enjoy growing their own desert gardens.

activity

30

GROW YOUR OWN BABY FERNS
10+

Show your children how to collect the spores from ferns and grow some baby ferns to plant out in the garden.

What You Need

- *Thick white paper*
- *Potting mix rich in humus*
- *Pots*

What To Do

Ferns grow in every size from minute ground hugging plants to giant tree ferns and climbers. They mostly love shady places and prefer a cool moist atmosphere under trees. Grow them in well-drained soil rich in humus. They can be propagated by dividing clumps, but it is much more fun to collect the spores with the children and grow new baby ferns.

Look at your ferns to see if there are any small brownish clusters of spores on the underside of some of the fronds. Pick the fronds and, with the children, lie them on the sheets of white paper for a day or so in a protected place until some of the spores have dropped onto the paper.

Fill several small pots or plastic containers with potting mix rich in humus and sprinkle the spore paper over them. The children will need to keep them moist, but not wet, in a cool, shady part of the garden.

Watch carefully to see the new baby ferns beginning to grow. In time the children will be able to plant out the new ferns into the garden and they will feel a wonderful sense of accomplishment when they rear their own baby ferns!

activity

31

GARDENING DIARY

10+

Encourage an interest in gardening and the environment by helping your children make a gardening diary.

What You Need

• *A good quality scrapbook or drawing book*
• *Glue, pencils, other drawing materials*

What To Do

Encourage your children to take an interest in the garden by making a gardening diary together.

Use a double page for each month of the year and they can draw, paint or press flowers that bloom in the garden at that time to put in the section for that month.

Use gardening books you have at home or access your local library for information about the plants they have featured. They may like to include where the plants originate, any special horticultural needs they have and their ideal growing conditions.

Encourage your children to look in other gardens or parks for plants they like that bloom in particular months, which could be added to your garden also.

The plant diary could be used as a school project or a special topic for a talk at school.

This could begin a life-long love of plants and gardens in your children. Who knows - perhaps one of them may be a botanist one day!

activity

32

HERBED VINEGARS

10+

Help the children make some delicious herbed vinegars to use at home or to give away as special gifts.

What You Need

• *Herbs from the garden*
• *Glass bottles with lids (suitable bottles can be bought cheaply)*
• *Good quality white wine vinegar*
• *Labels*
• *Coloured felt pens*

What To Do

Go for a walk in the garden with the children and pick a selection of herbs to use. Good herbs for vinegars are rosemary, sage, thymes, and marjoram.

Clean the bottles really well and the children can trim some herbs and add the sprigs to the bottles. Help them fill the bottles with vinegar and put the lids on tightly.

Next the children can decorate some labels with pretty designs and write the names of the herbs in the vinegar on the labels.

Give them away or use them up quickly for cooking or in delicious salad dressings.

activity
33

POTATO FEAST

10+

Nothing tastes so good as freshly dug baby potatoes from your own garden and they are so easy to grow. Show the children how to do this and they can grow some and sell them to Mum for pocket money!

What You Need

• *Seed potatoes*
• *Compost*

What To Do

Although potatoes do sprout and we have often found potatoes growing in the garden from old ones thrown out, it is better to start with special seed potatoes. You can buy these from your local nursery or garden centre.

Help the children thoroughly dig over a section of garden and add lots of lovely compost from your compost bin or heap. If you live in a flat or apartment they can grow their potatoes in a large pot or even a black plastic rubbish bag (with a few holes poked in the bottom for drainage). Just make sure you use a good quality potting mix with lots of mulch included in the mix.

To help your potatoes have the best possible start, leave them in a tray or shoe box lid in a sunny spot on the balcony or a window sill until they begin to sprout. Then plant out the potatoes about a metre (3 ft) apart in the garden or two or three in a large pot or rubbish bag.

Water them well and continue to do this regularly. Potatoes prefer heavy waterings at regular intervals but need good drainage. They should also be fertilized periodically.

In about three to four months the potato plants will begin to die off, and this is the time to dig them up and discover the wonderful potato treasure under the ground.

Yum! potatotoes in their jackets for dinner!

activity
34

SAVING SEEDS

10+

Recycling has been the catch-cry of the '90's. Help the children recycle seeds and save money.

What You Need

- *Fruit and vegetables*
- *Colander*
- *Baking tray*

What To Do

Encourage the children to save seeds that they can use to plant for their vegetable gardens. They will enjoy watching them grow into new plants.

When you eat fruit and vegetables that you could grow in your own garden, show the children how to save the seeds. They could save tomato, rockmelon, watermelon, pumpkin, peas, beans, and many other seeds.

They need to wash the seeds carefully and take off any of the fruit or vegetable matter so that the seeds won't rot. Then put them into a strainer or colander (depending on the size of the seeds) and run lots of cool water through them.

Dry them on a tray on a sunny window sill or on a table in the sun. When they are completely dry store them in well sealed screw top jars or plastic containers.

Label the containers with the name of the seeds and the date.

The children will enjoy growing their own fruit and vegetables from their seeds.

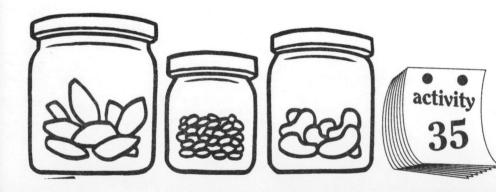

activity
35

DEVELOPING SKILLS

BALLOON FUN

2+ ✓

Blow up some balloons for the children to play with in the garden.

 ✓

 ✓

What You Need

• *Balloons*
• *Space to play*

  ✓

What To Do

 ✓

Blow up lots of balloons for the children to use for throwing, catching and kicking in the garden. Balloons are so cheap to buy and are a great way to begin teaching simple ball handling skills to young children. Balloons are softer and slower than balls and allow young children more time to catch. Sometimes younger children are frightened of balls if they have been hit with one, and playing with balloons can restore their confidence.

Some games to play with balloons are:

Balloon Volleyball
• String up a rope between two trees or posts and hit the balloon over the rope as in volleyball
• Keep it off the ground

Play a game where the balloon is not allowed to touch the ground. The other player gets a point if his opponent doesn't stop the balloon from touching the ground in a designated area.

activity

36

BATS AND BALLS

2+

 ✓

Developing eye/hand co-ordination skills early will help your children's ability to play sports such as tennis, cricket, golf, softball and baseball when they are older.

 ✓

 ✓

What You Need

- *Old tights*
- *Wire coathangers*
- *Masking or insulating tape*
- *Tennis ball*

What To Do

Bend the coathanger into the shape of a racquet and straighten the bent handle. Re-bend the handle over so it is narrower and longer than before.

Cut one leg off the tights and keep for later. Pull the other leg over the racquet until taut, then wrap the rest of the tights around the handle. Cover with the tape until the handle is firm and easy to hold.

Put a tennis ball in the toe of the spare tights leg and tie from a tree branch, the clothes line, or a hook.

Your children will have lots of fun hitting the ball backwards and forwards. Make two bats so your children can hit with you or a friend or sibling. As the bats are so soft, the children won't be hurt if they accidentally hit each other.

activity
37

FROZEN WATER PLAY

Great fun on a hot day.

2+ ✓

 ✓

 ✓

 ✓

What You Need

• *Large container for water play*
• *Balloons of various shapes*
• *Food colouring*
• *Eye droppers*

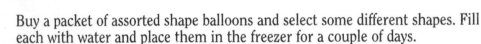 ✓

What To Do

Buy a packet of assorted shape balloons and select some different shapes. Fill each with water and place them in the freezer for a couple of days.

When they are frozen solid, cut away the balloon, leaving the frozen shape.

Place the iced shapes into your children's wading pool, large dish or even a baby bath. Your children will have lots of fun dropping food colouring onto the frozen shapes with the eye dropper and watching the colours change.

Another time you can fill plastic containers with coloured water for a different experience.

Your children will be fascinated by these colourful 'icebergs'.

activity

38

JUMP THE ROPE

2+

Very young children do not have the co-ordination to start to learn to skip with a rope. However fun rope activities like these will help develop your young child's co-ordination and balance and will lead on to learning to skip when they are a little older.

What You Need

• *A long rope*
• *A small cushion or a sock half filled with rice, dried beans or sand*

What To Do

Tie the cushion or sock onto the end of the rope. Swing the rope around you slightly above the ground and the children try to jump the rope as it comes around. If they are having difficulty, swing it a little slower until they master the skill.

With a few children you can turn it into a game and, if the rope touches anyone, they have to sit out for a minute, hop on one foot or jump to a particular spot in the garden.

It is also fun for children to jump over a still rope. Tie one end to your clothes line, a tree or a post and have the children run up and jump over the rope. With young children make sure it is very low until they have mastered this skill.

activity

39

BALLOON KICKS

4+ ✓

 ✓

Children love playing with balloons and they are so cheap to buy in your local supermarket. I always have a packet on hand for days when they are bored and can't think what to do.

 ✓

 ✓

 ✓

What You Need

• *Balloons*
• *Space to kick*

✓

✓

What To Do

Blow up a balloon for each child and send them outside. They will enjoy choosing their favourite colour balloon. The aim of this game is to kick the balloon and not let it touch the ground. Each player counts how many kicks they do without letting it fall to the ground. Give them some paper and a pen or a blackboard and chalk to record their scores and see who is the winner.

Another variation of this game is to hit the balloon with any part of the body - head, hands, feet, knees, shoulders and so on - to keep the balloon from touching the ground.

activity

40

BOX TARGET

4+

Visit your local electrical store and ask them for a large computer, stove or television box to make a throwing target.

What You Need

- *A large box*
- *A stanley knife*
- *Insulating tape*
- *Bean bags or old socks filled with rice, dried beans or sand to throw*
- *Balls for throwing*

What To Do

Use the stanley knife and carefully cut shapes from different sides of the box. Use a variety of shapes such as squares, triangles, diamonds and rectangles. Cut some shapes large and others small. Cut some shapes at ground level and some higher in the box.

Edge the shapes with different coloured insulating tape for strength and to make them stand out.

You could cut a trap-door in one side of the box to let the children retrieve the thrown items easily.

Give the children a variety of different shaped and sized balls and bean bags to throw. They will enjoy throwing and developing their aiming skills.

Older children can enhance their numeracy skills by writing down everyone's scores and keeping a running total.

activity

41

BOUNCING BALLS

4+

Children love bouncing balls. Try this game with them and see if they can beat you.

What You Need

- *Flat surface to bounce balls on - concrete or pavement tiles*
- *Tennis balls or other soft, bouncy balls*

What To Do

Count the number of times your children can bounce a ball in a row. Write down their scores so they can see if they can beat their 'PB'. (Personal Best!)

When they can bounce really well try these extra challenges:

Bounce with their right hand only
Bounce with their left hand only
Alternate hands
Twice with their right, then twice with their left and so on
Bounce under their legs - right then left
Clap between bounces
Bounce high then low, and so on

activity

42

BUCKET TARGETS

4+

Develop your children's throwing skills with a simple game of bucket targets.

What You Need

- *A plastic bucket*
- *Collection of tennis or other soft balls or bean bags*
- *A brick*

What To Do

Place the bucket on the ground at an angle, propped up by the house brick, so the bucket is tipped towards the throwers. Mark a spot a couple of metres away and the children take it in turn to throw the balls into the bucket.

Record their scores on some paper or a blackboard and improve their mathematics skills by totalling them up at the end to see who has the best aim. Handicap older children by making them stand further away from the bucket than the smaller children.

If the bucket is too small a target for younger children, a plastic garbage bin makes an excellent target too, or perhaps a plastic laundry basket.

activity

43

CHALK TARGETS

4+ ✓

Young children needs lots of practice to improve their throwing skills for games at school and organised sport. This simple game will provide lots of hours of fun.

 ✓
 ✓
✓
✓
✓

What You Need

- Coloured chalk
- Balls or bean bags
- A wall that is suitable for throwing against

What To Do

Mark a large circle on a wall of the house. In the middle of the circle mark a red target - use a saucer for the outline to make a perfectly round circle. The red circle in the middle is the target.

The children stand a few paces away. A hoop makes a good circle to stand in or else mark it with some of the chalk.

They score 10 or 20 points when they hit the bullseye and 5 or 10 when they hit in the bigger circle.

As they become more proficient with their aim they have to stand further away.

Handicap older children by making them stand further away than the littlies! Give them some paper and pencils or let them score on the concrete or pavers with the chalk; it will just hose off when they have finished.

activity

44

CLOWN CAPERS

4+

Boxes make great toys - they are cheap, easy to obtain, and it doesn't matter if they are wrecked eventually because you can always use another box.

What You Need

- *A large cardboard carton*
- *Felt pens*
- *Masking tape*
- *Scissors or a stanley knife*
- *A wooden box, stool or chair*
- *A brick or large book*
- *Soft balls or bean bags*

What To Do

Use the masking tape to close all the sides of the box. Draw a funny clown's face with a very large mouth on a strong side of the box. Cut out the mouth with the scissors or stanley knife and put the box on a chair outside. Put the brick or book inside the box to stop it falling over.

The children will love trying to 'feed' the clown with the balls or bean bags.

As their aim improves, make them stand a little further back to improve their throwing skills.

activity

45

EGG AND SPOON RACES

4+

 ✓

 ✓

Great fun for birthday parties or whenever you have a few children together.

 ✓

 ✓

What You Need

- *Teaspoons (plastic ones work well)*
- *Golf balls*
- *Starting and finishing lines*

What To Do

Each child has a teaspoon and an old golf ball to balance on it.

The children must keep one hand behind their backs at all times to resist the temptation to hold the ball on the spoon. The aim of the game is to walk or run as quickly as possible to the finishing line while still keeping the golf ball on the spoon.

If a child drops the ball he must go back to the starting line and begin again.

This game is a little like the old story of the hare and the tortoise - slow and steady usually wins this race!!!

activity

46

HOT POTATO

4+

A simple throwing game to play with a group of children.

What You Need

- *Children*
- *A medium sized soft ball*

What To Do

The children join hands to form a circle and then drop their hands.

Ask them to pretend that the ball is a sizzling hot potato and, when they get the ball, they have to pass it to the next player as soon as they can. This game is fast and furious and great fun!

activity

47

PING PONG BALL FUN

4+ ✓

If you have some space at home, a ping pong table is a great investment.

 ✓

What You Need

• *Ping pong balls*

What To Do

There are many activities children can do with ping pong balls; here are a few to try.

- Blowing the ping pong balls. This games needs two children, one at each end or side of a large table or flat surface. They take it in turn to try and blow the ping pong ball past each other. They have to be goalkeepers and try to defend their end by blowing it back to the other end or side.

- Roll ping pong balls along the side of a thick rope. The children will enjoy making the rope into interesting shapes.

- Make two bats out of rolled up newspaper or obtain two long cardboard tubes from lunch wrap, and use them to hit ping pong balls. Two cardboard boxes standing on ends make perfect goals.

- Put three fingers on a ping pong ball and pull them away fast and see how it goes then comes back to you like a boomerang.

- Play with ping pong balls in the bath or outside in a bowl of water or the swimming pool.

- Use them for throwing practice - throw them into a bucket or cardboard box.

- Use them to play with plastic racquets or ping pong bats on a flat surface - not the table.

activity

48

SCOOP BALL

4+

Make a cheap and simple game to help develop your children's eye-hand co-ordination and the visual tracking skills they need to play many types of sport.

What You Need

- *A few plastic milk or juice bottles with handles*
- *Tennis or other small soft balls*
- *Masking or insulation tape*

What To Do

With a stanley knife or sharp scissors cut the bottoms off some milk or juice plastic bottles. Tape over the sharp edges with some masking or insulating tape.

Hold the scoops by the handles and use them to catch and throw balls to your children. This game is not only lots of fun but also develops your children's eye-hand co-ordination as they move their scoops to catch the ball. Also, it develops their skills at visually tracking a moving object. Children need these skills later to play sports such as tennis, hockey, cricket and baseball.

activity
49

TIN CAN CLIP CLOPS

4+

Help the children make some simple stilts from tins to walk tall around the yard.

What You Need

- *2 large empty soup tins of the same size*
- *Clothes line or other thin rope*
- *Acrylic paint*
- *Hammer and nails*

What To Do

The children can help scrub the tins to remove the labels. Use the hammer and nail to punch two holes in the side of each tin very close to the filled-in end.

Now the children will enjoy painting the tins bright colours with some acrylic paints. (Some paint manufacturers now sell small sample tins of paint which are ideal for projects like this with the children.)

When the paint is dry, measure and cut the rope to fit the children. String a piece through each tin and tie a good knot in both ends so it can't come out.

The children stand on the tins and hold onto the ropes tightly as they walk on their tin stilts. This is very hard for some children and they will need many opportunities to practise.

activity

50

TREASURE HUNT

A fun party game for the small fry.

4+ ✔

 ✔

 ✔

 ✔

What You Need

• *Lots of players*
• *Some treasure - perhaps a coin*

 ✔

What To Do

Choose one child to be the first 'treasure hunter'.

 ✔

All the others sit in a circle on the floor with the treasure hunter in the middle of the circle. The players pass the 'treasure' around the circle from hand to hand and the 'treasure hunter' has to point to who has the treasure. Encourage the children to make it harder by all pretending to pass the 'treasure' even if they're not.

The 'treasure hunter' only has three guesses as this keeps the game moving and means everyone has a turn. (Young children find it difficult to wait for their turn.) The person with the treasure becomes the next 'treasure hunter'.

activity

51

WACK IT

4+

A cheap and fun game for two children or an adult and child to play in the back yard.

What You Need

- *A broom handle*
- *Thin rope or some strong string - 120 cm (4 ft) long*
- *A pillowcase, plastic shopping bag or tights*
- *Some soft rags from the rag bag*

What To Do

Hammer the broom handle into the ground in an open part of the garden. Very firmly tie one end of the rope to the top of the broom handle and attach the other end to the bundle. Make this by putting some rags into a plastic shopping bag, a pillowcase or even into the top of a pair of tights. Bundle them all in and shape it like a big, soft, ball.

The players take it in turn to thump the ball, one child using his right hand to hit the ball anti-clockwise and the other using his left hand to hit the opposite way. The players must stand opposite each other.

The aim of the game is to hit the ball so that the rope spirals around the pole and the ball eventually touches the pole, thus scoring a point for that player.

The opponent tries to stop the ball by hitting it in the opposite direction so it doesn't keep spinning around and eventually hitting the post.

The game is lots of fun and the more the children play it the better they will get and the wilder the fun! Mum might have to be around doing a little pottering in the garden or hosing to adjudicate!

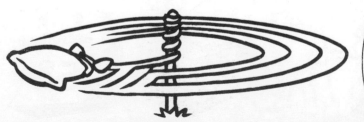

activity

52

WISHING WELL TARGET

4+

For a party or special event make a wishing well target for the garden for children to throw into and make a wish.

This is also a great idea for a fund raiser at a preschool or school fete.

What You Need

- *2 large cardboard boxes*
- *A plastic washing-up dish*
- *House paint*
- *Stones*
- *A tin of gold spray paint*

What To Do

Turn one of the boxes over and cut a circle out of the bottom in which to fit the washing up dish. Use the other box to make the top of the wishing well, with strong cardboard supports to hold it up. Paint the wishing well with house paint and decorate with glitter and flower cut-outs, fairies or anything else that takes your fancy.

Spray some pebbles or small stones gold or cover them with silver foil for throwing.

The children will love throwing their pebbles into the wishing well and making a wish.

This idea is great for the fairy birthday parties that are so popular with little girls.

activity

53

BALL CHASES

6+

A fun throwing game to play with a group of children.

What You Need

- *A group of children*
- *Two or more soft balls*

What To Do

The children join hands to form a circle, then drop their hands.
Space the children about a metre (3 ft) apart. Explain to them that they are going to be passing two balls around the circle and they have to see if the second ball can overtake the one in front.

Begin one ball and then, when it has been passed by a few children, begin the second ball.

The children really concentrate and this helps develop their throwing and catching skills.

activity

54

BALL SWEEP

6+ ✓

A fun game to play at a party, with a group of children, or with the family.

What You Need

 ✓

- *Brooms*
- *Large rubber balls*
- *Cardboard boxes*

 ✓

What To Do

Each player has a ball, a broom and a box to sweep their ball into. Spread the players out on the drive or in the backyard and when you say 'go' the players have to sweep their balls down to their boxes, which have been placed some distance away, as fast as they can.

The first player to sweep their ball into the box is the winner.

A variation of this game, if you don't have enough balls or booms for all the players, is to divide the children into relay teams. The first player in each team sweeps the ball into the box. The next player sweeps it out and back to the start and so on. Relays are lots of fun to play with children.

activity
55

BODY VOLLEYBALL

6+

This game is a variation on traditional volleyball, which is also a good game for the backyard. This is just a little trickier and lots of laughs.

What You Need

- *A rope or a net*
- *A soft ball or a balloon*
- *A few players*

What To Do

Tie the rope or the net between two trees or posts in the backyard. If you don't have the space take the children to a local park.

The players divide into two teams on either side of the net. The aim of the game is to toss the ball across the net, not letting it touch the ground. If the ball touches the ground the other team gets a point and the game starts again. The trick with this version is that they can't use their hands. They can use any other part of their bodies - heads, feet, knees, elbows, shoulders and so on - but if anyone uses hands the other team gets a point.

It is a very funny game and great to play with a balloon also.

activity

56

BOOK BALANCING

6+   ✓

 ✓

Long ago, young ladies were encouraged to walk around with a book on their head to improve their posture. Today this is a fun game to play with a few children at a party or just in the back yard.

 ✓

  ✓

What You Need

• *Books - hardcover picture books work well*

✓

What To Do

 ✓

Give each player a book to balance on their head. Let them have a few minutes to practise walking before the race begins.

When they are ready, line them up and they have to walk as quickly as possible to the finishing line with the book balanced on their head. They cannot touch the book at all with their hands. If it falls off, the player goes back to the start and begins again.

Some children find this very easy - for others it is almost an impossibility. Try it yourself and see how good your posture is!

activity

57

FLOWER POT RACES

6+

I first saw this at a school fun day but, for safety purposes, they used large flat bean bags. Traditionally, however, it seems flower pots were used.

What You Need

• *A pair of flower pots per child (or bean bags, smooth bricks of flattish stones could be used)*

What To Do

Each player needs two terracotta flower pots. They balance with a foot on each pot and go forward by moving the pot forwards with their hands, one pot at a time.

If they fall off or put a hand or a foot on the ground they have to go back to the beginning and start again. This is really hard and the children need a lot of strength in their arms to be able to do this game.

Using the monkey bars or flying foxes in your local park helps build arm strength in young children.

activity

58

FRISBEE FUN

6+ ✓

Frisbees are great for throwing and catching. Take one to the beach or to a park to throw with the children.

 ✓

What You Need

• *A frisbee*

✓

What To Do

✓

Frisbees are very cheap to buy at toyshops or chain stores.
However, you can use round plastic ice cream container lids or used disposable plastic plates as frisbees also.

Children need help to develop the action required for successful frisbee throwing. Show the children how to hold it horizontally, then swing with their throwing arm bent from the chest away from the body. They then let go of the frisbee when the arm is fully extended. With this technique the frisbee floats through the air and is easy to catch.

Have a frisbee throwing contest to see who can throw the longest distance.
Play 'catch the frisbee' and keep count of who has caught it the most times.

Frisbees are lots of fun to play with in the water too! Use them in the pool or at the beach.

activity

59

GOLF BALL TOSS

6+

A fun throwing game that all the family will enjoy playing in the garden.

What You Need

- *Golf balls*
- *Containers such as plastic washing-up dishes, large bowls, buckets, cardboard boxes, ice cream containers and so on.*
- *Ropes or hoops*
- *Cardboard and pencils*

What To Do

Arrange a throwing golf course around the backyard. Put out the containers and place a hoop or rope in front of each one so the players are all throwing from the same distance.

The players each have a golf ball and progress around the course trying to 'hole' each container in the least number of throws. Give each player a card so they can keep their own score.

If adults or older siblings are playing younger children, keep it fairer by using a handicap system.

activity

60

HOOPSCOTCH

6+

When your children have mastered hopscotch really well, give them a new challenge with a game of 'hoopscotch'.

What You Need

- *Some colourful plastic hoops (available from chain stores or toyshops)*
- *Plastic milk or juice bottles*
- *Strong masking or insulating tape*
- *A flat stone to throw*

What To Do

The children will enjoy helping you half fill the empty plastic bottles with water or sand so they won't over-balance.

In a clear grassy space in the garden set up a game of 'hoopscotch'. Place a hoop on two bottles and secure it with tape. Then place another hoop after it on more bottles and so on until you have a 'hoopscotch' track marked out. You can put two hoops beside each other so children jump into them with a foot in each hoop.

The rules are the same as hopscotch except the children jump instead of hop. One child begins by throwing the stone into the first hoop. They jump into the hoop, pick up the stone and throw it into the next one, and so on.

When they over-balance or their throw goes astray, the next player has a turn. When all the players have had their turn the first player begins where their turn ended.

This game is much harder because the hoops are raised and the children have to jump high. If two-litre bottles are too high, use small plastic juice bottles to support the hoops. Or, as an alternative, use the two sizes of bottles to make the game varied and more interesting.

This is a wonderful warming-up activity for the whole family on a cold winter's day!!!

activity
61

POTATO RACES

6+

This is similar to Egg and Spoon Races for the younger children but a little more challenging!!!

What You Need

- *Metal teaspoons*
- *Potatoes*
- *Starting and finishing lines*

What To Do

Give each competitor a metal teaspoon on which a potato is placed. (Plastic ones are not strong enough to hold the potatoes.) Line them up and on the word 'go', they set off as fast as they can for the finishing line.

However, if they drop their potato, they must scoop it up again with the teaspoon without using their hands, before they continue the race.

Again, slow and steady is often the way to go as the more intrepid racers usually manage to drop their potatoes.

Give the adults a turn too; it's not as easy as it sounds.

Finish with a sausage sizzle and lots of mash with the sausages to use up all the bruised potatoes.

activity

62

PRACTICE WALL TENNIS

6+ ✓

If your children are keen to learn tennis this is an excellent way to begin.

What You Need

 ✓

- *Tennis balls*
- *Tennis racquets*
- *A practice wall*

 ✓

What To Do

Children's tennis racquets are not very expensive and make a great gift. Grandparents are often glad to have practical suggestions for Christmas and birthday presents. Adult racquets are not suitable for young children as they are too big, too heavy, and the grips are too large for their smaller hands.

Most tennis courts have a practice wall where you can take children to have a hit together free of charge. Many schools allow public access to their courts on weekends and after school and, if they have tennis or multi-purpose courts, they usually have practice walls also.

It takes a long time for children to be consistent enough to hit to themselves on a practice wall but you can hit to them, taking it in turn to hit the ball.

As their skills improve, introduce some of the other shots such as volleys and smashes. If they are really interested and show some skill, think about tennis lessons. Most towns and cities have well-organised Junior Tennis Associations where kids can play in Junior Competitions, have a lot of fun and make lots of new friends. I have played tennis all my life and it is a great sport to keep playing well into your later years.

activity

63

SHADOW TIGGY

A fun variation on the old chasey game.

6+

What You Need

- *Two or more children*
- *Lots of space to run*

What To Do

One player is 'it' and he waits and counts to 10 while the other players scatter as far away as they can run.

The player who is 'it' chases them and tries to stand on their shadows. When someone is caught he joins the first guy who is 'it' to help chase all the others.

The last player to be caught is 'it' for the next game.

activity

64

SOCK BALL

6+

Make a simple sock ball for the children to have lots of fun with outside.

What You Need

• *Tennis ball*
• *A long sock - one of Dad's football socks is ideal*

What To Do

Put the tennis ball in the toe of the sock and tie a knot at the other end.

Your children will have lots of fun swinging it, throwing it, bouncing it against walls and catching it.

As my son says, 'They'll have a ball with this game!!!'

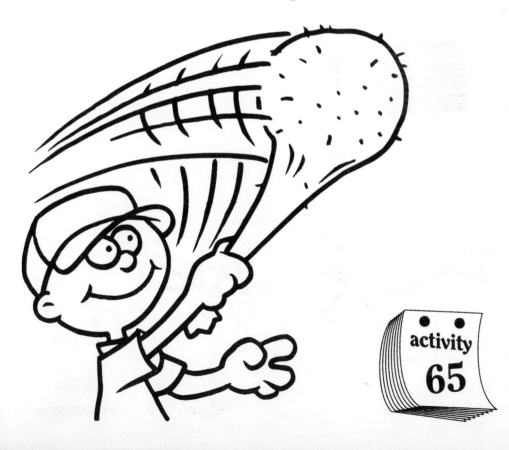

activity
65

VOLLEYBALL

6+

Young children need lots of fun games with balls to develop ball skills for more formal ball games such as basketball and netball.

What You Need

• *A large soft plastic ball or balloon*

What To do

String up a net or simply a rope from between two trees at just above your child's head height. Bat and throw the ball back and forward to your child. Whoever fails to catch the ball must give a point to the other player.

This game is great fun played indoors also, but with a balloon instead of a ball. Simply clear space in a room and tie a string between the backs of two chairs. If you have more players, add a few extra balloons to increase the fun (and the challenge!).

activity

66

BOUNCE WITH A PARTNER

8+

When your children are really competent ball bouncers, increase the challenge by using two balls and bouncing with a friend, sibling, Mum or Dad.

What You Need

- *Two tennis balls or other small bouncy balls*
- *A flat area to bounce balls outdoors*

What To Do

This is much trickier than simply bouncing balls on your own. The two players stand about one and a half metres (5 ft) apart and increase the distance between them as the go through the routine. The idea is to throw and catch using the two balls at the same time.

- Bounce the ball to your child and catch his ball with both hands.
- Bounce the ball to your child and catch it in your right hand with the palm up.
- Bounce the ball to your child and catch it in your left hand with the palm up.
- Bounce the ball to your child and catch it in your right hand with the palm down.
- Bounce the ball to your child and catch it in your left hand with the palm down.
- Bounce the ball to your partner and clap before you catch his ball.

Discard one ball and practice bouncing the ball to your child, who bounces it back without catching it. See how many times you can do this without stopping.

Now try to do it and clap once before you receive the ball.

Think of other skills you can try together.

activity
67

ELASTICS

8+ ✓

 ✓

 ✓

My primary school friends and I spent most lunch hours playing elastics!

If you remember how, teach it to your own children. ✓

 ✓

✓

What You Need

- *2-3 metres (6½ to 10 ft) of elastic knotted to make a big loop*
- *3 children*

What To Do

This game needs three players (although I can remember that my sister and I used to play it at home with a chair at one end).

Players take it in turn to be the jumper, the others stand inside the elastic and move apart until the elastic is taut. The elastic goes around their ankles and with their feet about shoulder-width apart.

The jumper starts outside the elastic and then:-
- jumps in
- jumps out again with a leg on either side of the elastic
- jumps inside again
- jumps onto both strands of elastic
- jumps onto one strand with both feet
- jumps out - to one side with both feet under a strand and then jumps over to the other side taking that strand with his feet
- jumps out so the elastic goes back into place.

Then the whole sequence is repeated from the other side. A player is out when they make a mistake in the sequence or they can't manage one of the moves.

They then become one of the supports at one end of the elastic and one of those children has the next turn.

Encourage the children to think of other variations to the routine. If you played this as a child you may remember some parts that I have forgotten!

activity

68

ELASTIC CHALLENGE

8+ ✓

When the children have mastered the basic moves of the game of elastic see if they can perform these moves.

 ✓

 ✓

What You Need

• *2-3 metres (6½ to 10 ft) of elastic knotted to make a big loop*
• *3 children*

 ✓

 ✓

What To Do

To increase the challenge elastics can be played with the elastic around the holders' knees so the player jumping has to jump higher.

The children may also like to try these moves:-

The jumper starts outside the elastic and then:-
• jumps in while the holders have their feet close together so the elastic is narrower
• jumps out again
• jumps in but the elastic is at knee level
• jumps onto one strand with both feet with the elastic at knee level
• jumps inside again
• jumps out - to one side wih both feet under a strand and then jumps over to the other side taking that strand with his feet - this is done with the elastic at hip level
• jumps out

If they really master this game they can try jumping with the elastic at waist level!!!

Have a turn yourself and see if you can still remember some of those old playground tricks!

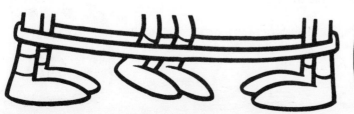

activity

69

HOSPITAL TIGGY

8+

A fun chasing game to play with a group of children.

What You Need

- *Lot of children*
- *Space to run safely*

What To Do

One player becomes 'it' and has to try and tag the other children. When he catches someone the person tagged has to hold the spot on his body where he was tagged and also become 'it'.

The children get better at this game and try to tag people in places that make it very, very, difficult to hold while running, such as feet!

activity
70

PLAYING ORGANISED SPORT 8+

Encourage your children to join a sporting club or team if they are interested.

What You Need

• *Time*

What To Do

Children need to have outlets for their physical energy and, while sporting team time can eat into family outing time, it is still great to encourage children to join and take an interest in sport. Lifetime hobbies and interests can be commenced in childhood.

Many adults are still playing sports such as bowls, golf, tennis and so on into their eighties and are healthier and more alert for it.

It may mean that, as parents, we drive our children to practices and spend precious weekend time watching soccer, football or netball games, but the physical and interpersonal skills our children develop by being part of a team make up for the commitment we put in.

I believe it is important for the years ahead that children learn to lose and win gracefully, to work as a team and to accept the knocks that sport can give. Just remember, however, that it still needs to be fun for them and we mustn't push on them our own agendas as parents.

activity
71

SEVENSES

8+   ✓

This was one of our favourite games at primary school. Your children will love playing it if you have a wall to bounce against at home.

  ✓

What You Need

- *Players*
- *A tennis or other soft, small, bouncy ball*

What To Do

The players take it in turns - when a player drops the ball the next person has a turn. There are many ways to play this game but the one I remember went like this:-

7 times   throw the ball against the wall and catch it with two hands

6 times   throw the ball against the wall and catch it with one hand

5 times   throw the ball against the wall, let it bounce and catch it

4 times   throw the ball under your leg against the wall then catch it

3 times   throw the ball, clap your hands once and catch it

2 times   throw the ball, turn around, let it bounce and catch it

Once   throw the ball, let it bounce, bounce it with your hand, and catch it

When you have another turn you start at the turn where you dropped the ball rather than have to begin all over again.

activity

72

FOOD FUN

BANANA PANCAKES

2+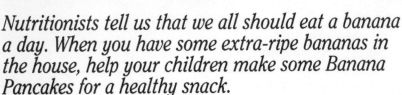

Nutritionists tell us that we all should eat a banana a day. When you have some extra-ripe bananas in the house, help your children make some Banana Pancakes for a healthy snack.

What You Need

- *2 ripe bananas*
- *1 egg*
- *1 cup of self-raising flour (use wholemeal if you wish)*
- *3/4 cup of milk*
- *1 tablespoon of butter*

What To Do

The children can help with the first step of mashing the bananas well. Next let one of them break the egg and whisk well into the bananas until smooth and creamy. Next measure in the flour and 1/2 of the milk and beat for 1 minute with a large spoon. Stir in the rest of the milk.

Cover the mixture with a tea-towel and allow it to stand for about half an hour.

In a frypan add a teaspoon of butter and pour or ladle in some of the mixture to form small pancakes.

When bubbles appear on the side turn carefully with an egg lifter and cook until golden brown on the other side. Banana Pancakes are delicious served warm with icecream and sliced bananas for dessert or cold for a snack. Makes about 12.

activity
73

BUTTERFLY SANDWICHES

2+

Even the pickiest eater in your family will love these sandwiches, especially if they helped in the making.

 ✓

 ✓

What You Need

- *bread*
- *cream cheese, cheese, or peanut butter*
- *decorations such as fruit or vegetable pieces, cheese slices, slices of sausage or ham, gherkins, celery, sultanas or anything else tasty and colourful*

 ✓

 ✓

What To Do

Stand your children on a chair beside you at the kitchen bench so they can help. Cut a slice of bread into either two or four triangles and face them outwards on a plate to form the 'butterflies'. Apply a spread to the triangles, then decorate - your children will love helping with this part and making suggestions. Cheese slices cut up with celery pieces are very tasty, or banana rings and sultanas on peanut butter are just great. Use strips of carrots, beans, or capsicums for antennae.

activity

74

CHEERIO KEBABS

2+

 ✓

 ✓

Cheerios are also called cocktail sausages. Children love them though, like most parents, I consider them party fare. However they will enjoy helping you make them into exciting kebabs for their own dinner or for a special occasion such as a birthday party or a sausage sizzle with friends.

What You Need

- *1 kg of cheerios (cocktail sausages)*
- *cherry tomatoes*
- *diced cucumber*
- *large can pineapple pieces*
- *can of baby corn cobs*
- *stuffed olives (if your children like them)*

MARINADE INGREDIENTS
- *1 tablespoon lemon juice*
- *1 tablespoon of brown sugar*
- *2 teaspoons of French mustard*
- *Reserved pineapple syrup*

What To Do

Make the marinade by combining the pineapple syrup, brown sugar, mustard and lemon juice in a saucepan. Bring the mixture to the boil and boil until it is reduced to a third.

The children can help by dicing the cucumber, cutting the cheerios in half and putting the other ingredients into dishes. Then they will have lots of fun threading their own kebab sticks. (If you soak the wooden skewers or kebab sticks overnight they will be less likely to burn on the grill or bar-b-que.) Use a pastry brush to brush their finished kebabs with the marinade mixture and baste some more as they are cooking. Any that are left are delicious cold in your children's school lunch boxes.

activity
75

CHOCCY BANANA ICEBLOCKS 2+

Children love bananas and they are very good for them. When you have a lot to use up, try this delicious recipe.

What You Need

- *Bananas*
- *Cooking chocolate*
- *Iceblock sticks*

What To Do

Your children can help by peeling the bananas and the older ones can cut the bananas in half across. Poke an iceblock stick into the end of each banana, then place them on a tray and freeze.

When they are frozen dip them in the melted chocolate. Enjoy!

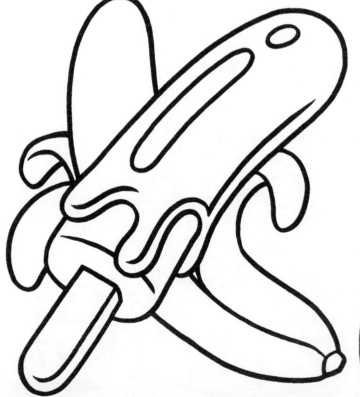

activity
76

CHOCOLATE CRACKLES

2+

A tasty treat to make with your children for special occasions.

What You Need

- *4 cups of Rice Bubbles*
- *3 tablespoons of cocoa*
- *1½ cups of icing sugar*
- *1 cup of coconut*
- *250 g of Copha*
  (solid coconut oil)

What To Do

You children will enjoy sifting the icing sugar into a large mixing bowl. Next they can measure and add the other dry ingredients. The can then mix these well. Meanwhile, melt the copha (solid coconut oil) gently in a saucepan and cool a little. Carefully pour the copha into the bowl of dry ingredients. Be careful that the children are safely away as you do this. When the mixture has cooled enough to handle they will love filling patty cases with the mixture. Cool on a tray in the refrigerator and enjoy!

activity
77

EGG FLIP

2+

Whenever my child is off his food, an egg flip is something I can always get into him. What's more, he likes to help me make it too!

 ✓

 ✓

What You Need

- *1 egg*
- *Sugar*
- *Vanilla essence*
- *Milk*
- *Nutmeg*
- *(Sometimes I add a banana also)*

✓

What To Do

Your children can help you collect all the ingredients and utensils, then they can break the egg into the bowl, add the vanilla and two teaspoons of sugar. Hold the bowl while they beat the mixture until it is frothy. Next, they pour in one cup of milk and then beat it again.

Help them pour the egg flip into a glass and sprinkle the top with a little nutmeg.

activity

78

FRENCH TOAST

A taste-tempting breakfast that is easy to cook together.

2+

 ✓

 ✓

 ✓

What You Need

Ingredients
- *1 egg*
- *1/2 cup of milk*
- *2 teaspoons butter*
- *4 slices of bread*
- *Honey, golden or maple syrup*

What To Do

Collect all the utensils and ingredients together. Help your children crack the egg and then they can beat it and add the milk. Mix well. Melt the butter in a fry pan and, when it is bubbling, dip two slices of bread in the egg and milk mixture and cook. Turn once.

Serve warm with honey, golden syrup or maple syrup. We like it with maple syrup best - a favourite Sunday morning breakfast in our house.

activity
79

FRUIT SMOOTHIES

2+

A great way to get fruit and milk into reluctant eaters.

 ✓

 ✓

What You Need

- *1/2 cup cold milk
  (children should always have full-cream milk)*
- *6 strawberries or 1 banana or any other fruit you may have that will blend well*

 ✓

- *1/4 cup flavoured yoghurt*

What To Do

Your children will enjoy helping you measure in all the ingredients. Blend well until nice and frothy. Pour into a tall glass, add a straw and watch it disappear! Makes enough for one serve.

activity
80

FUNNY EGG FACES

2+

Sometimes we have to resort to clever trickery to encourage our children to eat healthy food. Your children will love to help you make these funny egg faces and hopefully will enjoy eating them at the end.

 ✓

 ✓

 ✓

 ✓

What You Need

- *Boiled eggs*
- *Grated cheese, carrot or shredded lettuce for 'hair'*
- *Sultanas, pieces of tomato or beetroot for the facial features*
- *Mayonnaise or cream cheese for the adhesive*

What To Do

Help your children cut their egg in half and place the halves on a plate. They then use their imagination to make hair and facial features on their egg. Make a body with triangles or rectangles of buttered bread. Then they get to eat their creation!

Another alternative is to make a clown by cutting off the top of the egg and keeping it for the hat. Carefully scoop out the yolk and mix it with a little tomato sauce or perhaps some salmon and lemon juice, or mayonnaise. Pile the filling back into the egg and place the top back on to make the clown's hat. Tiny pieces of tomato or capsicum could make the face. Sit the clown on some shredded lettuce 'grass'.

activity

81

ALPHABET BISCUITS

4+

 ✓

 ✓

Help your young children learn their letters by making some Alphabet Biscuits together.

What You Need

- *1 cup of self raising flour*
- *1/2 tablespoon of cornflour*
- *1/3 cup butter or margarine*
- *1/4 cup castor sugar*
- *1 beaten egg*

 ✓

What To Do

Your children will be able to help with lots in this simple dough recipe. Begin by helping them sift the flour and cornflour into a mixing bowl. Next show them how to rub in the butter. Last of all they can help break the egg into a small bowl and beat it with a fork or whisk. Add the mixture with the sugar. Next lightly flour a board and with their hands they can knead the dough until it's pliable. Break it into small pieces and they can roll it into little sausages. Help them shape the dough sausages into the letters of their name. Perhaps they know how to spell some other words - Mum or Dad, or perhaps the names of their brothers or sisters. Ask if there are any other letters they would like to make and show them how to make them. 'Mum, can we make the letter that Bandy-dog's name starts with?', or 'Mum, what letter does Nanny start with, or Pa?'

Bake the letters in a moderate oven (180°C) (350°F) for about 20 minutes and cool on a rack. They are delicious plain or you might like to help the children ice them when they have cooled. Ours never last long enough to be iced! Makes about 12.

activity

82

BANANA DATE SQUARES

4+

A healthy snack your children will love helping you make, and all the family will love eating!

 ✓
 ✓

 ✓
 ✓

What You Need

- *3 bananas*
- *1/2 cup pecan nuts*
- *2 cups rolled oats*
- *1/2 teaspoon salt*
- *1 cup dates*
- *1/3 cup cooking oil*
- *1 teaspoon vanilla essence*

What To Do

Your children can help collect all the utensils and ingredients. Older children will also be able to chop the dates and pecans. Younger children can help with the measuring, pouring and mashing.

Your children can peel and mash the bananas in the bowl. Next add the chopped dates, nuts and oil and mix well. Add the vanilla, rolled oats and salt and again mix well. Let the mixture stand for 5 minutes so the oats absorb the moisture.

Push into a greased baking tray and bake for 25 minutes at 180°C (350°F).

Cut into squares while still warm. Very popular, but still healthy.

activity
83

BUTTER CHURNS

4+

Show your children how butter was made in the olden days with this simple butter churn.

 ✓

 ✓

What You Need

- *250 mls (1/2 pint) of pure whipping cream*
- *jar or plastic container with a secure lid*
- *1 marble*

 ✓

What To Do

✓

Pour the cream into the container and add the marble. Take turns with the children to shake the container (not too hard!). After about ten minutes the cream should have changed into butter. Taste the left-over butter milk. Compare the butter you have made with commercially made butter you have in the 'fridge. Can the children see and taste any difference? Explain how the butter was traditionally made into small pats and often printed with a simple design.

Make some bread and butter sandwiches with the butter you have made together.

activity
84

DOUGH SCULPTURES

4+

Make delicious dough creations that you and your children can really eat.

 ✓

 ✓

What You Need

 ✓

- 1 packet yeast
- 1 teaspoon salt
- 4 cups plain flour

- 300 mls (1/2 pint) warm water
- 1 tablespoon sugar
- 1 egg (beaten)

✓

✓

What To Do

Help your children measure the warm water and pour into a large bowl. They can then sprinkle on the yeast and stir it until it is soft.

Next, they can help measure and then add the salt, sugar and flour. Mix into a dough and form a ball.

Show your children how to knead the dough until it is smooth and pliable. They can then shape the dough into shapes, letters, animals and whatever takes their fancy. Put the shapes onto a greased baking tray and cover with a tea towel. Leave in a warm spot until they have risen to double in size.

Next, your children can 'paint' their shapes with the beaten egg and bake in a moderate oven for 10-15 minutes until the bread creations are golden brown.

They'll look almost too good to eat!

activity
85

GEOMETRIC SHAPE SANDWICHES

4+

 ✓

 ✓

Teach your young children their geometric shapes in a yummy edible way!

What You Need

- *Sliced bread*
- *Fillings such as egg and lettuce, cheese slices, ham, peanut butter and any other favourites* ✓

✓

What To Do

Your children will enjoy helping make the sandwich fillings. This is a great opportunity to introduce new taste sensations to them such as peanut butter and sultanas or avocado and sprouts.

After the sandwiches are made, help the children to carefully cut them into different shapes - triangles, rectangles, squares and use a scone cutter to make circles.

Take them outside on a rug in the garden with a large jug of juice and enjoy a shape picnic together.

activity

86

GINGERBREAD MEN

4+

Read or tell the story of the Gingerbread Man to your children and then make some together.

 ✓

 ✓

 ✓

 ✓

What You Need

- *1 cup of plain flour*
- *1/2 cup of sugar*
- *125 grams of butter (4$\frac{1}{2}$ ozs)*
- *1 egg*
- *1/2 teaspoon of baking soda*
- *2 teaspoons of ground ginger*
- *Mixed fruit for decoration*

What To Do

The children will love helping find all the necessary utensils and ingredients for the recipe and of course helping with the measuring.

Cream the sugar and butter, then add the egg and beat well. Let them help use the flour sifter to sift the flour and then add the baking soda and ginger.

Using a floured roller, roll out the gingerbread on a floured board. The children will love to help cut out the gingerbread men and then help lift them with a lifter onto a greased over tray.

Now for the fun stuff! Give them mixed fruit or even chocolate bits to decorate their gingerbread men. Perhaps a cherry nose, sultana eyes, some peel for the mouth and currant or chocolate buttons.

Cook the gingerbread men in a moderate oven for 15-20 minutes.

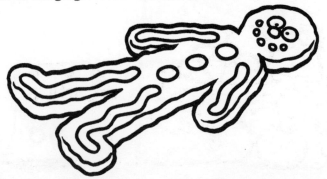

activity

87

HEALTHY APRICOT TREATS

4+

A tasty and easy recipe that's also healthy for them.

 ✓

What You Need

 ✓

- *1 cup of chopped dried apricots*
- *1/2 cup of orange juice*
- *4 tablespoons of honey*
- *1 cup of powdered milk*
- *1/2 cup of desiccated coconut*

 ✓

✓

✓

What To Do

Simmer the apricots, orange juice and the honey in a saucepan for about 10 minutes. Add the powdered milk to the mixture. Pour into a mixing bowl and mix well. Chill in the fridge until cool.

Later your children will enjoy rolling the mixture into balls and coating them with coconut.

Store in the 'fridge - but they won't last long. Makes about 24.

activity

88

HOME-MADE LEMONADE

4+

An easy drink recipe your children will enjoy making with you to share with the rest of the family.

What You Need

- 4 lemons
- 1/2 cup sugar or honey
- 1/2 cup of hot water
- 4 cups of cold water

- Ice cubes
- Lemon squeezer
- Large jug

What To Do

Ask your children to count out four lemons. Help them cut the lemons in half and they can then juice them with a juicer. (We have an electric juicer and my son loves making lemon and orange juice with it). Pour the juice into a large jug.

Your children can measure out the honey or sugar, but add the hot water to dissolve it yourself.

Next your children pour out and add to the jug the four cups of cold water. Add the honey or sugar solution and let them stir well.

Add some lemon slices and a tray of ice cubes for a decorative touch.

For a slightly fizzy lemonade you can substitute a bottle of spritzig mineral water or soda water for the plain cold water.

activity
89

HONEY AND ORANGE WHIP 4+

Make a delicious and healthy drink for the whole family on a hot day. This drink can also be poured into iceblock containers and frozen.

 ✓

 ✓

What You Need

- *1 dozen (12) oranges or a bottle of commercial orange juice and 3 oranges*
- *1/4 cup of honey*

✓

✓

What To Do

Cut the oranges and help your children squeeze them in a juicer to make six cups of orange juice. My four year old loves using our electric juicer to make orange juice for breakfast. Next peel the oranges and help them cut the oranges into segments, making sure you remove all the pips. Combine the orange juice, oranges, and honey and blend in a couple of batches until smooth.

This recipe makes about ten cups. Drink some now and freeze some for yummy good-for-them iceblocks later. Makes 4 glasses.

activity
90

JUNKET

4+

Junket is a yummy, healthy dessert that your young children will enjoy helping you make. We always loved it as children - try it with your own kids.

 ✓

 ✓

What You Need

- *1 junket tablet (Junket tablets are sold in packets in your supermarket)*
- *1½ cups of milk*
- *2 teaspoons of sugar*
- *food colouring*
- *nutmeg, coconut or sprinkles*

 ✓

 ✓

What To Do

Your children will enjoy watching the junket tablet dissolve in a teaspoon of water. Meanwhile, heat the milk in a saucepan - only until blood heat - the junket will not set if the milk is too hot. Stir the dissolved tablet into the milk. Your children can add a few drops of food colouring if they like. Pour the junket into serving bowls. Adults like nutmeg or coconut sprinkled on the top but my bet is the children will want colourful sprinkles or hundreds and thousands.

The junket needs a few hours in the 'fridge to become quite cold before serving. Makes four servings.

activity

91

PARFAITS

4+

 ✓

 ✓

 ✓

The whole family will love assembling (and eating) their delicious parfait desserts. They are traditionally made in tall parfait glasses but any long glasses will be fine. However, you will need spoons with long handles to reach all the delicious dessert at the bottom!

What You Need

- *A variety of fillings for the parfaits - the children can help prepare them*
- *Fruit - fruit salad works well or any tinned or fresh fruit chopped well*
- *Jelly - make up a jelly with the children in their favourite flavour*
- *Custard - make your own or buy a commercially made one*
- *Whipped cream*
- *Crushed nuts and wafer biscuits for the top*

What To Do

Set out the glasses and the fillings and let the family layer their own parfaits. They look great with contrasting layers of colour. Top with some toasted or crushed nuts and wafer triangles. They'll be coming back for more!

activity

92

PIKELET LETTERS

4+

 ✓

Cooking with children involves many learning areas - reading recipes together, following directions and measuring. As well making letter pikelets helps them learn the alphabet in a really fun way!

 ✓

What You Need

• *A basic pikelet recipe*

✓

What To Do

✓

Don't forget to involve your children in making the mixture - children always eat more if they have helped in the cooking process.

Make your pikelet batter in a jug for easy pouring. Carefully pour the batter into a hot greased pan in the shape of individual letters. Once the letters begin to bubble you can pour a little more batter onto the top of the letter to form traditional round pikelets and the letter section will stand out in relief when you turn it.

Otherwise just leave the letter shapes and turn them carefully. Your children will have great fun making their name as well as other words, and even more fun eating them!

activity

93

PIZZA

4+

A guaranteed culinary success with all the family.

 ✓

What You Need

 ✓

- *Pita bread or pizza bases*
- *Bacon*
- *Cheese*

- *Mild salami sausage*

 ✓

- *Tomato paste or pizza paste*
- *Vegetables such as zucchini (courgette), capsicum, mushrooms, onion, pineapple*

What To Do

Place the pizza base on a baking tray and your children can spread the tomato paste over it. Next, they grate the cheese and sprinkle that over the tomato paste.

Together, cut up the bacon and vegetables and sprinkle over the cheese.

Cook in a hot oven for 15-20 minutes.

activity

94

SESAME SNAPS

4+

A healthy, chewy snack that children adore.

 ✓

 ✓

What You Need

- 3/4 cup honey
- 1/2 cup sunflower seeds
- 1/2 cup skim milk powder
- 1 cup sesame seeds
- 1/2 cup shredded coconut

- Measuring cup
- Large saucepan
- Mixing spoon
- Flat dish or baking tray

✓

What To Do

Your children can help collect the ingredients and utensils needed for this recipe.

Bring the honey to the boil and then add all the other ingredients. Your children can help measure them, but you will have to do the pouring and mixing.

Pour the mixture into a flat dish and pop it into the 'fridge to set. When it's cold, slice into rectangles.

activity

95

SOUP FOR LUNCH

4+

Most children love soup and they will love this tasty, healthy soup even more because they have helped to make it. Bon appetit!

 ✓

 ✓

 ✓

✓

What You Need

• *Mixture of vegetables such as a carrot, a couple of celery stalks, a potato, peas in the pod, beans, a tomato, a parsnip and a zucchini (courgette)*
• *Bacon or ham pieces*
• *olive oil*
• *stock cube*
• *dry pasta*

• *vegetable peeler*
• *vegetable knife*
• *large soup pot*

What To Do

Involve your children as much as possible in preparing the soup, letting them peel the potato, scrape the carrot with the vegie peeler, shell the peas and so on.

Cook the bacon or ham in a little oil and your children will be able to then tip in the prepared vegetables carefully. Add some water, the stock cube and about 1/2 cup of dried pasta. Bring the soup to the boil and then let it simmer for about 30 minutes. Delicious served with crusty bread or toast fingers. Your children will enjoy the accolades of the whole family! Makes enough for 6.

activity

96

VEGETABLE TASTING

4+

Cooking together can help picky eaters develop an interest in food and try something new.

 ✓

 ✓

What You Need

- *Selection of raw vegetables*
- *Vegetable peeler*
- *Bowl of cold water*
- *Cutting board*

 ✓

What To Do

 ✓

Many parents complain that their young children won't eat vegetables but I have always found at preschool that they prefer raw vegies to cooked ones. Involve your young children in the shopping and preparation of a raw vegetable platter and I'm sure you will be surprised.

There is rarely a meal prepared at our home where my three year old is not standing on a chair beside me at the kitchen bench 'helping'. I am hoping that this early interest in food preparation will make him a better cook than his Dad!

Put your children up beside you and they can help wash the vegetables, peel cucumber and carrots and help break up vegetables such as cauliflower or broccoli. Older children can use a small sharp knife but always supervise carefully.

Vegetables can taste delicious on their own or even more interesting with a dipping sauce. Avocado Dip is usually popular, or just tomato or a mild soy sauce, mild sweet and sour or a packet of French Onion soup mixed with sour cream or yoghurt. Your child will be able to make up these simple sauces also.

Next time your children have friends to play help them make up a vegie platter and dipping sauce before the friends arrive and watch it disappear.

activity

97

CHEESEY BALLS

6+

A delicious, easy, savoury treat you can make with the children.

 ✓

 ✓

 ✓

 ✓

What You Need

- *1 tablespoon butter*
- *1½ cups of self raising flour*
- *1 cup instant oats*
- *1 cup milk*
- *1 cup of grated Cheddar cheese*

What To Do

Show the children how to rub the butter into the flour until it resembles crumbs. Next they can grate the cheese and add it to the flour and butter mixture. Then add the oats and milk and mix well. They'll enjoy rolling the mixture into small balls. Place them on a well greased scone tray and bake at 200°C (390°F) for 10-15 minutes until golden brown. Delicious warm but also great cold. Makes about 15.

activity
98

FRIED RICE

6+

A healthy tea to cook with your children that all the family will enjoy.

 ✓

 ✓

 ✓

 ✓

What You Need

- *1 1/2 cups rice*
- *Water*
- *1 onion*
- *2 eggs*
- *4 bacon rashers or ham*
- *Frozen peas*
- *Other vegetables the family likes: e.g. corn, capsicum, etc*
- *Soya sauce*
- *Oil for cooking*

What To Do

Bring about six cups of water to the boil and add the rice. When it is cooked, pour into a colander, let it drain and cool. Your children will be interested in the difference between a cooked and uncooked grain of rice.

Then they can help you chop up the onion, bacon and any other vegies you want to add.

Add some oil to a pan and cook the onion and bacon, then remove.

Let your children break the eggs carefully into a bowl and mix together with a fork. Pour into the fry pan and let it cook like an omelette. Cut into pieces and add the cooked rice, bacon, onion and the rest of the ingredients. Mix together and all enjoy.

I find my child (who is a fairly picky eater, like most three year olds) really enjoys eating the meals he has helped to prepare.

activity

99

JELLY FRUIT FLUMMERY

6+

I don't know where the word 'flummery' comes from but children love these delicious fluffy desserts, especially if they have helped make them.

 ✓

 ✓

 ✓

 ✓

What You Need

- *1 packet of jelly crystals in your children's favourite flavour*
- *1/2 cup of castor sugar*
- *1 egg*
- *1 cup of milk*
- *fruit - chopped bananas, pineapple or kiwi fruit or passionfruit pulp*

What To Do

Your children can help stir the jelly crystals in one cup of hot water to dissolve them thoroughly. Stand the jelly until it's cool but not set. Add one cup of cold water from the 'fridge. Let your children beat the egg with the sugar until nice and frothy and then add the milk. Help them cut up the fruit and add to the jelly mixture. Then add the beaten mixture, stirring thoroughly together. Put the jelly fruit flummery into a pretty bowl and put into the 'fridge to set. A favourite dessert for young and old at our place. Makes enough for six.

activity
100

MALTY BALLS

6+

A delicious and healthy snack to make together.

What You Need

- *1 cup skim milk powder*
- *1/2 cup powdered milk*
- *2 cups corn flakes*
- *1/2 cup sultanas*
- *1/4 cup coconut*
- *1 teaspoon carob or cocoa*
- *1/2 teaspoon vanilla*
- *Water or fruit juice to bind*

What To Do

Combine all the dry ingredients in a large bowl. Gradually add enough water or juice to combine.

Your children will enjoy rolling teaspoonfuls of the mixture in extra coconut. Keep them chilled.

Great for a picnic or a healthy snack at home.

activity
101

POTATO PRINTS

6+

Children of all ages love printing and you can use their colourful prints for wrapping paper.

 ✓

 ✓

✓

✓

✓

What You Need

- *potatoes*
- *small, sharp kitchen knife*
- *thin felt pen*
- *polystyrene trays*
- *paint made from food colouring and wall paper paste or commercial paint*
- *lots of newspaper*
- *paper or card*
- *kitchen sponges*

What To Do

Cut the potatoes in half and suggest to your children that they draw some simple designs with the thin felt pen on the potato halves. Next cut carefully around the shapes for them. Older children may be able to do this for themselves.

Put the kitchen sponges on the polystyrene trays and pour a little paint on each - a different colour on each one.

Put plenty of newspaper on a flat working surface and show them how to print by pushing down firmly on the sponge and then printing on their paper. If you have some cardboard, they could print some cards. Keep them for use in the future. The printed paper makes excellent wrapping paper and everyone will be impressed by the children's creativity.

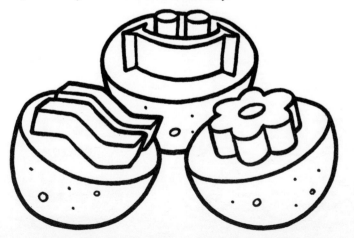

activity

102

CHRISTMAS RUM BALLS

8+
 ✓
 ✓

 ✓
 ✓

Make some Rum Balls with your children for the family or to give as gifts at Christmas time. Great for your children's teachers, the neighbours - our milkman even got some last year! Here's an easy but delicious recipe your older children can make on their own.

What You Need

- 9 breakfast cereal biscuits
- 2 dessertspoons cocoa
- 1/2 cup dessicated coconut
- 1/2 cup minced or finely chopped sultanas
- Extra coconut or chocolate hundreds & thousands for rolling
- 1 can condensed milk
- 2 tablespoons rum

What To Do

In a large bowl, your children crush the breakfast cereal biscuits with their hands or a rolling pin. Add all the other ingredients. The sultanas are best minced in a mincer (about the only time I use mine) or they can be finely chopped - you will have to help with this step.

Mix very well. Your children then roll teaspoonsful in their clean hands (make hand-washing a prerequisite for cooking). Then they roll the ball in the extra coconut or chocolate hundreds and thousands.

The Rum Balls make a decorative gift wrapped in cellophane and tied with Christmas ribbon.

activity
103

COCONUT MACAROONS

8+

Older children will love making these delicious biscuits and the whole family will love eating them.

 ✓

 ✓

What You Need

- *2 cups of desiccated coconut*
- *1 cup of castor sugar*
- *2 tablespoons of cornflour*
- *pinch of salt*
- *2 eggs*

✓

 ✓

What To Do

First your children measure all the dry ingredients into a mixing bowl. Next they beat the eggs well and add to the dry ingredients. Mix them together well. Grease your biscuit trays and cover with aluminium foil as macaroons tend to stick to the tray.

Place teaspoonfuls on to the trays, leaving room for the macaroons to spread.

Bake in a slow oven - 150ºC (300ºF) - for about 15 to 20 minutes.

Makes about 24.

activity
104

POTATO FRITTERS

8+

A favourite recipe from my childhood that your children will enjoy helping to make and eat!

 ✓

What You Need

 ✓

- *3 medium sized potatoes*
- *2 beaten eggs*
- *1/2 cup of plain flour*
- *1/2 teaspoonful of salt*

 ✓

 ✓

What To Do

Peel the potatoes and your children will enjoy grating them into a colander. Rinse and squeeze out the excess liquid. Next they will enjoy breaking the eggs into a mixing bowl and beating them with a fork or whisk. Add the potatoes to the eggs and then the flour and salt. Let the children mix them well. Shape into fritters. Add a small amount of cooking oil to a hot frypan and cook until golden brown. Makes 10-15.

activity

105

BAKED APPLES

10+

A lovely dessert your older children will enjoy making (with a little adult help) for the whole family. ✓

What You Need

 ✓

I'll give the quantities for one apple - it's a good maths lesson for your children to work out how much is needed for an apple per family member.

 ✓

- *1 Granny Smith cooking apple*
- *1 teaspoon of crushed nuts*
- *1/2 teaspoon sultanas*

- *1/2 teaspoon coconut*
- *1 tablespoon honey*

✓

What To Do

Wash the apple and carefully core it with an apple corer, making sure you don't make the hole go through to the other side or all the delicious filling will dribble out. Fill the centre with the crushed nuts, sultanas and coconut. (If you are making the apple for children under 5 it's best to leave out the crushed nuts in case they choke).

Next, your children can dribble the honey over the sides and into the centre of the apple. Bake the apples on a tray or in an oven-proof dish for about 45 minutes at 200°C (390°F).

Delicious served with ice-cream.

activity
106

SAUCY MEATLOAF

10+

Most children want to cook and, although it is often quicker to cook on your own, it is very important that you let them try. Think how great it will be when they are older and can take over and give you a night off! My sister and I used to love cooking on Sunday afternoons when our parents played tennis. When we were young we went with them but as older teenagers we often stayed home and cooked Sunday night dinner. Older children will be able to do most of this recipe on their own.

 ✓

 ✓

 ✓

✓

What You Need

- *500 g (1 lb) sausage mince* } *or use 1 kg (2 lbs) of minced*
- *500 (1 lb) minced steak* } *steak if preferred*
- *1 cup of fresh breadcrumbs*
- *2 onions, finely chopped*
- *2 teaspoons of curry powder*
- *salt and pepper*
- *1 egg*

- *1/2 cup of milk*
- *1/2 cup of water*
- *chopped parsley*
- *barbecue sauce*

What To Do

Heat the oven to moderate - 180°C (350°F) and grease a large loaf tin. Combine all the above ingredients in a mixing bowl except the milk and water and the barbecue sauce. When they are very well mixed add the milk and water and mix until smooth. Carefully spoon the mixture into the loaf tin and smooth down the top. Bake in the oven for 30 minutes. Remove and drain off any fat. (Parents will need to help with this part of the recipe). Invert the meat loaf onto the baking tray and cover with barbecue sauce. Bake for a further 45 minutes.

Delicious served with baked vegetables and greens. Makes enough for 6.

activity

107

HOME MADE MUSIC

BOTTLETOP TAMBOURINES

4+ ✓

 ✓

 ✓

 ✓

Children love percussion-type instruments and many of them are very easy to make. Make these simple tambourines with the children and start a home-made band.

 ✓

What You Need

- *Offcuts of pine*
- *Metal bottletops - beer bottletops are ideal*
- *Nails*
- *Hammer*

What To Do

The children will love helping you make these simple percussion instruments. Most timber yards or furniture manufacturers will let you have small offcuts of pine. Simply help the children hammer four to six bottle tops into each small piece of pine. Don't hammer the nails in all the way - leave some room for the bottle tops to shake around.

They can simply shake the wood in time to the music or bang it on their other hand to the beat.

Sing lots of songs you all know with strong beats - nursery rhymes are ideal or songs like 'Frere Jacques'.

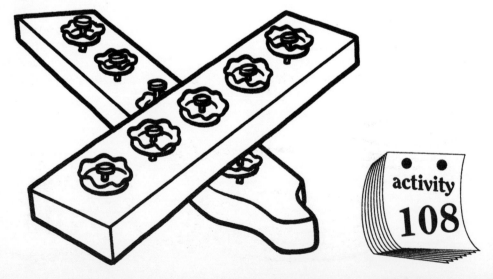

activity
108

DIFFERENT DRUMS

4+ ✓

 ✓

Make a variety of simple home-made drums for the children to play. Simple instruments will help develop your children's sense of rhythm.

 ✓

 ✓

What You Need

- *Containers - cardboard cylinders, tins, cardboard rolls from fabric shops*
- *A variety of 'skins' for the drums - plastic, thin rubber sheeting, greaseproof paper, wrapping paper and balloons*
- *Strong rubber bands*
- *Cord*

 ✓

What To Do

The children will love helping you make and decorate these simple drums.

Simply cover a variety of cardboard cylinders and tins with different 'skins' using the strong rubber bands to hold the skins on the drums.

To make some of the skins even tighter for higher sounds, you can dip paper in water first and stretch it on wet.

Show the children how to play the drums by tapping the skin with their fingers.

You can attach cord to the sides of the drums so they can wear them around their necks and be a marching band.

(One of the advantages of these home-made drums is that they are not noisy enough to have the neighbours up in arms!)

activity
109

MUSICAL JARS

4+

A simple way to make music together.

 ✓

 ✓

What You Need

 ✓

- *4-6 similar empty glass bottles (coffee jars are ideal)*
- *Metal spoons*

 ✓

What To Do

Leave one bottle empty, then fill the others with varying amounts of water, and fill one completely. Add a little food colouring to the water to make the water level easy to see.

Let your children experiment with the different sounds the bottles make by tapping them with the spoons. Arrange them in order so they can hear the notes go higher and lower.

After they have played for a while, ask them to close their eyes and listen carefully while you tap the bottles. Can they tell you which one is being tapped?

Later, they might like to tap (gently) other household items to hear the sounds they make.

activity
110

RICE MARACAS

4+

 ✓

 ✓

Children love making music. Make some simple rice maracas with them and they will love playing them and following the beat of their favourite songs.

 ✓

 ✓

 ✓

What You Need

- *Paper cups*
- *Felt pens*
- *Masking or insulating tape*
- *Uncooked rice*

What To Do

Fill a paper cup about half full of uncooked rice and then place an empty cup on the top. Your children can help hold them firmly and steadily in place while you join them together with tape. Now they can use their felt pens to decorate the maracas in bright colours.

Make a few with different amounts of rice in each one. For different sound effects you could use dried pasta, beans or split peas.

Shake out some different rhythms and see if they can copy them.

activity
111

SIMPLE GUITAR

4+

Help your children make a very simple guitar out of an old shoebox. It won't make the lovely sounds of a real guitar, but your children will enjoy strumming it just as much.

  ✓

  ✓

What You Need

  ✓

- *Shoebox with a lid*
- *Scissors*
- *6-8 rubber bands of different sizes (use thick ones that won't break easily)*

What To Do

Cut a hole in the lid of the shoebox about 8 cm (3½ ins) in diameter. Put the lid back on the shoebox and press down hard on the lid so the rubber bands won't actually touch it and deaden the sound.

Now stretch the rubber bands right around the box and position over the sound hole.

As your children pluck the rubber bands they will hear the different sounds.

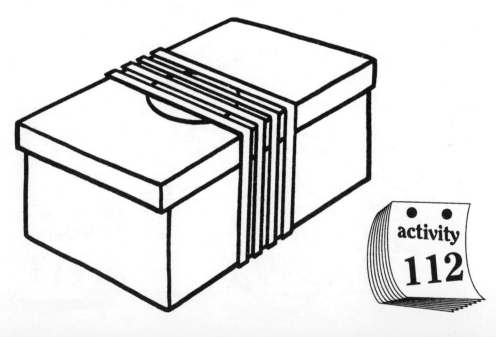

activity
112

COMB SYNTHESIZER

6+ ✓

Show your children how to make music with a comb and their lips!

 ✓

 ✓

What You Need

- *Comb*
- *Tissue paper*

✓

What To Do

Tell your children you are going to make a music synthesizer that does not need electricity. Wrap a few layers of tissue paper around a comb and hold it up to your lips and hum. See if your children can recognise the tune. Now it's their turn. Ask them if it tickles their lips! Make one for yourself and make a comb band.

activity
113

SOFT DRINK BOTTLE MUSIC 6+

Pre-schools and kindergartens have long been the best recyclers of junk. Plastic soft drink bottles have many uses - for storage, pouring in the water trough, for scoops in the sand pit and even for musical instruments. Save some and make a wind ensemble with your children.

What You Need

- *Plastic soft drink bottles*
- *Water*
- *Food colouring*

What To Do

Making music out of a plastic soft drink bottle is incredibly simple. Just hold it up to your lips and gently blow across the top of the empty bottle. You can vary the sounds by putting different amounts of coloured water into some of the bottles and making a whole range of sounds. Lots of cheap musical fun.

activity
114

INDOOR PLAY

BASH A BAG

2+ ✓

 ✓

Let your young children use up some energy and get rid of the 'Terrible Two's' aggression with this simple activity.

What You Need

• *A bag made of strong paper, plastic or fabric*
• *String*   • *Newspaper*   • *Wooden spoon* ✓

What To Do

Your two-year-olds will love helping you tear up the newspaper and roll it into balls to fill the punching bag. When it's full, tie it tightly with string and attach a string to hang it from a hook or doorway. (Make sure it will not hit anything precious.)

Your children will have a great time bashing away at the bag with a wooden spoon.

activity
115

BOX FUN

Lots of good fun, cheap creative play!

What You Need

- *Cardboard fruit boxes of all sizes*
- *Other props such as cardboard cylinders, broom handles, sheets, rugs*
- *Masking tape*

What To Do

On wet days when the children are driving you crazy, drive to your local fruit shop and they are usually happy to let you load up as many fruit boxes as you can fit in your car. Let the kids loose with the boxes and their imagination, and they will spend hours making tunnels, cubby houses, towers and other creations.

When they have lost interest in building cubby houses, save the boxes to make box cars or enlist their help to tidy up their toys and store some away in boxes for other rainy days.

activity

116

DETERGENT BOX BLOCKS

2+

Junk materials often make the best play toys for young children and, by recycling packaging, you are saving money and the environment.

 ✓

 ✓

 ✓

What You Need

 ✓

- *Square laundry detergent cartons*
- *Coloured or patterned Contact*

 ✓

What To Do

Many laundry detergents now come in block shaped cartons. They make ideal building blocks for your children. After wiping them out, tape the lid closed securely with masking tape and then cover with coloured or patterned *Contact*. (*Contact* can be bought by the metre from most hardware stores.)

Store the blocks neatly in the largest basket you can buy and add to the supply as you wash! My son uses his for building towers, making cities to go with his train set, making castles and other myriad uses.

Challenge your children to a competition to see who can build the highest tower before it falls down. If you have toddlers they will love it if your older children build towers for them to knock down!

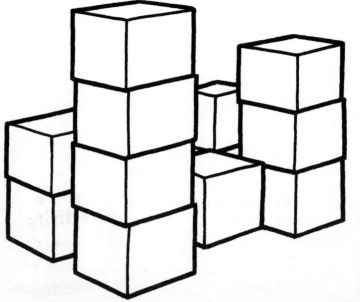

activity

117

DRESS-UPS

2+

Dressing up is an important part of young children's play. It is the way they practise for life. Provide a variety of dressing up clothes for them and they will play happily for hours acting out the family roles and relationships they see around them.

 ✓
 ✓
 ✓
 ✓
 ✓

What You Need

- *Cardboard box*
- *Glue*
- *Variety of dressing up clothes and props*
- *Scissors*
- *Old magazines*

What To Do

Your children can help decorate a cardboard box to hold the dressing up things. They can cut out magazine pictures and 'collage' them all over the box until it is totally covered. While they are busy doing this, collect the clothes and props to put in it.

Talk to the family; older relatives may have hats, wigs and beads to donate. Sometimes a visit to an opportunity shop can yield wonderful dressing up clothes for little expense. When choosing accessories and clothes make sure they can be put on easily and worn safely. You may have to take up hems, thread elastic through waistbands to make them smaller, and perhaps even replace tiny buttons and fasteners with velcro. This way, their dressing up play need not always involve an adult.

The dressing up collection might include - necklaces, bangles, clip on earrings, shorts and T-shirts, coats, trousers, ties, belts, dresses and skirts (the frillier the better), lacy nighties and petticoats, stockings or tights, shoes and boots, handbags, purses and wallets, scarves, shawls and glasses (without the lenses).

If you can sew you might like to sew some special dressing up clothes; look in the pattern books for dressing up clothes suitable for young children.

Birthday or Christmas gifts might include a special dressing up outfit such as a fairy costume, Bananas in Pyjamas, Batman or pirate gear.

Extend your children's imagination with dress-up clothes.

activity
118

KITCHEN PLAY

2+

As well as helping you in the kitchen with simple tasks, older toddlers love playing make-believe with some of your kitchen gadgets!

What You Need

- *Unbreakable bowls, spoons, ladles, baking trays, muffin tins, measuring spoons, plastic jugs and cups*
- *Playdough or water*
- *Large plastic sheet or plastic tablecloth*

What To Do

On a hot day your children will love 'cooking' outside with water - measuring, stirring, pouring and mixing. Add a few drops of food colour to the water and they will think it's great!

On cooler days, spread the plastic sheeting down, give the children some playdough and the kitchen items and they will 'cook' happily for ages. A cardboard carton turned on its side makes a great pretend stove. Draw some 'hotplates' on the top with a felt pen and put a biscuit rack inside for the oven shelves.

activity
119

SILLY WALKING

2+

This has been a favourite bedtime routine with our young child for some time.

 ✓

 ✓

What You Need

• *Time!*

What To Do

Bedtime routines vary in all families, but 'funny walking' is one we use that I thought I would share with you. If you bring routines into bedtime, it often makes putting young children down for the night easier.

When it's bedtime my child and I take it in turns to be the leader for 'silly walking'. As we go through the house playing 'follow the leader' he gets ready for bed - a small drink of water stop in the kitchen, a kiss for Dad in the lounge, toilet stop and then brushing teeth stop in the bathroom. Then he happily snuggles down for a bedtime story and kiss goodnight.

activity
120

SURPRISE BAGS

2+

There are many times when you will have to keep your young children amused and quiet, in an aeroplane or train, visiting someone in hospital, or perhaps just in a waiting room. Surprise bags are great for times like these.

What You Need

• *Fabric bag* • *Interesting things to put inside it*

What To Do

Make or buy a fabric bag to hold the surprises. Collect things as you see them and have a bag ready to take with you when you need it in a hurry.

Some suggestions for things to put in the bag are:

• A new paperback book to read together
• Notebook or scribbling block
• Packet of coloured pipe cleaners
• Large wooden beads and plastic thread for threading
• Peggi-beads and board for building towers
• A new jigsaw puzzle stored in a plastic bag
• Threading cards
• Finger puppet
• Magnifying glass
• New small toy or car
• Unbreakable mirror

activity
121

WET DAY OBSTACLE COURSE 2+

Going through an obstacle course helps develop body co-ordination, control and balance.

 ✓
 ✓

 ✓

What You Need

- *Furniture*
- *Pillows*
- *Towels*
- *Balloons*
- *Household items*

What To Do

On wet days when the kids are going 'stir crazy' why don't you set up an indoor obstacle course. (Make sure precious ornaments are safely out of the way first!)

Some ideas:-

- Crawling through the legs of the dining room chairs
- Under a coffee table (watch those heads)
- Tie a cord between two chairs to slide under on their tummies
- Make a tunnel out of chairs, cushions and a rug
- Play leap frog, stepping from towel to towel (only on carpet so they don't slip)
- Tie some balloons under a table and crawl through without moving any
- Roll up some towels and make a long 'balance beam'

For the older children (or when your children need new challenges) let them try the course balancing a bean bag on their heads, or do it holding a sock in each hand.

Time them to see who completed the course in the shortest time. Graph the results together.

Your children will enjoy altering the course but make sure you emphasize the safety aspect and check their alterations.

activity

122

ANIMAL SHADOWS

4+

  ✓

Lots of fun and great for the developing imagination of your children.

 ✓

What You Need

• *Lamp*
• *Hands*

What To Do

 ✓

Shine a light on to a wall in your children's darkened room. Try and make as many different sorts of animal shadows on the wall with your hands as you can. Start with simple ones and see if you and your children can create some more, or try some of the ones listed below.

For children who are frightened of the shadows and who often think they 'see' strange things in a room at night, this game might make them less afraid of the dark.

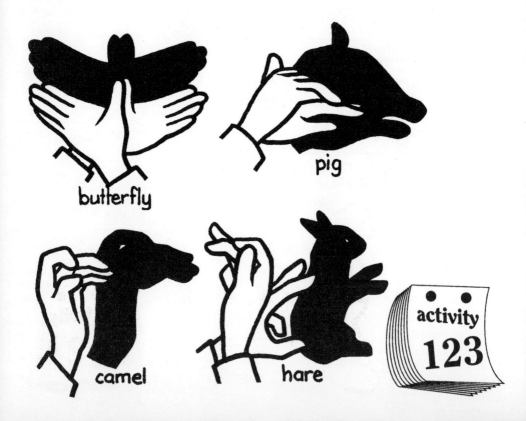

butterfly

pig

camel

hare

activity
123

BALLOON BOUNCING

4+

An activity to help your children learn their body parts and gain mastery of them.

 ✓

 ✓

What You Need

• *A blown-up balloon*

What To Do

 ✓

 ✓

Encourage your children to toss the balloon in the air and stop it touching the floor. Count together and see how many times they can tap it before it comes down.

Encourage them to keep it up using other parts of their body - head, elbows, knees, feet, back etc.

Challenge your children further by seeing if they can:-

• Keep two balloons up at once
• Lie on the floor and keep the balloon up with their feet
• Hop on one foot and use their knee to bounce the balloon
• Jump around holding the balloon between their knees

activity
124

CLOTHES PEG RACES

4+

A great finger motor pre-writing game to play with your children.

 ✓

What You Need

 ✓

• *Two players*
• *10 pegs each in two containers*
• *A clothes airer or clothes line strung between two chairs*

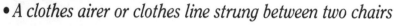

What To Do

Each player has a container with ten pegs. When you say 'go' they have to clip their pegs onto the line. They can only use one hand (the other hand stays behind their back).

If you have lots of children, you can divide them into two teams for this game and one players puts the pegs on and the next takes them off.

Lots of fun and a great activity to develop finger muscles ready for writing.

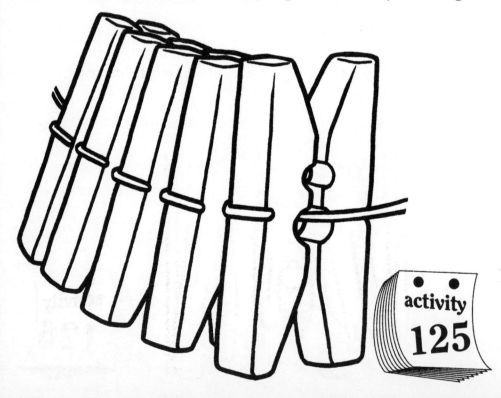

activity
125

CURTAIN PUPPET THEATRE 4+

Make a simple puppet theatre and your children will love putting on their own 'productions' with the home-made puppets they have been making.

What You Need

- *Calico or other cheap white fabric*
- *Hooks*
- *Stretch wire*
- *Your sewing maching*
- *Acrylic or fabric paints*

What To Do

To calculate the width of the puppet theatre, measure the width of your children's bedroom doorway and double it. For the height, have your children kneel in the doorway. Measure just above their heads so they'll be hidden and add enough for a hem at the top and bottom.

Sew up the curtain and thread the stretch wire through the top and attach to a hook on either side of your children's bedroom doorway.

I am sure they will want to decorate the puppet theatre with acrylic paints or fabric paints but take it down again to do it outside.

When it's dry, hang it up and 'on with the show'. When not in use, roll it up and store it in the wardrobe.

activity
126

DRESSING FAST

4+

Give your children practice in dressing themselves with this game. It's fun to do on their own, but even more fun to do if they have a friend over to play.

 ✓

 ✓

What You Need

• *Dressing-up clothes - Mum and Dad's old clothes work well for this game*

 ✓

What To Do

Give each child a pile of similar clothes - maybe a shirt, pair of long pants, socks and a hat each. Say 'go' and they must run to their pile of clothes, put them on over their own clothes, and do up all the buttons and fasteners. Then they run back to you.

Don't forget to have a camera handy! This game is lots of fun at birthday parties, as well as being terrific practice for doing up buttons, clips and zips.

If you are playing it with your children on their own, they can try to beat the clock, or use an egg timer.

activity
127

FOOTPRINTS

4+

A fun way to help teach your children right and left.

 ✓
 ✓
 ✓
 ✓
 ✓

What You Need

• *Cardboard* • *Pens* • *Scissors*

What To Do

Draw around your children's left foot and cut it out. Use this shape as a template and make at least ten more. Do the same with their right foot. Give them cutting practice by letting them help you cut out the shapes.

Blu-Tack the feet in a walking pattern around the house and your children have to follow them.

Sometimes it could be a treasure hunt with a surprise at the end!

Vary the difficulty by making the footprints further apart, or perhaps a hopping section.

activity

128

FUNNY FEET

4+

Make some 'Funny Feet' with your children for them to wear and add to their dressing-up box. Watch the imaginative games begin.

 ✓

 ✓

 ✓

What You Need

- *Egg cartons*
- *Strong cardboard*
- *Rubber gloves*
- *Pair of Dad's old socks*

✓

✓

 ✓

What To Do

You can make a variety of 'Funny Feet' or just one pair.

Cut two egg cartons in half and use the top halves to make some claw feet. Cut the tops in half again and cut triangular shapes around the sides (see below) so they look like claws. Your children can attach them to their feet (or hands) with rubber bands. Hey presto! Instant tigers!

Wearing old rubber washing up gloves on the ends of their feet, they can be a platypus, seal or a duck.

Make clown or 'big' feet by wearing a pair of Dad's old socks with some strong cardboard inside.

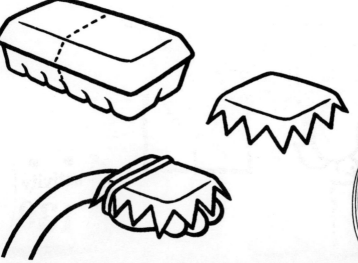

activity
129

NEWSPAPER WALK

4+

A good inside game to play with the whole family. (But don't play on the carpet or the newsprint may mark it!)

 ✓

 ✓

What You Need

- *2 or more players*
- *2 sheets of newspaper per player*

✓

What To Do

Mark out a starting and finishing line. Each player stands on the starting line with their two pieces of paper in front of them. When you say 'Go', the players must get to the finishing line without touching the floor. To do this they must walk on one piece of paper and then put the other piece in front of them. They then pick up the first piece, place that down in front and then walk on that.

The first player to reach the finishing line by only walking on their newspaper sheets is the winner. The children love watching Mum and Dad have a go at this too, so go on, be a good sport and give them a laugh. Think how good all the bending is for the waistline!

activity
130

PLAYING SHOPS

4+

Solve the problem of wet day boredom by helping your children set up a 'pretend shop'.

 ✓

 ✓

What You Need

 ✓

- *Large cardboard cartons or child size table*
- *Coins • Crayons • Paper • Scissors*
- *Items for the shop*
- *Props such as plastic bags, a toy cash register or a plastic shopping trolley*

 ✓

What To Do

Help your children make a shop with cardboard cartons or a table. Raid the pantry together for tins and packets they can borrow for the shop.

To make money, Blue-Tack some coins to the table, place a piece of paper over them and show them how to rub over the coins with a crayon to get the coin rubbings. Help the children cut them out. If they have a toy cash register they can use that for the shop, otherwise help them find a container for the takings.

Make a shopping list and visit their shop - they'll love serving Mum!

activity

131

EASTER EGGS

6+

 ✓

 ✓

Eggs are traditionally associated with our Easter celebrations. Decorate some eggs with your children and serve coloured boiled eggs for breakfast on Easter Sunday.

What You Need

- *Eggs*
- *Food dyes*
- *Birthday cake candles*
- *Masking tape*

What To Do

Make up strong solutions of red, yellow and blue food dyes. (White eggs dye best so try and find a carton at a supermarket with lots of white eggs.)

Boil the eggs for at least ten minutes. Hard boiled eggs are best to use with younger children and will last as decorations for the Easter period out of the 'fridge, (unless you live in the tropics). However with older children you can use blown eggs which of course, while more fragile to work with, will last much longer.

To blow eggs use a large tapestry or darning needle and make holes at both ends - larger at one end than the other. Use the needle to carefully pierce the yolk sac a few times. Blow from the smaller hole end making sure you get all the egg out of the shell or later the egg will smell. Save the egg for scrambled eggs, omelette or other cooking. Blown eggs must be decorated before blowing.

To decorate, give your children a thin birthday cake candle to draw interesting designs on the egg. If you want to have multicoloured eggs, wraps sections of the egg with masking tape. Then use a spoon to dip the egg in the food dyes. Remove the masking tape gradually and you will end up with multi-coloured eggs.

activity

132

INDOOR HOCKEY

6+

Hockey is becoming a very popular sport in our schools. Show your children how to play this simple table-top variety - great for bored kids on wet days.

 ✓

 ✓

 ✓

What You Need

 ✓

- *Table-top*
- *Books*
- *Iceblock sticks*
- *Paper*
- *Masking tape*

 ✓

 ✓

What To Do

On a large table position thick books all around the edges to form the sides of the hockey field. Leave a space at each end to be the goal to shoot through. Each player has an iceblock stick for a hockey stick. To make the ball, roll a piece of paper into a ball shape and wrap masking tape around it to secure it. Let the game begin.

The players stand at each end behind their opponent's goal and take it in turn to shoot the 'ball' towards their goal. Stay around because, like most family games, an umpire is often needed!

activity

133

MARBLE BOWLS

6+

Make a bowling alley for your children's marbles with them. A good game to play before bedtime or on wet days.

 ✓

 ✓

What You Need

- *A box - a shoebox is ideal, or a cereal box will do*
- *Scissors*   • *Marker*
- *Paper*   • *Marbles*

 ✓

What To Do

Cut arches out of the bottom of the box for the marbles to roll into. Above each arch mark the score. Mark a spot on the floor for the players to roll from.

The competitors take it in turn to roll six marbles towards the box. If a marble goes through an arch, the player earns that number of points.

Appoint a score-keeper (parents are great at this) so there will be no arguments. The first player to reach a certain score - perhaps 50 or 100 - is the winner or, if it's before bedtime, the player with the highest score at bedtime!

activity
134

PING PONG BLOW

This was a favourite game of my sister and I when we were younger. Like many families, we had a table-tennis table set up under the house and we both loved playing it. But we also loved this simple game of blowing the table tennis ball.

What You Need

- *A ping pong ball*
- *A large flat surface - a table is ideal*

What To Do

This game is almost incredibly simple and yet it will keep children occupied for hours. One child is at one end and another child at the opposite end. They take it in turns to blow the ball to the opposite end (or side of the table for younger players without so much puff!). If you can blow your ball past your opponent, you score a point. You cannot touch the ball with your hands - you must only blow to keep it from going over the end of the table.

Lots of simple fun and a great inside game on wet, boring days.

activity
135

COIN SPINNING

8+

I am indebted to my mother-in-law for this activity. She and her brothers and sisters loved playing this when they were children.

 ✓

 ✓

What You Need

• *Coins*   • *Pins*

 ✓

What To Do

Carefully hold the coin between two pins, exactly opposite each other, and gently blow on the coin to make it spin. See who can make their coin spin the fastest. When they have mastered the trick see if they can do it with other coins.

Make sure that the pins are put away safely when this activity is over and keep them out of the reach of younger children.

activity
136

COLLECTIONS

8+

Being a collector will help your children develop organisational skills and scrounging abilities.

What You Need

- *Try to encourage your children to collect more unusual items than football or basketball cards.*
- *Some things your child might like to collect:-*

Autographs	Shells	Rubbers
Badges	Keys	Drink coasters
Beads	Labels	Stamps
Book marks	Marbles	Stickers
Bottle tops	Match boxes	Matchbox cars
Crystals	Corals	Bus or train tickets
Buttons	Pencils	Dolls
Cards (greeting)	Postcards	Dolls clothes
Coins	Rocks	Tazos

What To Do

The most difficult part of any collection is finding the best way to store it.

Photo albums are great for storing items like bus tickets, postcards, labels and cards. Badges can be pinned on bedroom curtains, and a cork notice board in your children's room can display lots of items also. Large clear bowls (fish bowls or tanks are ideal) can hold other collections.

Encourage your children to be selective collectors - keeping double-ups for swapping with their mates or other collectors.

If you have a computer at home and are linked into the Internet, this is a great way to meet up with other collectors for swaps.

activity
137

PLAITING

8+

Many children have never learnt to master this interesting skill. Learning to plait will help develop your children's manual dexterity.

 ✓

 ✓

What You Need

• *Lengths of heavy wool, thin rope or twine or long strands of interesting fabric*

 ✓

What To Do

 ✓

Tie together three equal lengths of the plaiting material. It's a good idea when your children are learning to use three different colours to make it easier for them. Attach the plaiting material to the back of a chair or a door knob and separate the strands so there is a left, a centre and a right strand.

The left hand strand goes over the centre one and then the right hand strand goes over the new centre one, the original left strand and so on. Continue plaiting, left to the centre, right to the centre. Tie off when the plait is finished.

If your children are really 'into' this activity they could plait lots of lengths of fabrics (great way to empty the rag box) and later you can help them sew them together to make an old-fashioned rag mat to put beside their bed or use as a bath mat.

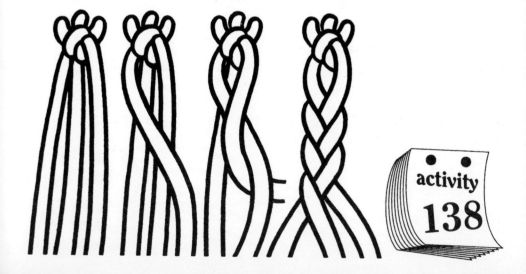

activity
138

SECRET MESSAGES

8+

Children love intrigue and mystery and writing secret messages to their best friend (so brothers and sisters can't read them) will become a favourite activity.

 ✓

What You Need

- *Paper*
- *Watercolour paint*
- *Cotton buds*
- *Birthday cake candles*
- *Lemon juice*

 ✓

 ✓

 ✓

What To Do

There are two ways to write secret messages. The simplest way is to write on a piece of white paper with a candle. When your children's friends want to read the message, they paint over the paper with a wash of water colour paint.

The other method is to write the message with lemon juice using a cotton bud. When it's dry, dip the paper in water and the message can be read.

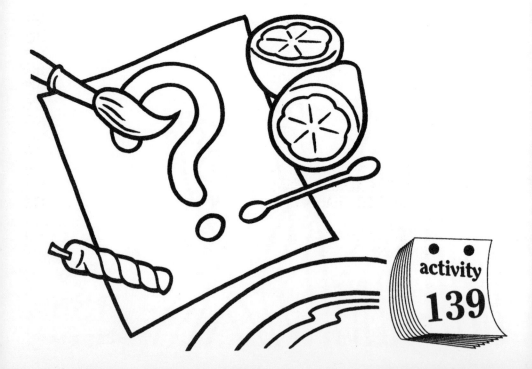

activity
139

LANGUAGE AND LITERACY

BAA BAA BLACK SHEEP 2+

Teaching young children lots of Nursery Rhymes helps improve their language and memory, and develops important rhythmic patterns.

What You Need

• *Time together*

What To Do

If you cannot remember the words of Baa Baa Black Sheep, they go like this:

Baa Baa black sheep
Have you any wool?
Yes sir, yes sir, three bags full.
One for the master and one for the dame
And one for the little boy
Who lives down the lane.

Teach them the next verse too:

Moo Moo Jersey cow
Have you any milk?
Yes sir, yes sir, three buckets full.
One for the master and one for the cat
And one for the little boy
Who wants to get fat.

Talk about wool together, how it is shorn off the sheep and what happens next. Find a woollen garment or blanket for your children to feel.

activity
140

HUMPTY DUMPTY

2+

Teach your young children lots of Nursery Rhymes. This will help develop not only their language but also their memory and sense of rhythm.

 ✓

 ✓

What You Need

• *Eggs, etc.*

What To Do

 ✓

If you cannot remember it, Humpty Dumpty goes like this:
Humpty Dumpty sat on a wall
Humpty Dumpty had a great fall
All the King's horses and all the King's men
Couldn't put Humpty together again.

There are some other funny ends you can use.
Two of my favourites are:
Humpty Dumpty sat on a wall
Humpty Dumpty had a great fall
All the King's horses and all the King's men
Had bacon and eggs for breakfast again.
Or:
Humpty Dumpty sat on a wall
Humpty Dumpty had a great fall
All the King's horses and all the King's men
Said 'Oh, not scrambled eggs for dinner again'.

After your children have learnt the rhyme, why not make scrambled eggs together for dinner. They will love beating the eggs, adding the milk and buttering the toast. My family loves grated cheese in our scrambled eggs, so your children can help grate the cheese too. Later, carefully wash up the egg shells, roll them with a rolling pin to break them into small pieces and help your children make an egg shell collage picture of Humpty Dumpty.

Or have boiled eggs for tea, then carefully wash the empty shells out and fill them with cotton wool Help your children to pour enough water onto the cotton wool to make it damp. Place the egg in an egg cup and together draw on Humpty's face with felt pens. Sprinkle the top with bird or grass seed, water regularly, and in time Humpty will grow a magnificent head of hair.

activity
141

'I HAD A LITTLE NUT TREE'   2+

When you teach young children Nursery Rhymes, you are building their foundations of literacy.

What You Need

• *Time together*

What To Do

If you cannot remember the rhyme, it goes like this. If you can remember the tune, sing it to your children too.

> I had a little nut tree
> Nothing would it bear
> But a silver nutmeg and a golden pear
> The King of Spain's daughter came to visit me
> 'Twas all for the sake of my little nut tree.

Macadamia nut trees are very easy to grow and are not only a most attractive small tree, but a useful culinary addition to your garden. If you live in a colder climate go to your local plant nursery and find out what sort of nut tree you could grow - chestnuts are wonderful trees to plant too. Make this your children's special tree and their responsibility to help water and care for it.

By the time the tree is big enough to bear, they will be old enough to help crack the nuts with a hammer or nutcracker or the vice in Dad's workshop.

activity
142

JACK AND JILL

2+

When you teach your children Nursery Rhymes you help develop not only their language, but also their memory and sense of rhythm.

What You Need

• *Time together*

What To Do

If you cannot remember the Nursery Rhyme, it goes like this:

> Jack and Jill went up the hill
> To fetch a pail of water
> Jack fell down and broke his crown
> And Jill came tumbling after.
>
> Up Jack got and said to Jill,
> As in his arms he caught her,
> You're not hurt, brush off the dirt,
> And now we'll fetch the water.

On a hot day, fill a large bucket with water in the garden. Your children will love pretending it is the well and filling lots of smaller buckets and containers from it. Give them some small stones, too, and they can improve their throwing skills by throwing them in the 'Wishing Well'.

Don't forget to always supervise water activities well!!

activity

143

LITTLE MISS MUFFET

2+ ✓

When you teach your young children Nursery Rhymes, you are helping to develop their language, memory and sense of rhythm.

 ✓

 ✓

What You Need

• *Time together*

What To Do

 ✓

If you cannot remember the Nursery Rhyme, it goes like this:

> Little Miss Muffet sat on a tuffet
> Eating her curds and whey,
> There came a big spider who sat down beside her
> And frightened Miss Muffet away.

Today's name for Curds and Whey is Junket. See 'Junket' (Activity No 91) in the book and make some together with your children.

Go for a walk in the garden together early in the morning and see if you can find some spiders' webs. They look beautiful sparkling in the early morning light with dew from the night on them. Keep watching them for a few days and see what the spider is going to have for his dinner!

activity
144

READ READ READ

2+

Young children love books and, as teachers, we know that children who have had lots of stories and books read to them at home are more likely to become good readers. They know what books are for and they want to learn to read for themselves.

 ✓
 ✓

 ✓
 ✓

What You Need

- *Time with your children*
- *Books*

What To Do

Make a special time each day to read to your children. My time with our four year old is before rest time in the afternoon and before bedtime at night, but any time is fine. It's nice to snuggle up together and enjoy some good stories. If you don't already belong, join your local council library. Going to the library was a tradition my parents started with me and I have continued with my child. He loves choosing books - last week he took out eleven and he would love me to read them all every day!

Books make great gifts and, as children get older, Gift Vouchers to bookshops make great presents as they can choose books that they specially want to read. Make reading together a part of every day with your children - no matter how old they are!

activity
145

COPY THE PATTERN

4+

Copying and recognising a pattern is an early reading skill. Children who have difficulty naming and matching colours often have difficulty learning to read. Provide lots of activities like this for your four and five year olds and read to them lots and you will make learning to read easier for them.

 ✓

 ✓

 ✓

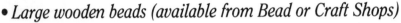

What You Need

 ✓

- *Large wooden beads (available from Bead or Craft Shops)*
- *Plastic threading string or long shoe laces (available from Craft Shops)*
- *White cardboard • Felt pens • Clear Contact*

What To Do

Work out some simple patterns with the beads - two long yellow beads, one round red bead, two long yellow beads and so on. Or perhaps three square blue beads, two long green beads and one small round brown bead, and then repeat. Copy the patterns onto pieces of the cardboard and then contact to make them last longer.

See if your children can copy the bead pattern card by threading the beads onto the strings. Make sure your children understand to copy the pattern from left to right - the same progression as reading. Can your children name all the bead colours and tell you what shapes the beads are? Can they continue the pattern.

Later, see if your children have gained an understanding of patterning by seeing if they can create their own patterns. Perhaps they could make some for you to copy.

activity

146

DROP THE PENNY

4+

A listening game to play with your children.

What You Need

- *Large glass jar*
- *Small items made from different materials to drop into the jar, for example: coins, comb, dice, pencil, plastic clothes peg, safety pin, marble, sinker*

What To Do

Show your children the small objects and let them listen while you drop them, one by one, into the bottle.

Then put a blindfold on them and drop the items in again, one by one, to see if they can tell you what has been dropped.

This activity is harder that it sounds - have a turn yourself and see how good your listening skills are.

activity 147

FAVOURITE STORY TAPES

4+

If your children have a favourite story that they want to read time and time again, turn it into a fun activity together and suggest you record the story on a tape so they can listen to it themselves.

 ✓

 ✓

What You Need

- *Cassette player that young children can use*
- *Blank cassette tape*
- *Story book*

 ✓

 ✓

What To Do

Suggest to your children that they might like to have their own special recording of their favourite story. Find a bell to use to indicate when it is time to turn the page. If there are any sound effects that could be added, experiment with these. Your children will love adding the sound effects. They could also ring the bell when it is time to turn the page.

When the taping is completed, play it back, and you will have a big laugh hearing the results.

Perhaps you could also tape some nursery rhymes or fairy tales for your children to listen to.

Nothing replaces reading books with your children and having a nice cuddle together, but good listening skills are essential for school and this activity will help develop your children's listening skills in a fun way.

activity

148

GO-TOGETHERS

4+

 ✓

An activity to help develop your children's thinking and language skills.

 ✓

 ✓

What You Need

 ✓

- *Objects that go together:*
cup and saucer	*pencil and rubber*
pen and lid	*knife and fork*
toothbrush and toothpaste	*hair brush and comb*
needle and cotton	*key and lock*
hammer and nail	*shoe and sock*

What To Do

Explain the object of the game to your children then put half the objects on a tray for your children to see. Place the other half of the 'go-togethers' in a pillowcase.

Your children have to reach in, feel an object, guess what it is and then say what it goes with.

'It feels like a sock and it goes with the shoe.'

activity
149

HICKORY DICKORY DOCK

4+

 ✓

 ✓

 ✓

 ✓

 ✓

When you teach your young children nursery rhymes, you are developing their language and listening skills as well as improving their memory and sense of rhythm.

What You Need

- *Time together*
- *Cardboard*
- *Marking pen*
- *Scissors*
- *Split pins*

What To Do

If you cannot remember Hickory Dickory Dock, it goes like this:

> Hickory Dickory Dock
> The mouse ran up the clock
> The clock struck one
> The mouse ran down
> Hickory Dickory Dock
> Tick! Tock!

Make a simple clock face and large and small hands out of the cardboard. Attach them with the split pin. Mark the hours on the clock and begin to show your children important times during the day - this is when we have breakfast, this is when Daddy leaves for work, this is when we go to Playgroup and so on.

They won't learn to tell the time until they're older, but activities like this will help their understanding of how time passes.

activity

150

'I SPY'

4+ ✓
 ✓

A good observation game that can be adapted for various age groups.

What You Need

• *At least 2 players*

What To Do

You can play this game anywhere with your children as it is a great boredom alleviator. Think of something you can see around you (if you are playing it in the car, it obviously can't be something that flashed past 5 kms (3 miles) back!).

Say 'I spy with my little eye something begining with "??" ' (whatever letter)?

For non spellers use a colour or a shape:

'I spy with my little eye something that's red or something that's round'.

For beginner readers, it may help to use the letter pronunciation, e.g. something with 'dee' (the letter D).

If your children can't guess the answer, give them clues.

With older children, increase the difficulty by using lots of words:
  'A T S I T C'
  (e.g. 'Anna's teddy sitting in the chair').

An oldie,
but a goldie!! !

activity
151

NURSERY RHYME RHYTHMS

4+

Listening to rhythms in rhymes and songs is a great activity for your children.

What You Need

• *Time*

What To Do

Clap out a nursery rhyme your children know well. If they cannot identify it after a few turns, give them some clues, for example: 'It's about two children going up a hill' or 'Its about a little girl who was frightened by something'.

When they guess correctly, they can clap one out for you to guess. A great game to play in the car on long family trips.

activity
152

ALPHABET SPOTTING

6+

A good game to play together when you are driving in the car or just a thinking game to play at home.

What You Need

- *Clipboard with paper*
- *Pen or pencil*

What To Do

Before you start out on a long drive, help your children write the alphabet down the side of the paper.

As you drive along, first look for something beginning with A, write it down, then B, then C and so on. Your children can be the scribes but help them with any difficult spelling. If you want to make a competition out of it, your children can write beside each word who spotted the item.

If you are playing it at home, make it more difficult by thinking of categories, e.g. animals, foods, clothing, etc. that begin with different letters of the alphabet.

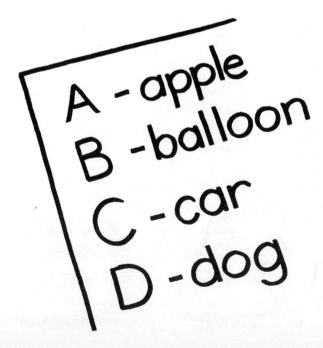

A - apple
B - balloon
C - car
D - dog

activity 153

ANIMAL, VEGETABLE OR MINERAL

A good guessing game to play with older children. **6+**

What You Need

• *Players*

What To Do

Think of an object or person 'IT'. The categories in this game are
Animal (people, animals, insects, etc.), Vegetable (plants) and Mineral
(iron, innate objects).

Your children can then ask twenty questions to try and determine what 'IT' is.
Except for the first question which traditionally asks if it is 'Animal, Vegetable or
Mineral' all the other questions are just answered with a 'Yes' or a 'No'.

The person being asked the questions keeps track of the number of questions asked.
If there is more than one person asking the questions, the first person to guess the
answer on or before the twentieth question has the next turn.

HINT!

If you find your children are getting 'bogged down' by the questions give them
some clues until they begin to understand the game!

activity

154

DIARIES

6+

A good way to start a lifetime habit of writing.

 ✓

What You Need

 ✓

- *Spiral notebook with blank page on one side and lines on the other*
- *Drawing and writing materials*

 ✓

 ✓

 ✓

What To Do

 ✓

Keeping a diary is a great way for your children to record their activities, thoughts and feelings. Starting young they can build an excellent writing habit for later life.

Writing in a diary each day may be too ambitious for younger children so perhaps an entry a week may be more realistic. Encourage them to draw a picture of something that happened that week and then write the events of the week on the page opposite. Younger non-writers can tell you what to write for them. Make sure each entry is dated at the top of the page. Remind other members of the family that diaries are private and only looked at with the owner's permission.

activity
155

'I CAN'

6+ ✓

 ✓

 ✓

 ✓

Make an 'I Can' book with your children to boost their self-esteem and their writing skills.

What You Need

- *Paper*
- *Stapler*
- *Drawing and writing materials*

What To Do

To encourage your children's increasing independence, talk together about things they can do now on their own. These might include dressing themselves, tying their shoelaces, keeping their rooms tidy, riding their bikes without training wheels, playing a sport, swimming or using a knife and fork correctly. I am sure you and your children will be able to do lots more.

Staple together pieces of paper to make a book. On the front they draw a picture of themself and write their name. (Don't forget to date the book so in years to come they can enjoy reading it again).

On each page they draw a picture of themselves doing something they can do on their own. Under the picture they write 'I can ?????...'. You will have to help them with some of the words.

Read it together, share it with the rest of the family and their teachers, who may like to try it with the rest of the class too. Then put it away in their special box to keep for the future.

activity

156

JOB CHART

6+ ✓

 ✓

 ✓

 ✓

 ✓

Begin a family job chart with your children to encourage them to help more and for all the family to share tasks.

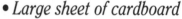

What You Need

- *Large sheet of cardboard*
- *Pens for drawing*
- *Paper*

What To Do

Together talk with your children about all the chores the family needs to do to keep your home running smoothly. List them together, e.g. ironing clothes, washing, vacuuming, dusting, cleaning the bathrooms, washing floors, shopping, putting shopping away, putting out the garbage, collecting the mail or papers, cooking, setting the table, mowing the lawn, gardening, hosing the garden, sweeping paths, cleaning the car, making beds, tidying up. I am sure you can think of lots more - it makes me exhausted just thinking of them all!

Your children then draw a small picture of each chore.

Rule the cardboard so there is a space for each family member and room for the chores. Your children can place the chore pictures beside the family member who does them. (At this stage in most families Mum will probably be doing a lot more than the rest!) If this is the case, talk to your children and the other family members about sharing more of the load.

A happy family works together.

activity

157

LETTER BINGO

6+ ✓

A fun game to teach letters to your children.

 ✓

 ✓

What You Need

- *Cardboard*
- *Pens*
- *Scissors*

What To Do

Cut the cardboard into bingo cards and divide each card into nine squares. Randomly, write alphabet letters on the bingo cards (use upper and lower case letters so your children learn both - for example 'Aa').

Cut up lots of small squares of cardboard and write the alphabet letters on them, making sure you have all the letters you have used on the bingo cards.

Give each child or family member a board and place the letter cards in a pillow case. Pull them out one at a time and hold them up for the players to see, as well as calling them out. This will help younger players. When a player has that letter on their board, they cover it with a token - buttons or small coins are ideal. The first player to cover their boards calls out 'Bingo'.

For older children make it more difficult by calling out words, and they have to place a token on the first letter of the word.

Another version is that the winner also has to think of a sentence made up of words that begin with the letters on the bingo board in sequence, e.g.

Tt	Hh	Cc
Ii	Ll	Uu
Dd	Oo	Bb

The sentences are usually very funny. The example above might be: 'The hairy cat is lying under Dad's old bomb'.

See if they can make the sentences as unusual as possible.

activity

158

MY BOOK ABOUT MY BIRTHDAY

6+

This activity provides a chance for your children to see the value of print. Making their own books will develop your children's vocabulary and counting skills.

What You Need

- *Notebook or scrapbook*
- *Writing pen*
- *Felt pens, colour pencils or crayons.*

What To Do

Like most parents we still talk about the joy and wonder of the day our son was born. Share this with your children and make a personalised book with them describing what happened that day.

Buy a scrap book and note book and help your children write the story or write it for younger ones. Your children can illustrate it or perhaps even use some of the photos taken that day (or have photocopies made very cheaply at your nearest photocopying shop).

This book is something your children will treasure especially in the years to come when they become parents. Together you have helped create a family heirloom.

activity
159

RHYMING CHARADES

6+

Listening to rhymes is an important pre-reading and reading skill. Make sure that from an early age you read your children lots of rhyming nursery rhymes, poems and books and encourage them to 'spot the rhyming words'.

 ✓

 ✓

 ✓

 ✓

What You Need

• *Paper* • *Pen*

What To Do

Together with your children think of rhyming word families, e.g.

Dog, log, frog, bog
Cat, mat, fat, pat, rat
Pen, men, ten, when

With younger non-readers just think of the rhyming words together.

Then say 'I'm thinking of a word that rhymes with Bill' and act out the rhyming word, e.g. taking a 'pill'.

See if your children can not only guess the correct answer, but write it down for spelling practice.

When they guess correctly it's their turn.

activity
160

DICTIONARY CODE

8+

Using their dictionary will seem like fun as your children unravel this fun code.

What You Need

• *a dictionary* • *paper and pencil*

What To Do

When your children are not around, use their dictionary. Begin by printing a simple message onto a piece of paper and then change the message into code. To do this you'll have to look up each word in the dictionary and then replace it with the word that immediately precedes it. For example 'What do you want for dinner tonight?' becomes (in my dictionary) 'Wharfinger djibba Yorkshire wanion fop dinky tonicity?'

Your children must use the same dictionary you have used or they will never be able to uncode the message. When they are proficient at this code they can make up some messages for you to uncode. They will love teaching their friends this easy code - see if their teacher can work it out too.

This activity is not only fun but will really increase your children's skill with their dictionary.

Wharfinger djibba Yorkshire wanion fop dinky tonicity?

activity
161

DIRECTORY ASSISTANCE

8+

Give your child practice at using a telephone directory.

 ✓

 ✓

What You Need

- *A cassette recorder and a blank cassette*
- *2 telephone directories*

 ✓

What To Do

Ask your children to pretend they are the telephone operator and, on a blank cassette, record five 'requests' for directory assistance. Use real names from both directories for these.

Leave enough blank tape between each request for your child 'operator' to give their name and respond to the request. This is not only great practice at using the telephone directories but also will help them become more familiar with using a cassette player.

When they are competent at the task, record some more for them to find, or perhaps they will enjoy looking up the names and addresses of businesses they know or friends at school.

activity
162

FAMILY TREE

8+

Help your children learn more about your family and understand family relationships by making a simple family tree together.

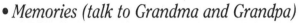

What You Need

- *Memories (talk to Grandma and Grandpa)*
- *Old family photos*

What To Do

Get a large sheet of cardboard and print in the names of your family with your children. Add dates of births, deaths and marriages. Go back through as many generations as you know about. Research together the ones you don't know by asking grandparents and older relatives.

If possible add photos to your family tree. Look for family resemblances and compare clothes and hair styles of today with those of your ancestors.

Encourage your children's awakening interest in the past by looking for historical books from the library or by visiting an historical museum together. Encourage your children to talk to their grandparents and great-grandparents about the 'olden days' so those memories are not lost.

Perhaps all of this might inspire you to oganise a family reunion!

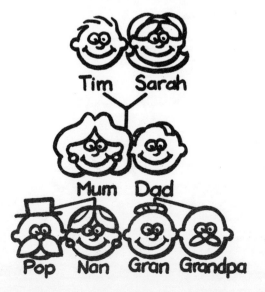

activity
163

FIND THE WORD GAME

8+

A game that tests the word skills of all the family!

What You Need

- *Pencils and papers*

What To Do

Find a long word and give all the players a pencil and paper. The players must try to make as many words as possible from the letters in the long word. The player who makes the most words is the winner.

A few rules - all the words must contain at least three letters; a letter may only be used more than once in a word if it is contained in the main word more than once; and it's a good idea to set a time limit for the game - perhaps ten minutes.

So, from the word CATASTROPHE you could make words such as:

TASTE, TROT, STAR, STRAP, TASTER, TOAST, PERT, TOTE, PEST, HAT and lots more!

activity
164

HANGMAN'S NOOSE

8+

A spelling game for older children - a great fun way to test your older children's weekly spelling list from school.

 ✓

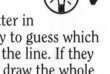 ✓

What You Need

• *Pencil* • *Paper* • *2 players*

✓

✂

What To Do

Select a word your children know and draw a line for each letter in the word at the bottom of the piece of paper. Your children try to guess which letters are in the word. If they are correct, write the letter on the line. If they are wrong, add a line to the hangman's noose drawing. If you draw the whole hangman they have lost!

activity

165

JUMBLED WORDS

8+

Help improve your children's spelling skills in a fun way.

 ✓

What You Need

 ✓

• *Weekly spelling list from school*
• *Pen* • *Paper*

What To Do

 ✓

Most schools send home a weekly spelling list for children to learn.
Ask your children for the list and jumble up the letters of each word. Write them down with a line beside each for the correct spelling. Your children will have lots of fun figuring them out.

Time them each week to see if they are getting faster at working out the solutions.

PLIGSELN	SPELLING
UFN	FUN
IHWT	WITH
UBEJMLD	JUMBLED
ODWRS	WORDS

activity
166

LETTER STEPS

8+

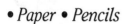

Help your children improve their spelling and word skills with this word-making activity.

 ✓

What You Need

• *Paper* • *Pencils*

 ✓

What To Do

Do a few of these word-making activities together first, then give your children some to try on their own.

 ✓

Choose any two words that have the same number of letters such as MINE and SAND. The object of the game is to change only one letter at a time until the first word is changed into the second. However, you must make a new word at each letter change. So, for MIND and SAND it might go like this:

  MINE / MANE / SANE / SAND

or SOAP to PEAR like this:

  SOAP / SOAR / SEAR / PEAR

Other words may take longer than three steps to change - try KITE to FAZE

  KITE / MITE / MATE / MAZE / FAZE

The person who can change one word to another with the least number of changes wins that round and chooses the words for the next go. Sometimes it simply cannot be done and that round is declared a draw.

LOOK AT WORDS

Making up anagrams (a mixed up word using the same letters) is lots of fun and a great way to improve your children's spelling ability.

 ✓

 ✓

What You Need

• *Paper* • *Pencils or pens* • *Dictionary*

 ✓

What To Do

Think of some words from which to make anagrams - beginning with one of your children's names perhaps. Our son's name is ANDREW, which can become WARDEN. If the names are short, your children could make anagrams with their middle name or surname.

The weekly spelling list from school is a good place to start, and encourage your children to use the dictionary to check their spelling, incorporating practice in a fun game.

Making up anagrams will help your children look at words in a new way.

Have a family competition to see how many words you can all make. Timing your children with the clock or the stove timer works well also.

Have them take their spelling list of anagrams to show their teacher, who might get the whole class involved.

andrew — warden
dust — stud
stage — gates
mate — tame

activity
168

SHOPPING LISTS

Encourage your children's writing skills by helping them make the shopping list before you go shopping together.

What You Need

• *Paper* • *Pen or pencil*

What To Do

Before you do your weekly grocery order, sit down with your children and together write the shopping list. Your children can do the writing - if they do not know how to spell a word, they might be able to look at packets in the pantry or advertising brochures - or just encourage them to have a go. Help them make the list in an organised fashion, with fruit and vegetables together, dry staples together, and so on.

Take the list when you do the shopping together and they can use it.

Shopping may take a little longer but your are helping your children learn an important life skill.

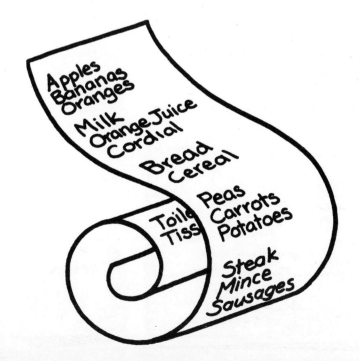

Apples
Bananas
Oranges

Milk
Orange Juice
Cordial

Bread
Cereal

Toile Peas
Tiss Carrots
Potatoes

Steak
Mince
Sausages

activity

169

SPELLING WORD BINGO 8+

Hearing children's spelling can be a fairly laborious task for parents night after night, and yet it is an essential one if we want our children to become competent readers and writers. Turn the Spelling Homework into fun by making some Spelling Word Bingo cards with the weekly Spelling List.

What You Need

- *Spelling homework list from school*
- *Cardboard*
- *Marking pens*

What To Do

Rule up a few boards divided into room for ten words. Choose words from the latest spelling list, as well as ones they have had to learn previously for revision. Make matching word cards with some more cardboard. Dad may like to play also.

Call out the words and the players put a coin or button, or other marker, on the correct word. The first player to match all the words is the winner and receives a small treat. Now take away the boards, call out the words and see how well they have been learnt.

Playing Spelling Bingo will help your kids learn their spelling in a really fun way.

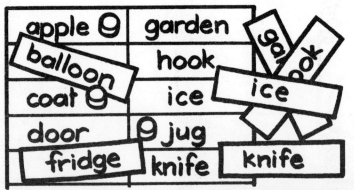

activity

170

SPELLING WORD CROSSWORDS

Make the weekly spelling homework more interesting by making up some crossword puzzles for your children to do.

8+

What You Need

- *Paper*
- *Pens*
- *Time*

(If you need help, buy a crossword book from your newsagent and this will give you some ideas for setting out.)

What To Do

Draw up a simple crossword and think of the clues. Don't use cryptic clues for younger children. As your kids get better at crosswords, you can increase the difficulty of the clues.

Give the crossword to your children to work out. When they have finished, see if they have learnt the spellings in a fun way. If they still need help, practise them together.

DOWN
1. It bounces
2. Boys name

ACROSS
1. It floats.
3. It's green.

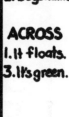

activity
171

TALKING TO GRANDMA

8+

Most children share a special bond with their grandparents. Encourage this and their interest in history by making a book about when Grandma or Grandpa was their age.

What You Need

- *Paper • Stapler • Glue*
- *Pens for drawing and writing*

What To Do

Next time you visit the grandparents suggest to them that they talk to your children about when they were their age.

They could talk about their favourite toys and activities, things they did together as a family, games they played with their brothers and sisters, their family, their home, differences between life then and life today. Your children will be fascinated.

Encourage them to write down what they learn. Their grandparents may have some photos they can have (or have copies made) to add to their book.

Keep it as a special family heirloom.

activity
172

ANIMAL FAMILIES

10+

Helps older children learn both dictionary skills and animal group names.

 ✓

What You Need

 ✓

• *Dictionary*
• *Paper*

 ✓

What To Do

 ✓

Do your older children know the names of animal family groups?
We all know a group of birds is a flock or fish a school, but what about some of the more unusual ones.

Write down the following words on a piece of paper.

Brace
Clouder
Drive
Flock
Gaggle
Herd
Kennel
Knot
Pace
Rather
Swarm

Your children can use their dictionary to find which animal group it describes. They can then illustrate the group.

School

activity
173

PENPALS

A way to encourage your children to write letters and also to learn about new places through a new friend.

 ✓

 ✓

What You Need

 ✓

- *Cousins who love far away, a friend from interstate met on a holiday, or friends who have moved away, can all be penpals. Ask your school's headmaster if you can't think of anyone - schools often have sister schools in other states or countries. Or help your children write to a school in their country or another country stating their name, age and that they are interested in finding a penpal. If you have a computer, look on the Internet!*

What To Do

When your children start writing their letters, keep a photocopy of each one and keep the originals of the ones they received in a large photo album. They will be fascinating to read in years to come.

Encourage your children to send lots of photos of themselves and family photographs to their penpal also. Hopefully, they will return the favour - photos of themselves, their family, home, school and environment.

Happy writing!

activity

174

LET'S CREATE

LET'S CREATE

LET'S CREATE

BOX CARS

2+ ✓

Making cheap play props like this together helps develop your children's imagination.

 ✓

 ✓

 ✓

What You Need

 ✓

- *Cardboard box*
- *Felt pens*
- *Paper plates, pieces of cardboard, foil pie plates*
- *Acrylic paint*

 ✓

 ✓

What To Do

Make a box car for your children. Cut the flaps off the top and bottom of a cardboard box except for the flap at the front. Your children can paint the box at this stage - maybe racy red, or British racing green! When it's done, stick paper plates on the side for wheels and foil pie dishes on the front for headlights. Straps go over your children's shoulders to hold it up and they're off and racing.

Boxes could also be aeroplanes or boats! Just use your imagination and, of course, your children's.

activity
175

BREAKFAST CEREAL THREADINGS

2+

 ✓

 ✓

Breakfast cereals can make pretty necklaces and bangles and keep the children amused while they make them. Threading is also an excellent eye-hand co-ordination activity.

What You Need

 ✓

- *Bodkin or a large tapestry needle*
- *Wool • Breakfast cereal loops*

What To Do

Help your children thread their needles or bodkins and tie a cereal loop at the end of the wool to secure it. If you don't want your younger children using needles, wrap some sticky tape around the end of the wool to make a firm threading and they thread with that.

Older children will enjoy making colourful patterns as they thread. Younger ones will enjoy eating their creations at the end!

activity
176

BUSY BOX

2+

Children are natural 'recyclers' and our junk is often their treasure. Make a 'Busy Box' together and start collecting.

 ✓

 ✓

 ✓

What You Need

- *Strong cardboad box with a lid (apple boxes are ideal)*
- *Glue*
- *Paper*

✓

✓

What To Do

Help your children decorate their 'Busy Box'. You could use some of their paintings or drawings, magazine pictures, wrapping paper or magazine illustrations to collage all over the box. Alternatively, they could paint it with bright acrylic paints or, after covering it with white butcher's paper, they could decorate it with crayons or felt pens.

Find a suitable place to store the Busy Box that's easily accessible for everyone - perhaps in a wardrobe or in the bottom of your linen cupboard.

In the busy box we keep a shoe box that contains the 'tools of trade' - good quality children's scissors (children will easily become frustrated with learning to cut if scissors aren't sharp), sticky tape in a good quality dispenser, masking tape, glue bottle or glue pen and a stapler. A pencil case could hold crayons, felt pens, and coloured pencils. Now you're ready to start collecting!

activity
177

BUSY BOX COLLECTION

2+

Here are some suggestions for junk, art, and collage materials you may like to collect and store in the Busy Box. Some smaller materials will be best stored in individual containers (margaine, butter, or take-away containers make ideal small storage containers).

What You Need

- *Aluminium foil, beads, bottle tops, bark, cardboard cylinders (lunch wraps and toilet rolls), cellophane, chalk, chocolate wrappers, confetti, corks cotton reels, cotton wool, cotton wool balls, dried flowers, egg cartons, egg shells, fabric scalps, feathers, grasses, gift wrappings, glitter, iceblock sticks, leather scraps, leaves, sweet wrappers, paint sample sheets, paper, paper bags, paper clips, patty cake papers, pebbles, pine cones, pipe cleaners, ribbons, rulers, sandpaper, seeds, sequins, scraps of lace, sawdust, straws, polystyrene, stickers, sponges, string, toothpicks, toothbrushes (old for painting), wallpaper samples or off-cuts, wool and yarn, anything else you can think of.*

What To Do

Having a collection of art materials and junk on hand is a necessity for many of the activities in this book. Children are natural recyclers and our junk is often their treasure. Make a Busy Box together and start collecting.

activity
178

COLOURFUL BLOB PAINTINGS 2+

Children love surprises and blob paintings really appeal to their sense of surprise.

What You Need

- *Paper*
- *Brushes*
- *Colourful paints (acrylic paint works well, or make up a strong paint with wallpaper paste and food dyes)*

What To Do

Help the children fold their papers in two. Next show them how to put blobs of paint on one side of the paper. Fold the paper over and press it down hard. When they open up the paper - wow! What is it? When the blob painting is dry they can draw around their picture and cut it out.

Maybe it's a butterfly or a monster! Anything is possible with children's imaginations.

activity
179

COLOURFUL PLAYDOUGH

2+

 ✓

 ✓

 ✓

Make up a batch of simple cooked playdough for your children. It will keep them occupied for ages and provide a great outlet for their creativity.

What You Need

- *1 cup plain flour*
- *1 cup water*
- *1 tablespoon cooking oil*
- *Food colouring or powder paints*
- *1/2 cup cooking salt*
- *1 tablespoon cream of tartar*

What To Do

Your children will enjoy helping you make the playdough. With a wooden spoon, mix the flour, water, salt and cream of tartar in a saucepan over a medium heat until thick. When it has cooled, add the oil and knead well on a floured board.

Divide it into at least six balls and add a different colour to each ball until you have blue, red, yellow, green, purple and orange playdough (or any other colours you would like).

Put each colour into a separate container and encourage your children to create playdough pictures or dioramas. When they have finished, help them sort out the colours to put back in their containers for another day, rather than mixing them all together. Happy modelling!

activity
180

CREATIVE PLAYDOUGH

2+

Playing with playdough gives children the opportunity to be creative while it helps develop their finger muscles, so important for writing at school.

What You Need

- *A batch of playdough (see activity 212)*
- *Objects to use with the playdough - choose any of these or think of others you may have at home: Plastic cutlery, plastic scissors, plastic hammers. Garlic crushers, potato mashers, rolling pins, tea strainers, pipe cleaners, old keys, patty papers and patty pans, cake and muffin tins, baking trays, iceblock sticks and biscuit and scone cutters.*

What To Do

Make up a batch of playdough with your children and give them all or a selection of the items mentioned above. They will play happily for ages. Make sure you are close by to admire their creations and to try making some of your own.

activity
181

EDIBLE PLAYDOUGH

2+

Make a simple edible playdough that younger children will enjoy playing with.

What You Need

- *Peanut butter*
- *Milk powder*
- *Sugar*
- *Edible food colouring*

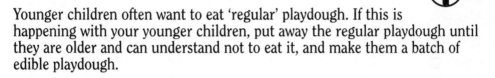

What To Do

Younger children often want to eat 'regular' playdough. If this is happening with your younger children, put away the regular playdough until they are older and can understand not to eat it, and make them a batch of edible playdough.

Simply mix one part of peanut butter to one part of milk powder and half a part of sugar. Double or triple the quantities depending on how much you want. Add some food colouring if desired.

activity

182

FINGER PAINTING

2+

Finger painting provides a wonderful sensory activity for young children. They love the squishy, slimy feeling as they draw with the finger paint.

What You Need

- *1 cup of cold water*
- *2.5 litres of boiling water*
- *1 cup of soap flakes*
- *1 cup of laundry starch*
- *1/2 cup of talcum powder*
- *Powder paints or food colouring*

What To Do

Begin by dissolving the starch in cold water. Add the boiling water slowly while stirring. Add the soap flakes and talcum powder and, last of all, the paint or food colouring. Allow to cool.

Carry a low table outside or spread a plastic sheet on the grass for the children to paint on. Make sure they are wearing a painting smock or an old shirt of Dad's over their clothes!

When they draw a special picture in the finger paint you can make a print of it by pressing a piece of paper on it.

Finger painting prints make great wrapping paper, too, so store some away for future birthday parties!

If you are game, feet painting is lots of fun, too! Make sure there is a bucket of soapy, warm water handy for cleaning up.

activity
183

FIRST LACING CARDS

2+

A new skill to teach your young children. A good pre-sewing activity and great for eye-hand co-ordination.
(See Hole Punch Pictures for older children - 242)

What You Need

• *Thick cardboard* • *Lacy materials*
• *A hole punch*

What To Do

Visit your local picture framer for a supply of the thick card they use for picture mounts. Cut the card into simple shapes or even shapes like toys or perhaps fruit. (You are only limited by your imagination and your art ability!!).

Now punch holes around the edge of the shapes at least 3 cm apart for your children to lace through.

With younger children it is safer not to use a bodkin so you will need threading materials that are stiff enough to thread without one. Old shoe laces are ideal, plastic lacing is cheap to buy by the metre from craft shops or most haberdasheries. You can even dip the ends of wool or string into melted candle wax or a strong laundry starch solution to stiffen them. Make sure you tie the lacing through a hole to start. When your children are a little older they will enjoy making their own Hole Punch Pictures. (See activity 242).

activity
184

HOBBY HORSES

2+

Children love pretending. Make a hobby horse with your little ones and it will be a favourite pet for years.

 ✓

 ✓

 ✓

 ✓

What You Need

- *A long cardboard cylinder or a broom handle*
- *An adult sock*
- *Cord or thin rope for the reins*
- *Wool*
- *Permanent felt pens of various colours*

What To Do

Using acrylic paint, coat the cardboard cyclinder or boom handle with your children outdoors. They will enjoy choosing the colours for their own special horse.

Next fill the foot of the sock with fabric, crunched-up paper or old tights. Decorate to look like a horse's head with permanent pens and sew or glue some wool on for the mane.

Next slip the sock onto the cylinder or boom handle and tie securely to look like a bridle. Attach the reins and the 'horse' is ready for riding.

Your children will love naming their own special hobby horse.

activity
185

PAINT PALETTE

2+

A cheap and easy way to provide paints for your children.

 ✓

 ✓

 ✓

What You Need

 ✓

- *A plastic egg carton or an ice cube tray*
- *Powder paints (available at toy shops)*
- *Fine brushes*

 ✓

What To Do

Water colour palettes can be quite expensive to buy but you can easily make your own at home.

Put some powder paint into the segments of the egg carton or ice cube tray and then add a little water to mix (**HINT!** make the colours quite strong). Allow to dry and harden for a few days.

Give your children some paper, small brushes or cotton buds and a jar of clean water to wash the brushes and they'll have lots of fun painting with their own home-made palette.

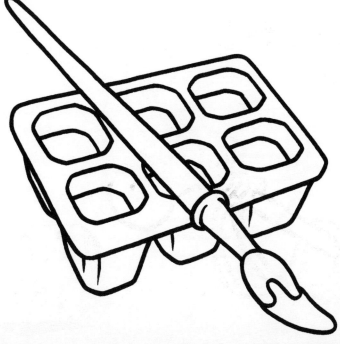

activity
186

PAINT POTS

2+

A cheap, fun outdoor activity to do on a sunny day.

What You Need

- *Bucket*
- *Elastic or cord*
- *Paint brush*
- *Food colouring*

What To Do

Young children love painting, but it is not always possible or practical to provide real paints. They also love painting with real brushes like Mum or Dad.

Attach a real paint brush to an old empty paint tin or small bucket. Half fill the bucket with water and add some food colouring. Now they can 'paint' the paths, driveway, concrete, or even the outside of the house, and you can rest easy knowing it can all be hosed off later ...!

activity
187

PHOTO PUZZLES

2+

Make some simple cheap puzzles for young children to put together.

What You Need

- *Large photos of your children, family or home*
- *Clear Contact (or have the photos laminated)*
- *Scissors or a Stanley knife*
- *Strong cardboard*
- *Craft glue*

What To Do

Use some large photos if you already have any or have some enlarged cheaply at your local photocopying shop. Your children will love doing a puzzle of their face, their whole body, one of the family, or perhaps their bedroom. Just use your imagination, or ask them?

Use craft glue to paste the photos onto the cardboard. When it is dry, contact over both sides or take it to have it laminated. Then use scissors or a *Stanley* knife to cut it into large puzzle pieces. As your children gain mastery of the puzzles, you can cut them into smaller pieces to increase the challenge.

Take photos of some of your friend's children and make them individual puzzles too - great cheap gifts, and everyone will be amazed at your creativity!

activity

188

SELF PORTRAITS

2+

Encourage your children to draw lots by always having lots of drawing paper, crayons, coloured pencils and felt pens available.

What You Need

• *Time together* • *Drawing materials* • *Paper*

What To Do

Ask your children to draw a picture of themselves or a self-portrait.
From an early age children should be encouraged to draw. Let them look in a mirror for inspiration or talk about the things they like doing best and they can draw themselves doing this. Another idea is to look at photos of them together and they can get ideas from these. Date and name these self-portaits and save them in a special place. You will be surprised when you look back together at how much their drawing changes each year.

activity
189

SOCK SNAKE

2+

Next time you find an odd sock, help your young children make it into a 'Sock Snake'. They will use it in their imaginative play and it will become a favourite friend.

 ✓

 ✓

What You Need

- *Old long sock*
- *Scrap paper to tear*
- *Coloured paper or stickers for the face*
- *Stong glue*

 ✓

 ✓

What To Do

Give your children a newspaper or other scrap paper to tear into small pieces for the filling. This is an excellent fine-motor activity to help strengthen their finger muscles.

When they have torn up enough, they fill their 'snake', pushing the paper right down to the toe.

They might like to use stickers to make a face on their snake or cut out pieces of paper. Stripes or spots of paper add interest also.

Together, think of a funny name for the snake - maybe 'Socks' or 'Snakey'!

activity

190

TEXTURED PLAYDOUGH

2+

Add interesting materials to a batch of playdough to introduce your young children to new textures.

 ✓

 ✓

What You Need

- *A batch of playdough (see recipe on activity 212)*
- *Sand • Rice • Confetti • Split peas*
- *Lentils • Dried beans • Glitter or small leaves*

 ✓

 ✓

What To Do

Make up a batch of playdough with the children and they will love helping you knead it when it has cooled a little. Then add one of the above texture materials to half the batch and another texture material to the other half. Try this with lots of textures and find out what the children enjoyed playing with the most.

activity
191

AUTUMN LEAF TREES

4+

Preserve the beauty of autumn leaves with this simple activity with your children.

What You Need

- *Autumn leaves*
- *Clear Contact (adhesive plastic sheeting)*
- *Scissors*
- *A hole punch*
- *String or thin ribbon*
- *A large bare branch*
- *A bucket or large tin*

What To Do

Next time you are in a park or garden admiring the magnificent autumn foliage, collect some different varieties of autumn leaves to make your own autumn decoration.

The children will enjoy pressing autumn leaves between clear pieces of *Contact adhesive* and then carefully cutting around the outside leaving a little border. At the top of the leaf, punch a hole and thread some string or ribbon through and attach the pretty leaves to the bare branch.

Stand it in a suitable container and enjoy autumn inside.

activity
192

BALLOON HEADS

4+

Make a whole family of colourful 'Balloon Heads' for your children's dramatic play. Simple, cheap and lots of fun.

What You Need

• *Balloons* • *Plain flour* • *Water* • *Funnel*
• *Teaspoon* • *Permanent marking pens*

What To Do

Together, blow up the balloons and then deflate them. Put the funnel into the balloon's mouth and carefully spoon in as much flour as you can. Add a little water to make the flour pliable and tie up the balloon.

Your children will love making faces on their balloon heads and moulding them to make funny facial features - big ears, squashed noses and fat cheeks.

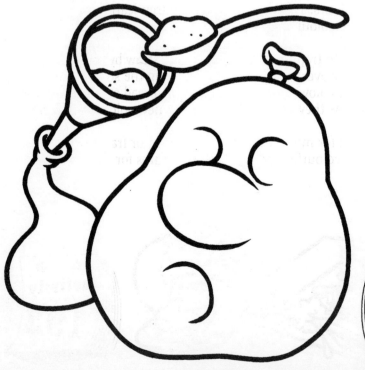

activity

193

BLOW PAINTINGS

4+

Children love making these paintings and watching the paint mix and change and form new colours.

What You Need

- *Drinking straws*
- *Food colouring or powder paint*
- *Plastic containers*
- *Paper*
- *Newspaper or plastic or vinyl tablecloth*
- *Painting smocks or old shirts of Dad's*

What To Do

Cover an outdoor table with newspaper, plastic or a vinyl cloth as this activity can be fairly messy. Make sure the children cover their clothes with a smock or an old shirt of Dad's.

Add some food colouring or powder paint to water in the containers to make nice strong primary colours. This activity helps children learn how new colours are made as the colours mix.

Show the children how to trap some water paint in a straw by putting it in the mixture, putting a finger over the top and then moving the straw to their paper. The next step is to blow gently. The paint will spread over the paper in spider-like formations. As they use different colours, new colours will form.

Save the blow paintings for interesting wrapping paper, or frame with some coloured cardboard for colourful and interesting pictures for the children's rooms.

activity

194

BODY CUTOUTS

4+

Children love looking at themselves in the mirror to see how much they have grown. Help your children see how big they are by doing a body outline with them to decorate.

What You Need

- *Large sheets of paper big enough for your children to lie on*
- *Felt pen*
- *Scissors*
- *Paints or collage materials to decorate*

What To Do

The children take it in turn to have their body drawn by Mum or Dad. They lie on the paper with their arms and legs out and you carefully draw around the body outline.

When it is finished they may like to cut it out. If they are still learning to use scissors, you could help them cut it out or, if they prefer, leave it uncut to decorate.

Hang it from the fence or *Blu-Tack* it to a wall outside and they can paint and decorate their body.

When it is finished and dry hang it on the door of their bedroom so everyone knows whose room it is.

HINT!

Your local newspaper sells the ends of rolls of newsprint very cheaply. A roll will give you years of great painting and drawing paper and is perfect for activities like this.

activity
195

BUBBLE PICTURES

4+ ✓

Help your children make beautiful bubble pictures. These colourful paintings make great wrapping paper for birthday presents, too!

 ✓

 ✓

 ✓

 ✓

 ✓

What You Need

- *Margarine containers*
- *Washing-up detergent*
- *Powder paints*
- *Paper*
- *Drinking straws*

What To Do

Half fill each container with water and add some powder paint and a little detergent. Place a drinking straw in each container. Show your children how to blow into the container until it is almost overflowing with bubbles. Press the paper on top of the container and when you take it off there will be beautiful bubble prints on it.

An alternative method is to place the straw in the bubble mixture and hold a finger over the end to retain some mixture, then your children blow lots of bubbles over the paper. As the bubbles burst they make colourful bubble prints on the paper.

Make sure that your children understand not to suck the liquid however!

activity
196

CLAY DINOSAUR WORLD

4+   ✓

 ✓

 ✓

 ✓

 ✓

 ✓

Children of this age are fascinated with dinosaurs and most have collections of small dinosaurs. They can use clay to make a dinosaur land for their dinosaurs to live.

What You Need

- *Clay*
- *Dinosaur models*
- *Books about dinosaurs*
- *Grass, leaves, twigs, stones*
- *Blue and red cellophane or a small mirror*

What To Do

Look in dinosaur books together so your children gain an understanding of the world the dinosaurs inhabited. Suggest to them that they might like to make a dinosaur world from clay for their toy dinosaurs.

They can use the clay to model mountains, volcanoes and other features. Help them add the cellophane for pretend water and for the flames from the volcanoes. Snippings from the garden make great jungles and, last of all, they can add the dinosaurs.

If they want to keep the 'dinosaur world' it can be left in the sun to dry, but usually with young children the fun is in the creating and playing. Why don't your take some photos for them to remember their great dinosaur land?

activity

197

CLAY PINCH POTS

4+ ✓

As children play and explore more with clay they will enjoy learning new techniques.

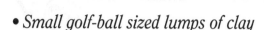 ✓

 ✓

What You Need

• *Small golf-ball sized lumps of clay*

✓

What To Do

✓

Show the children how to hold one of the balls of clay in the palm of one hand. Use your thumb to push a hole in the centre of the clay, but take care not to push it all the way through. Use your palm to support the ball of clay as your turn and push it out with your fingers. You are enlarging the pot by stretching the walls, but it is important to push and turn steadily so the pot sides are even.

This is harder than it sounds and your children will have to practise many times to perfect the technique. If they lose interest, let them just play with the clay and show them again some other time.

When the pot is round, push the base onto your table or board to make it flat so it will stand.

Show the children how you can use different fingers to make different shaped pots - thumb pots, Peter Pointer pots or even little pinky pots!!!

If your children want to save their pots, leave them in the sun to dry for a few days in a safe place and later they might like to carefully paint or decorate them.

activity

198

COLOUR MIXING

4+

Great fun and your children learn how colours are formed.

 ✓

 ✓

What You Need

 ✓

• *Lots of glass jars or clear plastic containers*
• *Plastic eyedroppers (cheap to buy, or save the ones that come with children's medicine)*
• *Red, yellow and blue powder paint*

 ✓

 ✓

What To Do

Help your younger children to half fill the containers with water (provide a jug for pouring the water, perhaps a new skill to learn). Older children will be able to manage it on their own.

Next help your children add some of the red, yellow and blue paint to three of the containers. They then add drops of colour to the jars with the plain water to make lots of new colours.

Arrange the finished containers on a shelf or table with the sun shining through them making rainbows.

Later they might like to add a mixture of cornflour and water to the jars and see the changes that occur:
• how the colours change
• the intensity of the shades
• how the clear colours become opaque.

Also see Eyedropper Painting - (activity 239) and
Rose Coloured Glasses - (activity 219)

activity

199

EGG SHELL PICTURES

4+

Help your children make an interesting texture picture from egg shells. They could also use them to decorate unique cards for birthdays and other special occasions.

What You Need

- *Dyed egg shells*
- *Strong glue*
- *Cardboard*
- *Plastic containers for storage*

What To Do

Save all the egg shells from cooking or from boiled eggs. Wash them well and dry in the sun before storing. When you have quite a lot you can dye them in batches, using strong solutions of food dye. Again, dry them well in the sun after dyeing. Your children will enjoy helping you with the dyeing, but don't forget to wear rubber or plastic gloves or your hands will look like the Incredible Hulk's!

Your children can then crush the egg shells with a roller or with a meat mallet. It is easiest to do this on a kitchen board covered with a tea towel. When they have finished, pick up the tea towel and pour the pieces carefully into a container for each colour.

Now they are ready to be creative with all the lovely dyed egg shells.

activity

200

FINGER PUPPETS

4+

Make some simple finger puppets with your children, then settle down with a cup of tea to watch the show.

What You Need

- *Old gloves (washing up gloves are fine)*
- *Permanent felt pens*
- *Strong glue*
- *Wool, sequins, small buttons, other decorations*
- *Shoe box*

What To Do

Cut off the fingers of a pair of gloves and help your children decorate them to make some finger puppets. Use the felt pens to draw faces or glue on small buttons or sequins for facial features. Make beards with cotton wool, dresses with scraps of fabric and hair with wool. You'll all have lots of fun thinking of details.

If your children want a puppet theatre for their puppets to perform in, this is easily made from a cereal carton or a shoe box. Stand it on end and then cut a window near the top for the puppets to perform in. Your children will enjoy decorating the puppet theatre too.

Gather the rest of the family, make some popcorn and sit back to enjoy the show.

activity
201

FLYING HELICOPTERS

4+ ✓

Make this fun flying object together. Launch it from the verandah and see how far it can fly.

✓

✓

What You Need

• *Scissors* • *Paper clip*
• *An old postcard or a small piece of cardboard*

✓

What To Do

Measure and cut together a strip off the postcard 3 cm (1¼ ins) wide. In this strip, make two slits 2/3 of the length of the card as shown.

Hold a corner in each hand and twist and then bring them together and secure with a paper clip.

The kids will love dropping the helicopter from up high and watch it as it whirls around.

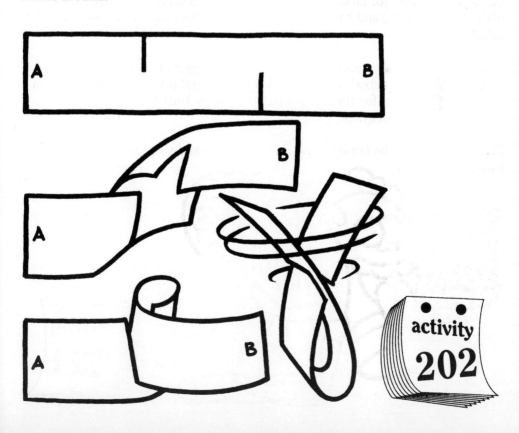

activity
202

FUN WITH CLAY

4+

Clay is one of the easiest art materials for children to use. It also provides great exercise for young hands to strengthen them for improving pencil grips for school.

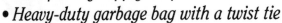

What You Need

- *Clay - very cheaply available from craft shops or your local pottery supply shop*
- *Heavy-duty garbage bag with a twist tie*
- *Individual work boards about 30 cm (12 inches) square made of lino or masonite (if required)*

What To Do

Clay is a great material for young children. They love the feel of it and the way they can quickly make great creations. It is very cheap, easily obtainable and can be used over and over again. It is a great outdoor activity and the kids will love helping clean up any mess with the hose.

I use an old plastic coated tablecloth on our wooden outdoor setting and when my son has finished I simply hose off the cloth or throw it in the washing machine to clean it for next time. $10 (£5) worth of clay has lasted him about a year and he comes back to it time after time.

Individual work boards are another alternative and old pieces of lino or vinyl flooring cut to size, or even plastic bread boards, would work well.

I keep our clay wrapped in an old damp towel in a strong plastic garbage bag, tied with a twist tie, and use a short length of fishing line to cut it into small blocks when required.

Special 'works of art' can be saved by leaving them out in the sun to dry for a few days and then they can be painted, but usually children are content to just model with the clay. Encourage them to explore and try new ways of working with the clay just for fun.

activity

203

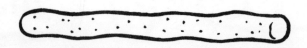

HAND GLOVE PUPPETS

4+

Make some simple fabric puppets for your children to decorate.

 ✓

 ✓

 ✓

What You Need

- *White cotton fabric (calico is ideal)*
- *Fabric glue • Felt pens*
- *Collage items such as sequins, buttons, wool, fabric scraps for decoration*

✓

✓

What To Do

Place your children's hand down on a doubled over piece of fabric approximately 20 cm x 15 cm (8 ins x 6 ins). Draw around the outline of their hand with a felt pen, leaving room for a seam allowance.

Stitch the puppet on your sewing machine and turn inside out and press flat with your iron.

Your children will have lots of fun decorating their puppet. (Why not make quite a few - they can make enough for a puppet show!) They might make the characters out of a fairy tale, perhaps Goldilocks and the Three Bears, or even their own family. Settle down in front of their puppet theatre for a great show (see Puppet Theatres - activity 126).

activity

204

HERB POSIES

4+

Children love smelling different types of herbs. Show them how to make a herb posy.

What You Need

- *Herbs and lavender flowers*
- *Rubber bands*
- *Pretty ribbons*

What To Do

With the children, gather some sprigs of different herbs from your herb garden. Posies are traditionally round in shape and the children will have to cut the stems so they have a mixture of lengths. Lavender smells wonderful and the flowers add colour to the posy, but other herb flowers look great, too, such as the bright red-pink of pineapple sage and the dainty thyme flowers. Use a variety of herbs with different leaf shapes for the posy, for example, the spiky leaves of rosemary contrasted with the soft round leaves of basil. Parsley looks pretty and soft around the edges. The children will enjoy selecting a variety of leaf shapes.

Help them wrap a rubber band firmly around the posy and then tie a pretty ribbon over the rubber band.

I love to pick some eau-de-cologne mint to scent our toilets and bathrooms. Try a herb posy as a gift or for your own home and enjoy the wonderful natural scent of herbs.

activity

205

JUNK THREADING

4+

A great eye-hand co-ordination activity. Older children will also enjoy making their own jewellery.

What You Need

- *Bodkins for younger children - tapestry needles for older ones*
- *Selection of different colour wools or embroidery cottons*
- *Fine hat elastic for bracelets*
- *Shapes cut from coloured cardboard or greeting cards*
- *Wide variety of threading materials such as:*
  milk bottle tops (punch holes in plastic ones with a hole punch)
  soft drink or beer bottle tops (use a hammer and nail to punch the holes)
- *matchboxes*
- *macaroni*
- *pieces of lace or other lovely woven fabrics*
- *cut up egg cartons (with holes punched in them)*
- *cardboard cylinder (cut into short lengths)*
- *straws*
- *dough or clay beads (baked in a slow oven)*
- *cotton wool balls*
- *patty cake papers*
- *paper beads (roll brightly coloured paper strips around a pencil, glue and leave to dry*
- *buttons or old beads*

What To Do

Thread the bodkin or tapestry needle and knot near the top. Thread an object on to the wool and knot at the bottom. Your children then thread.

Keep all the threading items in take-away food or margarine containers for easy packing away.

activity
206

KEY WIND CHIMES

4+

 ✓

 ✓

 ✓

Make a tinkly key wind-chime with the children to hang in the garden so the whole family can enjoy the music of the breeze.

 ✓

What You Need

• *Old keys*
• *Fishing line*
• *Driftwood or pieces of wood*

What To Do

Ask your friends and family for any old keys they may have which are no longer used.

The children will enjoy cutting pieces of fishing line and tying them onto each key.

Experiment with hanging the keys from a piece of wood or a piece of driftwood from the beach. The keys need to hang at different heights to balance but still be able to hit each other as they swing in the wind. Hang the wind chime from a branch of a tree or under a pergola.

The key wind chime will make a lovely musical sound in your garden as it swings and sways in the breeze.

activity
207

MAGIC PLAYDOUGH

4+

A fun way to help your young children learn how to make new colours.

What You Need

• *Basic recipe for cooked playdough
  (see Colourful Playdough - activity 212)*
• *Food colouring or powder paint*

What To Do

Make up the cooked playdough recipe with your children. When you have finished, divide it into six balls. In the middle of each ball of playdough hide some food colouring or powder paint (two balls each of red, yellow and blue).

First, give your children a ball with yellow paint hidden in it and one with red. As they play, the colours will appear and then combine to form orange. Magic!

Later, they can combine red and blue to make purple and blue and yellow to make green. All the balls combined will form brown playdough.

Talk with them about what they have learnt and about the new colours they have made.

activity
208

MAKE A MOBILE

4+

Young children love watching mobiles swing in the breeze. Help your children make one for their room or as a special gift for a new baby.

 ✓

 ✓

 ✓

 ✓

 ✓

What You Need

- *Wire coat-hanger or ice-cream container lid*
- *Bodkin*
- *Wool or embroidery cotton*
- *Junk for threading (see Junk Threading - activity 229)*

What To Do

After your children have threaded four or five lengths of threading, tie them securely to a wire coat hanger or through holes punched in an ice cream lid. Make sure it is balanced, then hang on a hook in the ceiling of your children's room.

Mobiles are also great to hang above a baby's change table.

activity

209

MAKE A PLACE MAT

4+

Your fussy eaters may enjoy meals more when they eat off their custom made place mat.

 ✓

 ✓

 ✓

 ✓

 ✓

What You Need

- *A piece of thick cardboard cut to the desired size*
- *Clear Contact (adhesive plastic sheeting)*
- *Crayons, felt pens, collage materials*

What To Do

Leave decorating the place mat entirely up to your children. They could decorate it with collage materials, magazine pictures, draw or paint on it or even use dried leaves or flowers from the garden.

Fringing the edges can add a nice touch as well as provide useful cutting practice for younger children.

When the decorating is finished, cover completely with contact (top and bottom to protect against spills) or have it laminated. (Many photocopying shops or even your children's school or kindy have laminators and will do it for a small fee).

Perhaps your budding artists might like to make a complete set for the whole family and be responsible for setting the table too!

activity
210

MAKE A SOCK PUPPET

4+

Children love making puppets for imaginative play.

 ✓

 ✓

 ✓

 ✓

 ✓

What You Need

- *Old socks*
- *Buttons*
- *Bits and pieces from your sewing box*
- *Permanent felt pens*
- *Needle and cotton*
- *Craft glue*

What To Do

If your home is like mine, whenever I clean out the drawers (particularly my husband's) there are always quite a few odd socks. It is one of life's little mysteries as to their mates - does my washing machine gobble them or perhaps the dog? Anyway, your children will think it's great fun making them into puppets.

Younger children will need your help with the craft glue to glue on buttons for eyes and other bits or pieces, or mark a mouth with a felt pen.

Older children will enjoy the challenge of sewing on buttons and other decorations from your sewing box.

Sock puppets are limited only by your children's imagination, but one of the creatures I have found they most enjoy making out of socks is dinosaurs. Take your children to see the dinosaur exhibits at your local museum or read books about dinosaurs together, and their ideas will just flow.

It is also a great opportunity to teach your older children how to sew on their own buttons!

activity

211

MARBLE PAINTINGS

4+

Make some colourful wrapping paper with marbles for paintings.

What You Need

- *Marbles • Paper • Teaspoons*
- *Containers of different colour paint*
- *Shirt or cereal boxes or a large plastic box*

What To Do

Put the paper in a large box. Put a few marbles into each different colour paint and use a teaspoon to lift out one marble at a time and put it in the box on top of the paper. Now show your children how to lift the box to roll the paint covered marble all around the box until all the paint has come off the marble and made marble tracks all over the paper. Your children repeat this until the paper is covered with bright tracks of colour. Keep the marble paintings for unusual wrapping paper for gifts.

activity
212

MESH WEAVING

4+

Young children love weaving and this simple activity helps them understand how fabric is made.

What You Need

- *Plastic mesh - available from hardware stores*
- *Natural materials such a grasses, strips of bark, long leaves, as well as strips of paper, cloth and pieces of string, twine, rope and wool*

What To Do

Show the children how to weave in and out of their pieces of mesh with the materials. They will have lots of fun making up interesting patterns and using a variety of materials for simple weaving.

activity
213

NOODLE NAMES

4+ ✓

Children not only love eating pasta, they also love playing with it and creating with it. However, like many messy art activities, it is best done outdoors!

 ✓

 ✓

 ✓

What You Need

- *Pasta of various shapes*
- *Strong wood glue*
- *Cardboard*

✓

✓

What To Do

Children love names on their bedroom doors and messages too. My son has 'NO GIRLS ALLOWED' on his bedroom door, which gives me a great excuse not to go in there, so he has to tidy it himself! Help the children make their messages with pasta so they not only look great but feel interesting too.

Decide with them on the message, cut some cardboard into the shape they want and then they paint on the letters carefully with the glue. Next, they position the pasta onto the glue before it dries. Let the pasta dry for a day or so and then punch holes in the corner of each sign and thread with string or ribbon to hang on the children's bedroom door knobs.

HINT!

Pasta can even be coloured with paint and left to dry if they want to use coloured pasta for this activity.

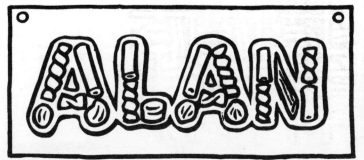

activity
214

PAPER BAG PUPPETS

4+

Help your children make a whole collection of these and then put on a puppet show together for the rest of the family.

What You Need

- *Paper bags*
- *Scissors*
- *Scrap paper or other collage materials*
- *Glue*
- *Felt pens*

What To Do

Today, most supermarket bags are made of plastic, but some stores are becoming environmentally conscious and are again using large brown paper bags. These make fantastic puppets. Otherwise, buy a pack of brown paper lunch bags.

Your children can make their puppets any way they like, but perhaps they might like to cut or tear long strips of coloured paper for hair, add a cellophane mouth and draw large eyes. Don't forget that the bottom of the puppet is where the hand goes in!

Older children like making funny faces cut from different photos in magazines.

When it is finished, your children put their hand in and make the puppet talk!

Fat puppets are fun to make too. Stuff the paper bag with newspaper, insert a lunch wrap roll and staple or sticky tape the bottom. Hold the puppet by the cylinder and make it move.

Don't forget to take a photo of your children's great puppets and the puppet show for your family album.

activity

215

PERFUMED PLAYDOUGH

4+

Playdough gives children the opportunity to be creative and to explore a new medium.

What You Need

- *A batch of playdough (see Colourful Playdough - activity 180 for the simple recipe)*
- *Essences such as strawberry, lemon, peppermint, vanilla, or chocolate (look for these in the baking section of your supermarket)*

What To Do

Make up a batch of playdough and colour it to match the essence you are going to add - yellow for lemon essence, pink for strawberry and so on. Add plenty of essence so the smell stays in the playdough.

Make sure your children understand that this is a smelling experience and not a tasting one!

activity
216

PET ROCKS

An oldie but a goldie!

4+

What You Need

- *Smooth creek or river bed rocks*
- *Paints or collage materials for decorations*

What To Do

We often have picnics near creeks or river banks covered with lovely smooth rocks. Help your children select a rock to bring home for a 'pet'. Younger children will be especially enchanted with this idea.

At home your children can characterize their pet rock with a painted face, or use collage materials glued on - perhaps some wool for hair, a button for his nose, a ric-rac braid mouth and so on.

It makes a great paper weight and the easiest pet to look after I know.

activity
217

PRINTING PLAYDOUGH

4+

Playdough is a simple, cheap medium that provides children with the opportunity to create and explore new materials.

 ✓

 ✓

 ✓

 ✓

What You Need

- *Batch of playdough (see Colourful Playdough - activity 180)*
- *Materials for printing, such as old keys, leaves, flowers, nuts and bolts, parts of the body such as toes, fingers and elbows, toy parts of Duplo, Lego or Brushblocks, stones, and kitchen items*

What To Do

Show your children how to make interesting patterns and prints in their playdough with a selection of the materials suggested above.

activity
218

ROSE COLOURED GLASSES

4+

Children are fascinated by how looking through new colours changes their world.

What You Need

- *Cardboard toilet rollss or lunch wrap cylinders*
- *Scraps of different coloured cellophane*
- *Sticky tape or glue*

What To Do

Help your children use different coloured scraps of cellophane to cover one end of some cardboard cylinders to make coloured telescopes. Look through them to see your familiar world in a different way.

You can also cut the middle out of paper plates and replace it with cellophane to make a good 'view finder' or even take the lens out of old sunglasses or reading glasses to make 'coloured ones'.

See Stained Glass Windows - activity 258 for more colour ideas with cellophane.

activity
219

SAND PAINTINGS

4+

Children love the texture of sand and they will enjoy the novelty of painting with coloured sand.

What You Need

- *Fine beach sand*
- *Powder paints*
- *Large salt shakers (the sort you take on picnics are fine for this activity) or plastic containers without lids*
- *Glue*
- *Paper or card*

What To Do

Put some fine sand into each of the plastic containers or large salt shakers and mix a little of the powder paint with the sand so you have a few colours of sand.

Next the children use the glue to 'draw' a picture. If younger children find this difficult, have them draw with a pencil first and then glue over their drawing. Now they sprinkle or shake the coloured sand over their glue picture. When they have dried, display them proudly.

HINT!

Make some large numerals and alphabet letters on paper with the sand. Children enjoy tracing around these textured numbers and letters with their fingers and will learn them easily.

activity
220

SAWDUST MODELLING

4+ ✓

Make an interesting modelling mixture for the children from sawdust and glue.

 ✓

What You Need

 ✓

 ✓

 ✓

- *Sawdust (available fron your local sawmill, timberyard or hardware store)*
- *Wallpaper paste*
- *Water bowl*
- *Drinking straws, toothpicks, pipe cleaners*

What To Do

Mix two cups of the sawdust to 1 cup of wallpaper paste in a bowl and slowly add enough water to form a modelling dough.

The children will love making it into interesting shapes and figures and using the straws, toothpicks and pipe cleaners. They might like to model animals, dinosaurs, aliens or anything they can imagine.

This is a messy activity and is best done out of doors.

Leave the models in the sun until they are dry and then the children will enjoy painting them.

activity
221

SHOE PRINTS

4+ ✓

 ✓

 ✓

 ✓

 ✓

Children are fascinated by shoe prints. Try this with your kids to compare the shoe patterns on your family's shoes.

What You Need

- *A collection of shoes*
- *Plain white paper*
- *White candle or white crayon*
- *Food colouring or powdered paint*

What To Do

Many shoes have interesting textured patterns on the soles. To help your children compare the textured patterns, turn the shoes upside down and press a sheet of paper firmly onto the sole of each shoe.

To see the pattern help the children rub over the paper with a candle or the white crayon.

Make up some water paint by mixing some food colouring or powdered paint with water. Next, the children use a brush to apply a wash of the water paint to the paper. Then the pattern on the sole of the shoe will be clearly visible.

Put some sheets of paper near the door so the family have to walk on them and the kids will have fun comparing and matching the shoe patterns left with the family's shoes. 'Playing shoe detectives!'

activity
222

SPLATTER PAINTINGS

4+ ✔

A quick and easy way to decorate paper.

What You Need

 ✔

- *Containers of acrylic paint*
- *A brush per container*
- *Newsprint paper*

 ✔

What To Do

 ✔

Spread out the paper on the grass outside or peg some paper on an easel if you have one.

Show your children how to dip the brush in the the paint and flick the brush with their fingers so the paint flies onto the paper.

Make sure your children wear a painting smock or an old shirt of Dad's over their clothes because this activity is fairly messy.

The splatter paper makes great gift wrapping paper or is also good for covering school books.

activity
223

SPRAY PAINTINGS

4+   ✓

Save all your old household spray bottles for this fun, painting activity.

 ✓

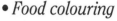

What You Need

 ✓

- *Food colouring*
- *Spray bottles*
- *Pegs*
- *Water*
- *Paper*

✓

✓

What To Do

✓

This is definitely an outside activity and only to be done on a very still day! Mix up some food colouring and water in the spray bottles (make sure they have been very well washed out first).

Peg up some paper outside - if your children have an easel use that, otherwise peg the paper between two trees or on the fence. Show them how to spray with short, fine bursts and encourage them to use lots of different colours to see how the colours mix and new colours are made. Discourage them from spraying too much on each piece of paper - if the paper becomes too wet it will fall to bits. Keep the spray paintings for sensational, bright, wrapping paper.

HINT!

If you don't have a painting smock to cover your children's clothes, put them in an old shirt of Dad's, done up back-to-front. On hot days let them spray paint in their togs - but don't forget the sunscreen.

activity
224

STOCKING BABY

4+

With a little help your children can make their own 'stocking baby' to love and cuddle.

 ✓

 ✓

What You Need

- *Tights*
- *Elastic bands*
- *Scissors*
- *Needle and cotton*
- *Filling - this could be cushion filling, cotton wool or old fabrics*
- *Buttons*
- *Wool*

 ✓

What To Do

Cut off the lower part of the tights below the knees and keep. Stuff and then knot the ends to form the baby's 'feet'. Use the lower legs to make the arms and, after filling them, sew the openings.

Take the rest of the tights and fill with the stuffing. Sew or knot the waistband to make the top of the baby's head. Twist a rubber band below its head to make its neck and, lastly, sew the arms onto the body.

Your children can help you make the baby's face. Buttons look great or perhaps embroider or felt pen on a mouth. Wool can be sewn on for its hair.

Your children might like to dress their baby in some of their own tiny baby clothes.

activity

225

TWINKLE TWINKLE

4+ ✓

 ✓

Take your young children outside at night to look at the stars and teach them the old song Twinkle Twinkle Little Star. Next day, try this 'star painting'.

 ✓

 ✓

What You Need

 ✓

- *White paint*
- *Black paper*
- *Cardboard for stencils*

 ✓

What To Do

Carefully cut out some cardboard stencils for your children to paint inside. Help them position the stencil on the black paper and paint the inside of the stencil with the white paint. Do this with lots of star shapes until they have their own beautiful starry nightscape to hang in their bedroom with *Blu-Tack*.

activity
226

WET CHALK DRAWING

4+

 ✓

 ✓

 ✓

Children love drawing with chalk - it's perfect for outdoors as it can be easily washed off walls, pavement tiles and paths. But they will really love this new way of drawing - with wet chalk.

What You Need

- *Sugar*
- *Water*
- *Container for the sugar/water*
- *Chalk*
- *Paper*

What To Do

Help the children make up a solution of sugar and water, about $\frac{1}{4}$ of a cup of sugar to a cup of water, and soak some coloured chalk in it. You can leave the chalk in the solution for a few hours, or the children can just dip the chalk tip in as they draw. Either way the chalk becomes much, much brighter and doesn't smear as much.

If you want to keep some of the children's chalk drawings for posterity you can spray them lightly with hair spray when they are dry.

activity

227

WRAPPING PAPER

4+

Save the cost of wrapping paper for gifts by making some with the children in the garden.

What You Need

- *Spray bottles*
- *Food colouring or powder paint*
- *Water*
- *Large sheets of butcher's paper*
- *Pegs*

What To Do

The children will enjoy helping you make up some water paint and filling up some spray bottles. Make up fairly strong mixes of colour with the powdered paint or food colouring. You can buy spray bottles quite cheaply from supermarkets or discount stores, or use old household cleanser bottles that have been washed very thoroughly.

Put a painting smock or old shirt of Dad's on the children as this is a fairly messy activity.

Peg some paper to the fence or, alternatively, string a piece of thin rope or cord between two trees and peg the paper to that.

Show the children how to spray the paper with thin bursts so the colours mix and look beautiful. Don't let them spray too much on each piece as the paper will become so wet it will fall apart. Change the paper often until they tire of the activity and you will have a wonderful supply of wrapping paper for all those special occasions.

activity
228

APPLE PRINT BOOK PAPER

6+

Make some cheap and unique wrapping paper for your children's school books in the holidays.

What You Need

- *Apples*
- *Vegetable knife*
- *Poster paint (available from chain stores or craft shops)*
- *Plate*
- *Newspaper*
- *Butcher's paper or a role of newsprint*

What To Do

Go to your local newspaper office and for a small sum you can buy the end of a roll of newsprint paper. This will last the children for years and is ideal for drawing, painting and printing.

Children's school books look better covered and last longer too. If you cover them all in the same paper, small children can recognise them fast.

Cover an outdoor table with some newspaper and help them cut some apples in half. Pat dry the cut side of the apple. Then dip the apple in a thin layer of paint and the children print all over the paper. Use a few different colours if they wish - red, yellow or green.

When the paper is dry they will love helping you cover their school books. Slip on a plastic cover or cover over with clear *Contact* to make them even stronger.

HINT!

Vegetables such as mushrooms, carrots, onions and potatoes are great for printing, too.

activity

229

ART IN THE DARK

6+

A good family activity to play at night, especially in storms when there is a power failure!

 ✓

What You Need

- *Pencils* - *Paper*

 ✓

What To Do

Hand everyone a pencil and paper and make sure they can draw comfortably. Turn out all the lights.

First, they write their name at the top of the paper, then tell them what to draw - perhaps a cow, or your house or Mum, or anything else you can think of. When everyone is finished, turn the lights back on and have a laugh at the results.

Move over, Picasso!

activity

230

BAKED BEADS

6+

Help your children make colourful necklaces for themselves or original gifts for others with this simple recipe.

 ✓

 ✓

 ✓

What You Need

- *4 cups of plain flour*
- *1 cup of salt*
- *1 ½ cups of cold water*

- *Acrylic paints*
- *Brushes*
- *Fishing line*

What To Do

Mix together the flour and salt and then add the water. Knead for at least ten minutes on a floured board (let your children help with the measuring and kneading). Measuring is a great maths activity and kneading is good for small muscle development. Knead until the craft dough is pliable and will not fall to bits.

Help your children mould it into interesting bead shapes. Use a nail, skewer or kebab stick to make a hole through the centre of each bead.

Bake the beads in a slow oven for 2-3 hours until they are hard and completely dry.

They look great painted in bright colours. Thread with fishing line when the paint is totally dry.

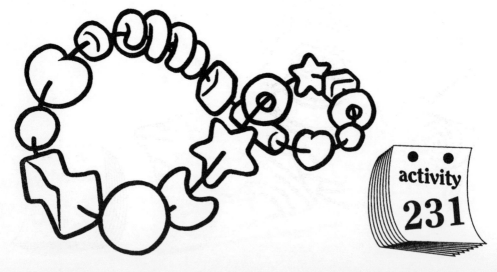

activity

231

BATIK FOR KIDS

6+

Conventional batik needs hot wax and this is dangerous with young children. Use this safe batik to make interesting fabric designs.

What You Need

- *Old detergent container*
- *Cold water dyes (available from chemists and supermarkets)*
- *White cotton fabric (sheeting material is fine) or T-shirts*

- *Flour*
- *Water*
- *Brushes*

What To Do

Together, make up a paste from flour and water and pour it into an old detergent bottle. Your children can squeeze the paste onto the T-shirt or fabric in whatever design they like. When the paste is dry, make up the cold water dyes, provide the brushes and they can paint the glue-free areas.

When the garment or fabric is dry they will have their own fabric art work. You could make the fabric into some great big comfortable cushions on which to read books in their bedroom.

activity
232

BEACH ART

6+ ✓

Collect lots of beach treasures with the children to enable them to enjoy creating some beach art at home.

 ✓

 ✓

What You Need

 ✓

• *Cardboard*
• *Strong wood glue*
• *Bits and pieces from the beach such as seaweed, sponges, shells, small stones, little pieces of driftwood, beach grass, and so on*

 ✓

 ✓

What To Do

Take some buckets or other containers to the beach and, before you go home, go for a walk with the children to gather lots of treasures. Save them for a rainy day or a day when everyone is tired or bored. Spread them out on a table and provide some wood glue in small dishes or plastic containers with brushes and a variety of cardboard.

This messy activity is ideal to do on a table out-of-doors and any left over bits and pieces can simply be hosed or swept into the garden.

You will be amazed at the wonderful creations they will make, and they will be very special momentos of a day or holiday at the beach for your children.

activity

233

BEATIFUL FLOWER PICTURES 6+

Preserve the beauty of spring flowers with your children.

What You Need

- *A selection of small spring flowers*
- *Grease proof paper*
- *A cool iron*
- *A tea towel*
- *Hole punch*
- *Thin coloured satin ribbon*

What To Do

Go for a walk in the garden with the children and gather a selection of small, dainty spring flowers and leaves.

Spread them out on a table outdoors (so the remaining flowers and leaves can simply be swept or hosed into the garden) and select flowers that go well together for pictrures.

Cut out pieces of the grease proof paper and lay the selected flowers and leaves on one piece and cover with another. Put the tea towel over the top and iron carefully with a cool iron. The wax in the paper will melt the paper together sealing in the flowers and leaves.

Help the children cut around their pretty pictures, punch a hole at the top of each picture and thread some ribbon through for hanging.

A lovely bedroom decoration and a way to keep spring in your home all year.

activity

234

CAMERAS

6+

Cameras make great gifts for children to record the important events in their lives.

What You Need

- *An easy-to-use camera*
- *Film*
- *Photo album*

What To Do

Recently I bought my son a small camera of his own at our local post office. It only cost a few dollars and he is really enjoying taking his own shots. Another option is to buy one of the disposable cameras with the film included. They would be great for a child to take on holidays, a school camp or for a special excursion and, again, are easy to use.

We made a few rules with our son about his camera:

• we will buy him the film but he has to pay for the developing from his pocket money

• we have taught him how to hold the camera still and looked at his photos to help him learn how to frame and choose good shots.

• he is responsible for putting his photos in his own album.

Older children will also be able to write down their own stories about their photos. You will have to write down the stories for younger children.

Encourage your children to take their cameras along to important events such as a school sports day or other notable event at school, a special family outing, or a club sports game, so they can record all the wonderful happenings in their lives.

activity

235

CLAY PRINTING

6+

Children enjoy seeing the prints that different objects can make in clay.

What You Need

- *Clay*
- *Individual boards to work on or a sheet of plastic or a plastic tablecloth*
- *Objects for printing with such as shells, small toys, construction materials, cutlery, screws, biscuit cutters, nails, stones, sticks, or clay tools*
- *Paints*
- *Paintbrushes*

What To Do

The children can knead their clay until they are happy with the shapes they want to print into. Using the printing tools they can make interesting prints and patterns in their clay. The might like to keep these finished pieces for paperweights or just for decorations or they may have just enjoyed the experience of printing.

After the pieces have dried for a few days they can be painted if wished, or sealed with some clear varnish.

activity
236

DINOSAUR PUPPETS

6+

Kids are absolutely fascinated by dinosaurs. Research them together and help your children make a Dinosaur Puppet Stage and Dinosaur Puppets.

What You Need

- *Stiff cardboard*
- *Felt pens*
- *Glue*
- *Scissors*

What To Do

Fold a large piece of cardboard at both ends so it can stand on its own (see the diagram below). Your children can use their imagination to decorate it with dinosaur 'scenery' - rocks, mountains, perhaps a volcano, water, etc. Look in books about dinosaurs together for ideas.

They then draw or trace pictures of dinosaurs onto more cardboard and carefully cut them out. Tape stiff cardboard tabs about 10 cms (4 ins) long and 3 cms (1 inch) wide onto the dinosaurs to hold them. Cut slits in the puppet theatre where your children want the dinosaurs to move.

Place the puppet theatre on the edge of a table. Your children stand or sit behind the theatre and move the dinosaur puppets as they tell the story.

Help them work out a little play to perform for the rest of the family or for their class at school.

activity

237

ENVIRONMENTAL WEAVING

6+

Show the children how to make a wonderful environmental weaving to decorate an empty wall at home.

What You Need

- *A large tree branch*
- *Wool*
- *Natural items such as feathers, grasses, leaves, strips of bark, seed pods, corn husks, wheat, etc.*

What To Do

Go for a walk and find a suitable branch with at least two or three small branches coming out of it to form a triangular shape.

Tie the wool onto the branch and wrap around the other branches to form the warp. Show the children some loosely woven fabric such as hessian so they understand about weaving and the warp and the weft.

Collect lots of natural materials to form an interesting weft. The children will enjoy weaving the items they find in and out of the warp threads. Coloured wool and strips of fabric could be used also.

When it is finished the weaving looks great hanging from a wall or hung securely from the ceiling. Everyone will be very proud of this unique piece of family art.

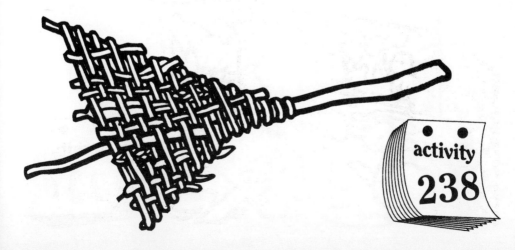

activity

238

EYE DROPPER PAINTING

6+ ✓

Teaches your children how to mix the three basic colours to form new ones.

 ✓

 ✓

What You Need

 ✓

- *Plastic eye droppers (cheap to buy or save the ones that come with the children's medicines)*
- *Red, yellow or blue powder paint or food colouring mixed with water*

 ✓

What To Do

A good activity to do on a table or tarp outside or, if it's going to be an inside activity, spread lots of newspapers on your table.

Provide three jars or paint pots with the basic colours, red, yellow and blue and three eye droppers. Provide plenty of paper and let your children experiment with making new colours.

Encourage them not to make the paper too wet with paint or it tears when hung up. Wet paintings can be hung on a clothes drier to dry or even on the clothes line.

Sometimes it is fun to wet the paper first with plain water and see what happens when the colours are squirted on. (Use small bottles of food colouring.)

(Also see Colour Mixing - activity 199 for more eye dropper fun).

activity
239

FINGERPRINT CRITTERS

6+

Your children can use their imaginations to create interesting 'critters' from their fingerprints.

 ✓

 ✓

What You Need

 ✓

- *Stamp pad or coloured felt pens*
- *Pens or coloured pencils*
- *Paper*

 ✓

What To Do

 ✓

Show your children how to make fingerprints by pressing their index finger in the stamp pad, rolling it from side to side and then carefully place it on the paper and again roll it from side to side to produce a clear print.

If you don't have a stamp pad, they can colour their index finger with a non-permanent felt pen and then make a print. (Have a cloth nearby to wipe fingers on - you don't want fingerprints all over the walls.)

Then they add details to turn their fingerprints into whatever they like, such as birds, flowers, people, bugs, monsters or anything else they can think of. Think of some of your own too!

activity
240

FOOTPRINT CASTS

6+

Go for a walk and find some interesting animal footprints with your children. They will have fun making permanent records of them.

What You Need

- *Animal or people footprints*
- *Small spade*
- *Cardboard boxes*
- *Plaster of Paris or casting plaster*

What To Do

Check in your garden, at the park or on the beach for interesting footprints. Dig up the prints with a small spade taking enough dirt to stop it falling apart. (This activity works best when there has been some rain and the ground is nice and moist.) Carefully place the footprint inside a box and take it home.

At home help the children mix up some plaster following the directions carefully. (Be careful not to tip any liquid plaster down drains as it may clog them up.)

Pour the liquid plaster carefully into the footprint and smooth off the top with an old knife. Leave it until it is dry and hard. Brush off the dirt and you should have an exact replica of the footprint.

The children may enjoy painting their interesting footprints.

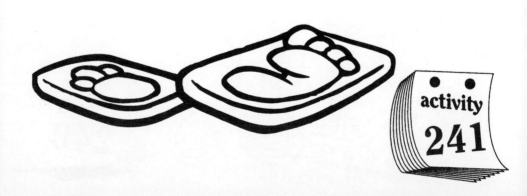

activity
241

HOLE PUNCH PICTURES

6+

A new skill to teach your children that helps develop their fine motor skills.

 ✓

 ✓

What You Need

 ✓

- *Polystyrene trays (butchers and greengrocers often use these) or thin card*
- *Felt-pens*
- *Hole puncher*
- *Threading materials*

 ✓

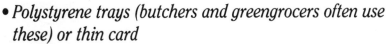 ✓

What To Do

After your children have drawn a colourful picture on the card or polystyrene, show them how to punch holes around either the outline of the picture or the border. The holes should be about 3 cm (1 inch) apart.

Your children will then enjoy lacing in and out of the holes. Use a bodkin (blunt ended large needle) threaded with wool or thin embroidery cotton. If you don't want them to use a needle they could lace with plastic lacing (available by the metre (yard) from craft shops and haberdasheries), old shoelaces or wool or string that has a strengthened end made by dipping it into melted candle wax or a strong solution of laundry starch and allowed to dry.

The pictures can be hung up with another length of the threading material.

activity

242

ICEBLOCK STICK CREATIONS 6+

Collect iceblock sticks or buy them cheaply from craft or junk stores and your kids will love creating all sorts of exciting things from them.

What You Need

- *Strong PVA or craft glue*
- *Iceblock sticks*
- *Newspaper*
- *Paint*

What To Do

Spread some newspaper on a table so the glue won't stick and work out what they would like to make. They could make something they could use, like a small box, by laying sticks in a square shape and gradually building it up, or they could simply create something like a plane or an animal. Most children are far more inventive than us 'oldies' and they will have lots of fun making wonderful creations. Just remind them that the glue does dry clear if it looks messy and that PVA and craft glue will need some time to dry. When the creation is dry they will enjoy painting it.

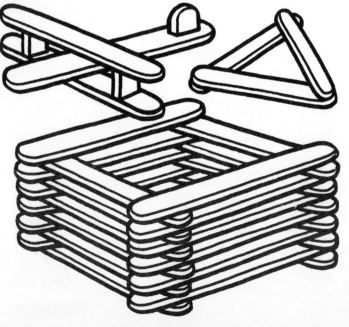

activity
243

JUMPING JACKS

6+

Make some Jumping Jacks with the children and give Dad a big surprise.

 ✓

 ✓

What You Need

 ✓

- *Strong paper - typing or photocopying paper is ideal*
- *A strong, wide rubber band*
- *Scissors*
- *Glue*

 ✓

 ✓

What To Do

Measure two 10 cm (4 ins) squares on the paper and your children can cut them out. Roll each square tightly into a thin cylinder and glue in place so they do not unroll. When the glue has dried, bend each cylinder in the middle and then wrap them together with the rubber band around the middle.

Hold one of the cylinders firmly while you wind the other up as tightly as possible. Carefully place the Jumping Jack inside a box or perhaps a book. Ask someone to open it and watch their face!

activity
244

LEAF PLASTER CASTS

6+

Preserve the interesting textures and shapes of leaves by imprinting them in plaster.

What You Need

- *Leaves of all shapes and textures*
- *Plaster of Paris*
- *Plasticine*

What To Do

Go for a walk in the botanical gardens, park or in your own garden and collect a variety of leaves from the ground.

Roll out some plasticine and carefully press some leaves into it using the side of the leaves where the veins are the most prominent. Form a wall of plasticine around the impressions and pour some Plaster of Paris into the mould. Leave this to set for a few days, remove the plasticine and the children will have a permanent record of the lovely leaves they collected.

They may enjoy painting their leaf moulds in interesting colours.

activity
245

PAINTED ROCKS

6+

Paperweights are useful for everyone. Help your children make some for gifts or their own use.

What You Need

- *Small rocks of a suitable size*
- *House or acrylic paints*
- *Small brushes*

What To Do

Next time you have a family picnic at the beach or near a creek or river, see if you can find some nice smooth rocks that would be suitable for paperweights. Take some home and keep them for a rainy day or for when the children are bored and looking for something different to do.

Cover an outdoor table with newspaper or an old cloth and find a selection of small brushes.

They will need to use acrylic or house paints for this project. You can now buy small sample tins of some brands of acrylic paints from hardware stores or paint shops and they are ideal for activities like these. Otherwise, visit a craft store to buy some acrylic craft paints.

The children will have great fun painting and decorating their rocks and, when they are dry, they can give them to friends and family for gifts.

HINT!

Acrylic paint is often difficult to wash out of clothes. Avoid this problem by giving the children old adult sized shirts or t-shirts to wear over their clothes.

If they do get some on their clothes, soak in warm water before washing and do not spray with a pre-wash spray as this often sets the paint.

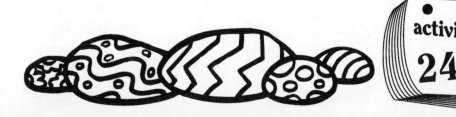

activity
246

PAPIER MÂCHÉ BOWLS

6+

My friend, Kerenne, a primary school teacher, makes these bowls with the children in her class to give to their mums for Christmas. A useful and colourful gift idea she has shared with us.

 ✓

 ✓

 ✓

 ✓

 ✓

 ✓

What You Need

- *Picnic set bowl or plate*
- *Newspaper and butcher's paper*
- *Glue (wallpaper paste is excellent)*
- *Acrylic paint*

What To Do

Any shaped bowl or plate can be the basic mould for your children's papier mâché creation, but Kerenne prefers to use plastic in case of accidents. Cover the bowl really well with Vaseline before applying the papier mâché so it can lift off well when it is dry.

Apply the newspaper in strips. Dip into the wallpaper paste and stick on. Papier mâché is a slow process - do a few layers each day.

When the bowl is nearly thick enough, help your children to make the last few layers from white strips of butcher's paper.

When it is all dry, they paint the inside and outside well with white acrylic paint. Kerenne says that large bright designs look great painted on the bowls and she gets the children to draw on their designs, first with a felt pen, then paint after. Maybe your children could colour co-ordinate the bowl to your kitchen or family room decor for a cheap designer look!

activity
247

PLASTICINE PLAY

6+

A different medium for creating. Cheap to buy but lots of fun.

 ✓

 ✓

What You Need

- *Plasticine (available from newsagents, school suppliers and toy shops)*

 ✓

What To Do

 ✓

While playdough is cheap to make at home, buying plasticine will give your children a different medium for modelling. Because it is firmer than playdough, it keeps its style better and is a great way to strengthen finger and hand muscles.

It usually comes in a variety of colours too, which adds another interesting dimension to creating. Sit down with your children and show them how to model people, animals and other shapes. They might like to create a whole plasticine environment - a dinosaur landscape or perhaps a farm.

For added interest, pipecleaners, matches, paddlepop sticks, beads and other things can be used with the plasticine.

activity
248

POTATO MEN

6+

Potatoes have such interesting shapes they make wonderful 'men'! Show your children how they can do this with a few bits and pieces and lots of imagination.

 ✓

 ✓

What You Need

- *Large potatoes*
- *Small scrubbing brush*
- *Toothpicks*
- *Playdough or plasticine*
- *Bits and pieces to decorate with - lace, felt, fabric scraps, coloured paper, ribbons and so on*

 ✓

 ✓

What To Do

Give the children a large bowl of warm water and they can begin by scrubbing all the dirt off their potatoes. Next they dry them with a tea towel. Now they are ready to begin making Potato Men.

Help them use the toothpicks (some may have to be shortened) to hold the playdough or plasticine in place for the facial features - eyes, nose, mouth and ears.

Now they can use the fabric, paper and so on to make bow ties, hats and other clothes. Cotton wool dyed black or brown could be the hair or perhaps a moustache. Lady Potato People might like a ribbon or bow in their hair. Help the children make a whole family of Potato People.

When they've finished the project they can scrub some more potatoes for a tasty snack. Show them how to rub the skins with some olive oil and bake in a fairly hot oven. When they are crispy on the outside, and soft in the middle take them out. Cut off the tops, scoop out some of the middle and mix with grated cheese and ham. Pop them back in the oven for a few minutes and take out.

A very 'more-ish' snack or a simple and easy tea.

activity
249

POTPOURRI POUCHES

6+

Help the children make some of these as gifts or to use in your own home.

What You Need

• *Fine squares of fabric such as lawn or muslin*
• *Alternatively, use ladies' or children's handkerchiefs*
• *Pinking shears*
• *Rubber bands*
• *Fine satin ribbon*
• *Potpourri*

What To Do

Potpourri pouches are best made out of doors so any spilt potpourri can simply be swept or hosed into the garden.

If you have made some Lavender potpourri (see activity 375) use some of that, or buy some commercial potpourri from craft or florist shops.

If you are using fabric rather than handkerchiefs, show the children how to cut the fabric into squares using the pinking shears. The serrated edges look most attractive.

Then the children simply spread out a handkerchief or fabric square, measure out three tablespoons or so of potpourri onto the handkerchief and twist the bottom of the handkerchief to form a little sack.

Help them wind a rubber band around the twist in the handkerchief until it is tight and then tie some ribbon over the rubber band to hide it.

Potpourri pouches are perfect to put in drawers to give your clothes a lovely scent, or tie them to coathangers to add perfume to your wardrobe.

activity
250

RUBBER BAND BALL

6+ ✓

 ✓

A fun recycling activity that will also help develop your children's fine motor skills.

 ✓

What You Need

• *Rubber bands*

What To Do

We seem to get rubber bands every day around the papers and the mail and they certainly can accumulate. Recycle them by making rubber band balls with your children. They will love a bouncing ball they made themselves.

Scrunch together a few rubber bands or even tie them and begin stretching the others around this core as many times as necessary. Keep building it until it is the size you want. You can make lots together or your children and their friends might like to have a competition to see who can make the biggest - maybe an item for the Guinness Book of Records!!!

activity
251

STAINED GLASS PICTURES 6+

A way to use up old crayons to create beautiful colourful pictures.

What You Need

- *Old broken wax crayons*
- *Grease proof paper*
- *Iron*

What To Do

Help your children grate old wax crayons into separate piles of colours.

They then make a design or picture on the waxed paper with the crayon gratings. Cover this with another piece of waxed paper and iron the two pieces together using a cool iron.

You can frame their creation or just *Blu-Tack* it on a window where the sun will shine through to give it a 'stained glass' window effect.

activity

252

STAINED GLASS WINDOWS 6+

Another activity with cellophane scraps to help your children learn about colour mixing and making new colours.

What You Need

- *Scissors*
- *Scraps of cellophane*
- *Glue or sticky tape*
- *Paper*

What To Do

Your children may need help to fold a piece of paper three times. They then cut interesting shapes out of the sides of the paper. Open it up to see what they have made. Now help your children glue or tape pieces of cellophane over the cut out shapes for a very colourful effect. Hang these 'stained glass' pictures on their bedroom windows with the sun shining through. Perhaps you could visit a local church or cathedral so they can see real stained glass windows.

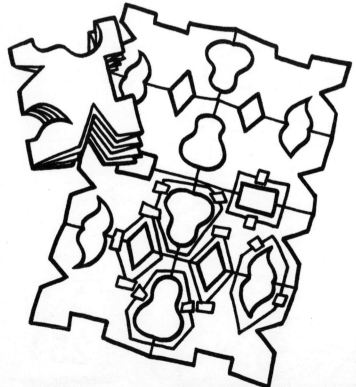

activity
253

STENCILS

6+ ✓
 ✓
 ✓
 ✓
 ✓
 ✓

Like most people, I buy a lot of the family's meat and chicken on polystyrene trays. Wash these up and save them because they make excellent stencils for the children to paint with.

What You Need

- *Polystryrene trays*
- *Pencils or pens*
- *Scissors or a Stanley knife*
- *Paints*
- *Brushes*
- *Paper*

What To Do

Have your children draw a simple design on the trays with a pencil or ball point pen. Use sharp-pointed scissors or a *Stanley* knife to cut out the design. Your children put the stencil over a piece of paper and paint inside the cut-out section. Lift it off carefully and admire their design.

HINT!

Make wrapping paper or cards with stencils. Perhaps heart shapes for Valentine's Day cards, bells, trees or holly leaves for Christmas wrapping paper or cards, or balloons for birthday wrapping paper. I'm sure your children will be able to think of lots more great ideas!

activity
254

STREAMERS

6+

Children love making these colourful streamers for sports days, processions, or just to use as dancing props.

What You Need

- *Pieces of dowel, rulers, chopsticks or long unsharpened pencils*
- *Crepe paper of all colours*

- *Strong glue*
- *Scissors*

What To Do

Help the children cut out long lengths of crepe paper. Choose a few strips of different colours and glue them from the end of a piece of dowel or ruler, pencil or chopstick. Roll up the streamers tightly and then unwind. Show the children how to wave the streamers around to create colourful displays. They can hold a streamer in each hand and let the colours mix. Put on some dancing music out in the garden and let the kids dance with their streamers.

HINT!

Streamers are great for school Sports Day made in their school or house colours. Volunteer to go to your children's classroom the day before Sports Day, take all the makings and help the children make streamers in their own house colours. You'll be a very popular person.

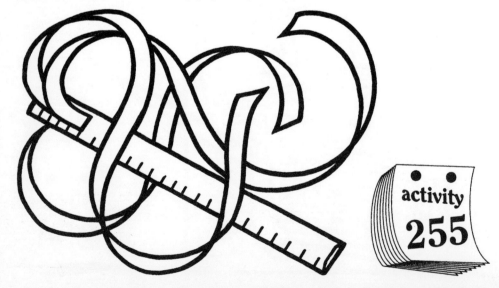

activity
255

TENNIS BALL PAINTING

6+

Children love watching the patterns and new colours form as the balls roll around.

What You Need

- *Old tennis balls*
- *Baking dish*
- *Paper*
- *Poster or acrylic paints*
- *Plastic yoghurt, margarine, or take-away containers*
- *Dessert spoons*

What To Do

Lay a sheet of paper inside the baking dish and spoon a little paint of each colour into the plastic containers.

Put a tennis ball into each container and the children can use the spoon to cover it with paint.

They then lift a couple of the balls into the baking dish and tilt it from side to side so that the balls roll around, mixing the paints, making new colours and spreading it into interesting shapes and patterns.

If you only use primary colours this will help teach younger children about how new colours are made. Yellow and red - orange, yellow and blue - green and red and blue - purple.

Keep the paper for very individual wrapping paper for gifts.

activity
256

TOOTHPICK MODELS

6+

Children will spend hours modelling with toothpicks and some clay, plasticine and matchsticks. Bring out all these things on those wet, boring days and they will be happily occupied for ages. (Well at least for long enough for you to read the paper and have a cup of coffee!)

 ✓

 ✓

What You Need

 ✓

 ✓

- *Toothpicks (for younger children you could substitute dead matchsticks or the brightly dyed matchsticks available at craft or junk stores)*
- *Plasticine, clay or playdough*

What To Do

Show the children how to roll small balls of the plasticine, playdough or clay and then stick the toothpicks in them. Use the balls as the corner stone of the houses and other buildings they make. They can stick in lots of toothpicks to form the walls and then make doors, windows, and roofs out of pieces of paper or cardboard.

Bring out some small props and they could make farms for their farm animals, houses for Lego or Duplo people or perhaps an airport or bridge for small planes and cars. They'll think of lots of creative ways to use the toothpicks once you get them started.

Don't forget to find the camera to take some photos of their wonderful creations before they fall to pieces. Who knows - you may have an architect in the family one day!

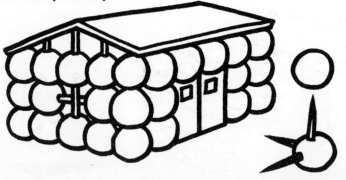

activity

257

TREASURE CHESTS

6+

Children love having special little boxes in which to store treasured possessions. Show your children how simply they can be made out of household junk.

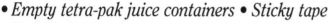

What You Need

- *Empty tetra-pak juice containers* • *Sticky tape*
- *Stanley knife or scissors* • *A ruler and a pen*
- *Paint and other materials for decoration*

What To Do

Decide together with the children how large they want their special box to be. Measure the distance from the bottom of the juice container and draw a cutting line with the ruler and pen. Cut along the two sides of the pack and the front at this point, but not the back.

Next, form the lid from the remaining long piece at the back of the box. Measure the depth and width of the box, add them together (older children can do this - it's great maths practice), and mark this on the lid flap. Cut carefully and then bend the lid over in the appropriate places.

Your children will enjoy decorating their own special box. They can begin by painting it - household paints work well, or acrylic paints - and then decorate the boxes with glitter, sequins, bits of ribbon, lace or fabric offcuts, pretty flowers or leaves from the garden, pictures cut from greeting cards or magazines or their own art work.

To keep the box closed, use some adhesive velcro (available from sewing shops) or a button and a loop at the front.

activity
258

TWIG WEAVINGS

6+

Introduce your children to the concept of weaving with this fun activity.

 ✓

What You Need

 ✓

- *Twigs about 30 cm - 40 cm (12 ins - 15 ins) long*
- *Pieces of wool, ribbons, strips of fabric, etc.*
- *Something to hang it from*
- *Sharp knife*

 ✓

 ✓

What To Do

Explain the concept of warps and weft to your children. Together look at some loosely woven fabric such as hessian or linen so they understand.

Cut about 20 pieces of wool of equal length for the warp. With the knife, cut notches in the sticks at equal distances so the wool doesn't slide. Tie the threads to the bottom and top sticks and, with another piece of wool, hang it to a door handle, a hook or a tree branch.

Anchor the bottom stick to a brick so it stays steady while your children are weaving. Your children then use the rest of the wool or other materials to make an interesting weaving.

Later, they can cut the weaving off to use as a mat or hang it up in the frame.

activity

259

WET CHALK DRAWINGS

6+

Soak sticks of coloured chalk in water to provide a different drawing medium for your children.

 ✓

 ✓

What You Need

 ✓

 ✓

- *Coloured chalk sticks*
- *Water*
- *Paper (if you want to spend a little money, buy some black paper - the effect is terrific)*

 ✓

 ✓

What To Do

Your children can help you soak the chalk sticks in water for about ten minutes. Warn them not to press too hard as they draw because the chalk can break easily.

Drawing with wet chalk on black paper looks especially effective, but it's just as interesting on white.

Happy drawing!

activity
260

BATH FIZZ!

8+

Help your children make some deliciously scented bath salts to use or give away as gifts. Add some excitement to bath time!

What You Need

- *Bicarbonate of soda*
- *Cornflour*
- *Cream of tartar*
- *Essential oils such as lavender (available from Health Food Stores)*

- *A glass bottle with a lid*
- *A measuring cup*

What To Do

Measure three-quarters of a cup of bicarbonate of soda, two tablespoons of cornflour and half a cup of cream of tartar. Put them all into the jar and stir well to mix and break up any lumps.

Add a few drops of an essential oil or perfume and mix really well again.

When your children are in the bath, drop in spoonfuls of the Bath Salts and they will enjoy the fizzy sensation and the delicious smell.

activity
261

BOX PUPPETS

8+

 ✓

Help your kids make a marionette puppet that works really well out of household junk.

 ✓

 ✓

What You Need

 ✓

• *A milk carton*
• *Paper*
• *String*
• *Felt pens and other materials to decorate the puppet*
• *Glue*
• *Sticks*
• *A pencil*

What To Do

Help your kids make a hole in each side of the top part of the milk carton for the puppet's arms. To make movable arms, wrap strips of paper tightly around a pencil and then glue the strips in place. Thread a long piece of string through the milk carton and then thread the paper cyclinders onto the string to make arms on each side. Next tie more strings onto the arms and attach to sticks that make the puppet work. Next make two legs in the same way.

The children will enjoy decorating the milk carton and finally attaching a string to the top of the milk carton to make the 'head' move.

Tie the crossed sticks together and make the puppet move by moving the sticks.

Help them make a few marionette puppets and put on a puppet show together.

activity
262

CITRUS PEEL JEWELLERY 8+

Help your children make some creative and individual jewellery from citrus fruit to give as gifts or for themselves.

What You Need

- *Oranges, lemons, grapefruit, mandarins, limes*
- *String or leather thonging*
- *Sharp knife*
- *Pencil or knitting needle*

What To Do

Help your children cut interesting shapes from the citrus peel. (Eat the rest of the fruit or make some delicious juice.)

Make holes in each piece while it is still soft and leave to dry. Flatten some pieces by leaving a weight on them while they are drying. Make cylindrical pieces by winding strips around the pencil or knitting needle.

When they are all dry, your children can thread them onto string or the leather thonging. Make the designs different by alternating small beads (available from bead or craft shops).

activity
263

COLOURFUL BOTTLES

8+

Your children will love your help to make these colourful bottles. They make useful and decorative storage, look great just for display, or give them away for gifts.

What You Need

- Bottles of different shapes and sizes
- Metallic spray paints (available from hardware and craft stores)
- Masking tape
- Scissors
- Newspaper

What To Do

Help your children cut out shapes from the masking tape and use them to decorate the bottles. Stars, moons, hearts, fish, shells, flowers and geometric shapes all look great.

Next, spread an area well with newspaper and help them carefully spray the bottles. When they are dry, peel off the masking to reveal the interesting patterns they have made.

Help them name their work (like all artists) by writing their name on the bottom of their bottle art!

activity
264

DOT PAINTINGS

8+

To encourage colour awareness and an appreciation of art in your children.

 ✓

 ✓

 ✓

What You Need

 ✓

• *Drawing paper (e.g. computer paper, etc.)*
• *Paints and a fine brush (only primary colours)*
• *Coloured pencils (red, blue, yellow)*
• *Fine pointed felt pens*

What To Do

Encourage your children to draw or paint using only a technique of tiny dots of primary colours. Your children may prefer to use a lead pencil to lightly pencil in the drawing and then colour it with the dots.

Show your children Impressionist paintings that use this technique, e.g. Vincent Van Gogh, Seurat, Monet and others. Your local library will have lots of art books you can borrow to look at with your children, or perhaps you are lucky enough to live in a city/town with an Art Gallery you can visit together.

As your children can only use dots of primary colours, they will have to think carefully about what dots to mix together to produce other colours, perhaps yellow and red to produce orange.

activity
265

ETCHINGS

Older children will love this new way to make colourful drawings.

 ✓

 ✓

What You Need

 ✓

- *Paper*
- *Crayons or craypas*
- *Match sticks, spoons, broken pencils*

 ✓

 ✓

What To Do

Show your children how to fill a whole piece of paper with every colour crayon except black. It is important that this first layer of colour is quite thick, so make sure your children press down heavily and apply the colour all over. Next, take a black crayon and, using it on its side, cover all the colours with black.

Then show the children how to use a pointed implement such as a spoon handle, paint brush end or match stick, to scratch a picture on the paper. The black is scratched away, leaving the bright colours revealed.

activity
266

FRAMED FLOWERS

8+

Older children who enjoy the garden will love making their own framed flower pictures as gifts.

What You Need

- *Thick books* • *Flowers, leaves and grasses* • *Frames*
- *Good quality white or cream whiteboard*
- *Latex adhesive or clear plastic adhesive spray*

What To Do

Many flowers retain their colour and beauty when pressed and make wonderful pictures. Cut the plant material the children wish to press on a dry day and place between two pieces of blotting or kitchen paper and then in a heavy book. Position the book under a chair cushion or mattress, or under a pile of other heavy books. The length of time it takes plants to dry depends on the weather and the individual plant material, but check after two weeks.

Help the children position their dried flowers and other materials on the cardboard, which should be cut to size to fit the frame, with the border outlined with a light pencil marking. Smaller flowers or petals can be used to make decorative borders; rose leaves and ferns make very effective borders.

When the children are satisfied with their design it is time to secure them in place with a little dab of the latex-based glue on the back of each flower or leaf or by spraying with the adhesive spray.

When the glue on the dried flowers is completely dry, place the pictures in the frames and secure. Choose simple and fairly light frames to ensure they don't detract from the delicate flower pictures.

activity
267

GOD'S EYES

8+

Show your children how to make this simple form of folk art. They originated in South America and were religious symbols.

What You Need

- *Brightly coloured wool*
- *Two sticks about 15-20 cm (6 ins-8 ins) long*

What To Do

Hold the sticks while your children tie them together to form a cross. You then show them how to hold the two sticks together where they join and loop the wool around the first stick close to the knot. Wrap the wool first around one stick, then the next, to keep forming X's. Remind them to keep turning the god's eye as they work.

Change wool often, tying one colour to the next to make it is bright as possible. Finish the god's eye off by tying the wool to the stick.

Bells and tassels are often added to make them even more colourful and decorative.

Your children might like to make a few to decorate a wall in their bedroom.

activity
268

INSECT BROOCHES

8+

Older children with some basic sewing skills will enjoy making some insect brooches to decorate a plain sweatshirt or T-shirt or to give to special friends as a gift.

What You Need

- *Oddments of felt and lace*
- *Safety pins*
- *Old tights*
- *Sequins*
- *Felt pen*
- *Chalk*
- *Mug*
- *Craft glue*
- *Scissors*
- *Needle and thread*

What To Do

Begin by making a ladybird. Draw a small circle on some red or orange felt or fabric and help your children cut it out. Show then how to sew large running stitches as close to the edge of the fabric as possible. Next, help them gather up the running stitches and put some pieces of cut-up tights in the centre. Pull the stitches up really tight and tie off the ends. Mould it into a long oval shape and sew carefully over the gap to close it.

Your children will enjoy marking on the ladybird's spots with a black felt pen. Add a safety pin to attach it.

To make a bee, follow the same steps using black felt or black fabric. Then glue on with the craft glue some strips of yellow felt to make the bee's stripes. Some scraps of lace make great wings and again attach a safety pin at the back.

To make a butterfly brooch, use purple or pink felt or fabric and add some beautiful lacy wings and glue on some bright sequins. Again, add a safety pin at the back for attaching.

activity

269

KNOCK KNOCK CARDS

8+

Help your children make their own joke cards to give to their friends. Lots of creative fun and saves money too!

What You Need

- *Paper*
- *Scissors*
- *Stanley knife*
- *Glue*
- *Felt pens*

What To Do

Measure together two blank pieces of paper about 20 cm by 14 cm (8 ins by 5½ ins). Your children cut them out carefully and then fold each one in half.

Draw a square about 5 cm by 5 cm (2 ins by 2 ins) on the front of one of the cards and then cut it out on three sides so it opens like a door. It is easier to cut this with a *Stanley* knife, but if your children want to do it all themselves, start off the cut with the cutting knife and let them do the rest with scissors.

Next, glue the uncut card to the inside of this card, except where the window is. When it is dry your children can decorate the card with a Knock-Knock joke and put the answer inside the card.

activity
270

LET'S MODEL

TENNIS BALL PAINTING

8+

A great way for older children to make models that last for ever.

 ✓

 ✓

What You Need

- *Plaster of Paris (available from hardware stores or craft suppliers)*
- *Plain flour*
- *Water*
- *Paint*

 ✓

 ✓

What To Do

Your children can help you make up a modelling mixture using one part Plaster of Paris, three parts of flour and enough water to make a dough consistency.

This mixture will remain workable for about an hour. Your children will enjoy making models with the mixture. Dry them in the sun until very firm and then the children can paint them.

Who knows, they may become sculptors one day!

activity
271

MODELLING DOUGH

8+

This simply-made dough is good for making small jewellery and ornaments.

 ✓

What You Need

 ✓

- *White bread*
- *Glue*
- *Lemon juice or eucalyptus oil*

 ✓

 ✓

What To Do

✓

Cut off the crusts from half a dozen slices of the bread and break into little pieces. Add two tablespoons of glue and the juice of half a lemon or a few drops of eucalyptus oil.

Mix it all thoroughly until it is ready for your children to use for modelling.

Making beads is a simple activity but make sure any holes are made before the object dries.

Place the finished pieces on a tray covered with grease proof paper.

The dough items will take at least two days to dry and should be turned frequently.

Later your children will enjoy painting their creation with some acrylic or water paints.

activity
272

ORANGE POMANDERS

8+

Revive an old-fashioned craft by making fragrant pomander balls with your children.

What You Need

- Oranges with thin skins
- Cloves
- 1 tablespoon of cinnamon
- 1 tablespoon of orris powder (available from chemists)
- Skewer or thin kebab stick
- Ribbon
- Paper bag
- Tissue paper or kitchen wrap paper

What To Do

Show the children how to make holes in the oranges with the skewers. Make holes all over and then insert a clove in each hole. Do this until the orange is totally covered with cloves.

Then, help the children combine the cinnamon and orris powder in a paper bag, and shake the oranges in the mixture until they are quite powdery. Wrap the oranges in the tissue paper and leave for a month. Leave them in a warm place, and in a month they will be ready.

They look great tied with Christmas ribbon.

Grandmas and Aunts will love one for a gift to hang in their cupboards!

activity
273

PAPIER MÂCHÉ

8+

A long term project for older children that has heaps of uses!

What You Need

- *Non-toxic wallpaper paste*
- *Balloon*
- *Strips of newspaper about 4 cm (1¹⁄₂ ins) wide*

What To Do

Blow up the balloon and simply dip strips of newspaper into the wallpaper paste and place on the balloon.

Papier mâché must be done slowly and allowed to dry well between each application so it won't mildew. Don't apply more than three or four layers at a time. Peg the balloon on the clothes line so it dries quickly. When the papier mâché is strong enough, burst the balloon inside with a pin and it can be cut and used for something special.

Make some masks out of your papier mache or a collection of funny animals.

activity
274

SHOE BOX DIORAMA

8+

A special way to display small objects or make a favourite story come to life.

 ✓

 ✓

 ✓

 ✓

What You Need

- *A shoe box*
- *Playdough, plasticine or Blu-Tack*
- *Ice block sticks*

What To Do

Help your children cut out the side of the shoe box. Decide what scene you are going to make and think of what you can use.

They could paint the sides and back of the shoe box first with colours suitable for the scene they are going to make.

Small mirrors or cellophane make excellent ponds, crepe paper can be used for trees and grass. Ice block sticks can be decorated for people and the playdough, plasticine or *Blu-Tack* can hold objects in place.

Your children may like to make a farm, a dinosaur world or perhaps their favourite fairy tale or nursery rhyme!

activity
275

STABILES

8+

Stabiles are lots of fun to make.

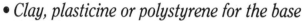

What You Need

- *Clay, plasticine or polystyrene for the base*
- *Toothpicks, ice block sticks, pipe cleaners, pasta, polystyrene pieces, leaves, flowers*
- *Coloured paper or cardboard*
- *Sticky tape or Blu-Tack*

What To Do

Using the clay, plasticine or a piece of polystyrene as a base, your children poke the sticks, pipe cleaners or toothpicks into it.

They then decorate them with leaves, flowers or shapes. If they need to secure them, use small blocks of *Blu-Tack* or sticky tape.

Fun to make at Christmas time also, using pictures cut from old cards, bits of tinsel and small decorations. Make one with your children for a centrepiece for the Christmas dinner table.

activity
276

T-SHIRT ART

8+

Your children will proudly wear a T-shirt that they have decorated themselves.

 ✓

 ✓

 ✓

 ✓

 ✓

What You Need

- *Plain T-shirt*
- *Fabric crayons (available at fabric and craft shops)*
- *White paper*
- *Iron and ironing board*
- *Tea towel*

What To Do

Suggest to your children that they work out their design before drawing it with the fabric crayons. When they have done that, they draw the design on the white paper, colouring as heavily as they can.

Put a tea towel on the ironing board and pull the front of the T-shirt through the board. (This will stop the design going through to the other side of the T-shirt.)

Place the drawing face down on the fabric and do the ironing yourself. Press down with a warm iron all over the design (don't move the iron back and forward or the design will blur). The crayon picture will transfer to the T-shirt.

Remove the piece of paper and see how the wax has melted the design onto the T-shirt.

Your children may like to decorate the back of their T-shirt also!

activity

277

DRY FOOD JEWELLERY

10+

 ✓

 ✓

Older children will enjoy making unusual jewellery from dried foods. A cheap new trend!

 ✓

What You Need

- *Dried fruit, such as dried apple rings*
- *Dried beans*
- *Macaroni*
- *Needle and thread*
- *Clear varnish and a brush* ✓
- *Paper clips* ✓

What To Do

Help your children work out a pattern with the dried fruit, beans and macaroni. Then they carefully sew through the dried fruit, the macaroni and, last, the beans.

When the necklace is finished, help them attach a paper clip to each end so they can link together to fasten the necklace.

Your children can even make matching earrings and a bracelet.

The varnish adds to the appearance as well as making the jewellery last longer too.

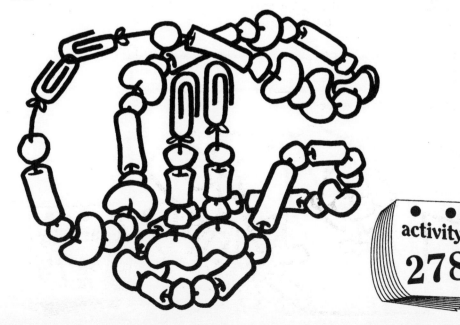

activity
278

PAPER JEWELLERY

10+

Older children will enjoy creating their own jewellery from colourful paper to match an outfit for a special event.

 ✓

 ✓

What You Need

 ✓

• *Colourful paper - can be bought from the newsagents, but old wrapping paper, advertising brochures, envelope insides and brown paper work well too.*

What To Do

To make a colourful bracelet, take two long strips of contrasting paper. Glue the ends together at right angles and then fold one piece over the other, then over the other and so on. (Your children will probably have made Christmas streamers using this method.) Glue the ends togther when it is finished. This bracelet expands like a concertina so the children will be able to slip it over an arm easily.

Make a matching necklace by cutting long, thin paper triangles. Begin wth the wide end and roll the triangle as tightly as possible around a pencil or knitting needles. Put a spot of glue at the end to hold it in place. Thread the colourful beads onto some wool or cord.

Instant chic!

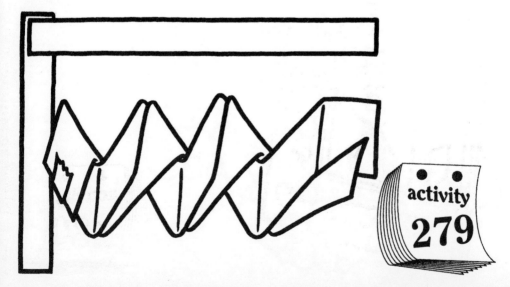

activity
279

PASTA PHOTO FRAMES

10+

Help your children make some interesting photo frames for their room or to give as gifts.

What You Need

- *Strong cardboard*
- *Strong glue*
- *Variety of pasta shapes (bows, twirls, etc.)*
- *Gold or silver metallic spray paint*

What To Do

Select the photos first for size, then cut a piece of strong card to double the size you need, with room for a border. Score with a knife and ruler and then fold in half carefully. Cut out the section for the photo, leaving a border of at least 4 cm (1½ ins) (although the 'in' look for frames now is to have a much wider border!).

Help your children decorate the frame with the pasta shapes and strong glue. Leave to dry. If you wish, spray with the gold or silver paint, but make sure you do this outside on a still day.

Glue the photo in the frame and glue together. Attach a small piece of strong card at the back so your frame can stand up.

activity
280

POMPOMS

10+

Older children will be able to make lots of small animals once they have mastered the knack of making woollen pompoms.

 ✓

 ✓

What You Need

- *Scissors*
- *Wool*
- *Strong glue*
- *Needle and cotton*
- *Cardboard*

 ✓

 ✓

What To Do

Help your children cut two round circles from cardboard - whatever size they want the finished pompoms to be. Next, cut a small hole in the centre of each cardboard circle. Your children then wrap wool around and around the circles until the centre hole is completely full.

With the point of the scissors, they cut the wool between the two circles. Take a length of wool and help your children tie it between the circles and knot firmly. Then they cut away the cardboard, trim and tie and are left with a pompom.

They could join lots of pompoms together to make a caterpillar, make a pompom teddy or mouse, or attach it to hat elastic and a paper cup and use it for a catch game. Pompoms also make great decorations on hats and clothes.

activity
281

TIE-DYED T-SHIRTS

10+

Help the children dye their own very fashionable tie-dye t-shirts.

What You Need

- *White cotton t-shirts*
- *A large non aluminium pot for dyeing*
- *Commercial fabric dyes*
- *String*
- *Large wooden spoon*
- *Water*
- *Towels*

What To Do

Spread newspapers all over an outdoor table and cover the children and yourself with painting smocks or large old shirts.

Help them tie the t-shirt in tight knots or tie pieces of the string around parts. Make up the dye according to the directions on the packet. Use the wooden spoon to stir the t-shirts around so they are well covered.

After dyeing help them rinse the t-shirts very thoroughly in cold water. Then untie the knots or string and rinse again very well. Squeeze out any excess water and spread the shirts on a thick towel to dry.

If the children wish, they can re-tie or use more string to re-knot the t-shirts and dye them with another colour.

When they have finished dyeing, help them rinse again well and dry the t-shirts. Cover with a clean cloth and iron to help set the dye.

The children will love wearing their trendy tie-dyed t-shirts. Why don't you get them to dye one for you?

activity

282

TWIG FRAMES

10+ ✓

The country look is still very popular and twig frames are very easy, as well as cheap and fun, for the children to make.

 ✓

 ✓

What You Need

 ✓

• *Twigs of different size, colour and texture*
• *A cardboard box*
• *Strong scissors*
• *Wood glue*
• *Ruler and pencil*

 ✓

 ✓

What To Do

Cut out the bottom of the cardboard box with the children, and when they decide what size they would like their frames to be, measure out a rectangle or square shape for the back. Cut two the same size. Then cut out the middle of one and glue it on top of the other leaving the top unglued. This space at the top is where you slide your photo or picture into the frame when it is finished.

Now the children will enjoy cutting their twigs to size and gluing them onto the frame. It looks more interesting if they cut the twigs into different lengths. Encourage the children also to choose a variety of textures and colours in the twigs for interest.

When the twigs are dry help them cut out a large triangle from the strong cardboard. Make a fold in the long side of the triangle and then glue it onto the back of the twig frame so it can stand. If they want to hang it, screw in a couple of tiny cup hooks and tie some fine string or fishing line between them to hang the frame.

The children's twig frames will be much admired by everyone.

activity

283

WOOL BALLOONS

10+

Help the children make some wool or string balloons to hang from the ceilings in their rooms.

What You Need

- *Balloons*
- *Plaster of Paris*
- *Lengths of colourful wool or string*

What To Do

Cover a table outside with some newspaper or a plastic or vinyl cloth. The children can each blow up a balloon.

Mix up some of the plaster with water in an old container.

The children soak the wool in the plaster and wrap it around the balloon. Use lots and lots of lengths of wool.

When they have done enough, leave until the string hardens and then burst the balloon and pull it through a hole.

They look great tied to the ceiling.

activity
284

MATHS IS FUN

MATHS IS FUN

CLOTHES PEG SORTING

2+ ✓

A simple colour sorting game to play with your children. Sorting colours is the first step in learning to name them.

 ✓

 ✓

 ✓

What You Need

• *Plastic clothes pegs of different colours*
• *Ice cream containers*

✓

What To Do

✓

Have a container for each colour peg. Clip a different coloured peg onto the side of each container.

Your children will then enjoy sorting the pegs by colour into the correct container. When they have finished this, show them how to clip the pegs around the side of the container. (This will be difficult for some children, but persist over time as they need strong finger muscles to begin writing.)

Later, you can help them count which container holds the most pegs. Can they name their colours yet? See which ones they are not sure of and play colour-learning games together as you dress, bath and play with them through the day.

activity
285

FISHING FUN

2+

A fun way to practise counting and to make size comparisons.

What You Need

- *Ruler or a short length of dowel*
- *Magnet*
- *Coloured cardboard*

- *String*
- *Paper clips*
- *Scissors*

What To Do

Cut out lots of cardboard fish. Be imaginative and make them different shapes, sizes and colours. Slide a paper clip onto each fish's 'mouth'. Tie a magnet onto the ruler or length of dowel with some string. Your children will love catching the 'fish' and telling you about them. Ask them to show you all the red fish, or all the blue or green fish. Next see if they can show you the largest or smallest fish. Talk about all the colours and do lots of counting.

Follow up the fishing game with fish and chips for tea!

activity
286

GARAGES

2+

Learning how to sort objects into sizes is an important mathematical skill. This activity will help teach your young children how to do this in a fun play way.

What You Need

- *Toy cars of various sizes*
- *Boxes of various sizes*

What To Do

Match the boxes to the sizes of the cars or else cut doorways in the boxes to fit the different sized cars.

Your children will have lots of fun driving the cars into the right garages. See if they can order the cars from the smallest to the largest. Practise counting how many cars there are altogether too!

activity

287

GARDEN DETECTIVES

2+ ✔

Encourage your children's thinking and questioning skills with this fun activity.

 ✔

What You Need

• *Time*

What To Do

Play a guessing game in the garden with the children. Tell them you are thinking of something that they can all see. Provide a few clues, and then it is up to them to ask the questions until they get the answer.

Younger children may need more help, so start with a couple of clues and they will ask for more.

This game can be played in the car, at the beach, or anywhere with any number of children. The child who guesses correctly has the next turn to think of an item.

activity
288

LARGE AND SMALL

2+

An activity to help younger children begin to sort and classify.

 ✓

 ✓

What You Need

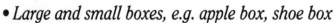

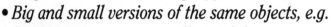

- *Large and small boxes, e.g. apple box, shoe box*
- *Big and small versions of the same objects, e.g.*

large toy car	*small match box car*
large comb	*small comb*
large brush	*small brush*
tablespoon	*teaspoon*
large stone	*small stone*
large leaf	*small leaf*

 ✓

 ✓

What To Do

Place all the items your have found on a tray. Your children find an item, then its smaller or larger version, and then puts them into the correct boxes, i.e. small items in the shoe box, large ones in the apple box.

Talk lots about big and little or large and small in everyday situations with your young children. Fun play situations like this are the way young children learn.

activity
289

MATCHING GAMES

2+

Make sure your children have lots of opportunities to try matching objects - this is an important mathematical step.

 ✓

 ✓

What You Need

Find lots of objects to match:
- *Pair of socks*
- *Clothes pegs*
- *Buttons*
- *Toys*
- *Shoes*
- *Cutlery*
- *Gloves*

What To Do

Simply collect all the pairs in a large box and have your children look through it to find all the pairs.

Your children will enjoy helping you sort the washing, and also finding everyone's pairs of socks.

activity
290

OUTLINES

2+

An activity to help younger children learn to compare size and to order according to size.

What You Need

- *Paper*
- *Pencil*

What to Do

Have your children place their hand down on a piece of paper and spread their fingers. Trace around the outline of their hand. Help them cut it out.

Now do the same to your own hand and other members of the family so your children can compare them and then put them in size sequence. Talk about bigger than and smaller than.

Do the same with the family's feet (after they have bathed or showered!). Your children might have fun putting out the footprint line to follow.

Keep their hand and foot outlines so you can compare them with new ones in a year or so. You'll be amazed at how much they've grown.

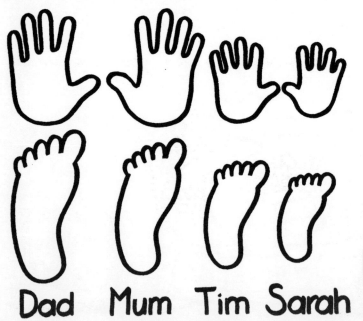

Dad   Mum   Tim   Sarah

activity

291

POURING AND MEASURING 2+

A fun activity which can be extended to a measuring activity for older children.

 ✓

 ✓

 ✓

What You Need

- *A sheet or table cloth*
- *A large plastic tub*
- *Mixture of rice*
- *Any or all of the following - different sorts of pasta e.g. shells, tubes, macaroni and spirals, rolled oats, sago, dried beans*

What To Do

Spread out the sheet on the family room floor, fill the tub and let them go. Provide toys from your children's sandpit as well as funnels, cups, spoons of different sizes, strainers and jugs.

As well as simply enjoying playing in and manipulating the material, your children may enjoy using trucks, cars, diggers and animals in the tub. The different mixtures make great loads for small trucks and backhoes.

Encourage your children to create mountains, valleys and other interesting landscapes for toy animals, or even a moonscape or dinosaur world.

Make sure the tub is securely covered after playing or better still transferred to larger sealed containers to discourage vermin sharing the fun.

activity

292

SEED SORTING

2+

Sorting and matching are important mathematical skills.

What You Need

• *A mixture of seeds*
• *A muffin or patty pan tin or an egg carton*

What To Do

Buy a few packets of seeds or use a bag of soup mix. Model for your children how to sort out the seeds into different categories, but encourage them to think of their own sorting criteria.

The children can put the different categories of seeds into the holes in the muffin tin. When they have finished sorting talk to them about what they did and why. See if they can count each pile to see which one has the most seeds.

Plant a selection of the seeds in a pot or in the garden so they can enjoy watching their seeds grow.

activity
293

SORTING TIME

2+

Sorting things into groups or sets is a very early basic mathematical skill. As your toddlers help you sort the washing they are gaining important sorting skills.

 ✓

 ✓

What You Need

• *Washing to sort*

 ✓

What To Do

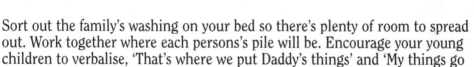 ✓

Sort out the family's washing on your bed so there's plenty of room to spread out. Work together where each persons's pile will be. Encourage your young children to verbalise, 'That's where we put Daddy's things' and 'My things go here'.

Then your children can help you put the items in the correct piles and find pairs of socks. When all the sorting is completed they can help carry each person's pile to their bedroom.

activity
294

ZANY MATCH-UPS

2+

A fun matching game you can make yourself for younger children.

 ✓

 ✓

 ✓

✓

✓

✓

What You Need

- *Collect a variety of small items such as:*
  comb, bobby pin, pencil, pen, spoon, knife, screwdriver,
  pegs, rubber bands, safety pin, scissors, buttons, small
  blocks, match box, cotton reel, small pins
- *A large sheet of cardboard*
- *Contact (adhesive plastic sheeting)*
- *Small box or container for the objects*
- *Fine, coloured felt pens or coloured pencils*

What To Do

Trace around the objects, if they are coloured, use the same colour for the outline. Keep all the objects in a container for matching. Cover the cardboard with *Contact* to keep it clean.

Your children match the objects to the outlines. Ask them questions such as:

How many red things are there?
How many are made from metal?
Can you find me something that's made from plastic?

Later they might like you to time them to see how fast they can match the objects or see if they can beat an egg-timer.

activity
295

BIG FEET

4+ ✓

 ✓

 ✓

 ✓

 ✓

 ✓

Another fun mathematics activity that helps your young children compare sizes and learn mathematical terms such as largest, smallest and bigger than and smaller than.

What You Need

- *Plastic ice-cream container lids or strong cardboard*
- *Elastic*
- *Felt pen*

What To Do

Draw around your own feet (or your husband's). Cut out the feet and attach elastic so your children can discover what it's like to have BIG FEET.

When you are walking on the beach or in the sandpit compare all the family's footprints. Can they tell you who has the largest feet, the smallest, etc.?

activity

296

BUTTONS

4+

*A sorting game which helps your children work out
similarities and differences for themselves.*

What You Need

- *Lots of assorted buttons in a container*
- *Egg cartons or ice cube trays*

What To Do

If you don't have lots of different size, shape and colour buttons in
your button box, charity shops always have them for sale for a small price.

Give them to your children to sort out according to their own criteria first. Ask
them to explain to you what they have done.

If they are having difficulty with this, offer some suggestions such as:

- Could you sort them out into different colours?
- Could you find all the ones with two holes in first and then the ones with
  four holes?
- Could you put all the metal ones together?

For younger children who are having difficulties matching colours, colour the
bottom of an egg carton with different colours and your children sort the
buttons into the correct hole.

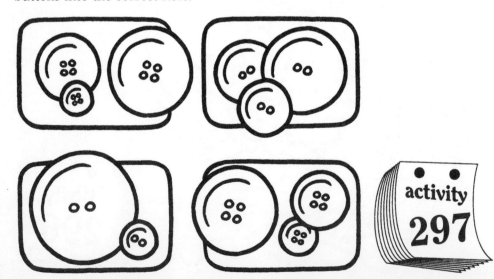

activity
297

COMPARING WEIGHTS

4+   ✓

Young children often find it difficult to understand weight; usually, they equate with size.

What You Need

 ✓

• *Two household bricks*
• *Short wide length of wood*

 ✓

What To Do

Walk around the garden with your children and find some things they would like to compare. You might find some wood, rocks, clumps of soil, feathers, different sized leaves, flowers, and so on.

Balance the wood over the bricks like a see-saw and compare the weights. Bring out your kitchen or bathroom scales to weigh them also.

Compare some wet and dry objects also, such as wet and dry soil, or a wet and dry sponge.

activity
298

ENVIRONMENTAL NUMBER CHART

  ✓

 ✓

Go for a walk around the garden or to a local park and collect lots of interesting leaves, seeds, flowers, gumnuts, twigs, small pebbles, grasses and other materials to make an environmental number chart with your children.

 ✓

 ✓

 ✓

 ✓

What You Need

- *Large sheet of thick cardboard*
- *Strong glue*
- *Brush*
- *Felt pens*
- *Environmental materials*

What To Do

When you come home from your walk, your children can sort out all the things you have collected into groups. Draw up a number chart together (see below).

Help them glue on the correct number of items beside each numeral. This way they will learn to match the numeral with the number of objects.

Hang it in a special spot in their bedroom and practise counting together before they go to sleep each night.

Andrews Number Chart	
1	🥜
2	🌸 🌸
3	twigs
4	seeds
5	pebbles
6	gumnuts

activity

299

ESTIMATION

4+   ✓

 ✓

 ✓

 ✓

 ✓

Estimating and trying to guess what is going to happen next is an important aspect of mathematics and science. Develop your children's powers of estimation by asking them questions like those listed below.

What You Need

- *Building blocks*
- *Large jug of water*
- *Measuring cups*
- *Egg timer*
- *Marbles in a container*
- *Hammer, nails, and a block of wood*

What To Do

Use the materials above and pose questions to your children, such as:

- How many blocks do you think you can build up into a tower before they will fall?
- How many yellow blocks do you think you will need to lay them end to end right across the doorway?
- How many cups of water do you think you will need to fill up the jug?
- How many marbles do you think you will need to fill a measuring cup?
- How many times do you think you will need to bang the nail with the hammer to hammer it right into the piece of wood?
- How many times do you think we will have to turn the egg-timer before you have tidied your room, put away that game, or picked up those blocks?

After your children have given you their estimations, work them out together and see how close they were.

activity

300

MY DAY

Young children find learning to tell the time very difficult. Before they can understand, they must acquire a sense of event sequence. Activities like 'My Day' will help.

What You Need

- *A long strip of paper*
- *Felt pens or coloured pencils*

What To Do

Discuss with your children the sorts of things they would do in a normal day.

Begin by suggesting to your children they draw a sun at one end of the paper and the moon and stars at the other, for the beginning and end of their day. Next, they draw in their day - when they get up, have breakfast, get dressed, go to preschool, things they do there, come home, play outside, have their bath, have dinner, play or watch TV, brush their teeth, have stories, go to bed. Hang their 'My Day' picture in their bedroom and talk about it together.

Hang a calendar in their room and if they are looking forward to a particular event, perhaps a birthday party or having a friend sleep over, together you can cross off the days as they pass.

Children need to have a good grasp of the sequence of daily events and days before they can tell the time from a clock.

activity
301

MY WEEK

Help your children understand more about the passing of time and learn the days of the week with this activity.

 ✓

 ✓

What You Need

 ✓

- *A long piece of paper divided into seven and marked with the days of the week*
- *Felt pens or coloured pencils*

 ✓

What To Do

Start the week on a Sunday. Discuss the days of the week with your children as you write their names on the paper. Talk about things you do regularly on certain days:

> On Mondays you come to tennis with Mum
> On Wednesday you to go kindergarten
> On Saturday Dad takes you to gym classes

At the end of each day have your children draw in the space the things they enjoyed doing most on that day.

At the end of the week hang it in their bedroom and talk about it together using language like 'yesterday', 'tomorrow', 'last week', 'next week', 'night', 'day' and so on.

activity

302

NUMBER MATCH

4+

 ✓

 ✓

 ✓

A simple activity to help young children learn numerals.

What You Need

 ✓

• *Paper*
• *Coloured felt pen*

What To Do

 ✓

Write lots of numeral pairs 1-5 all over a piece of paper. Your children have to draw lines to match up a pair of numerals the same. Make it even harder by drawing the numerals in different colours - a blue 5 and a yellow 5, a green 3 and a pink 3.

Can they tell you what the numerals are called? Can they find three yellow objects in their room? Five blue pegs in the peg basket? Two green leaves in the garden?

Turn counting and learning numerals into lots of fun. When they know their numerals to 5 add 6 to 10 also.

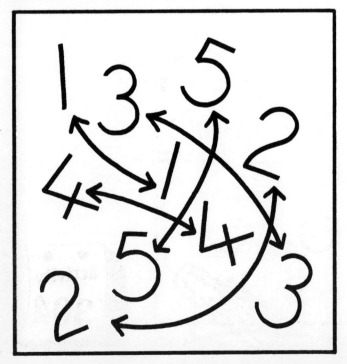

activity
303

PAPER CLIP COUNTING

4+

A fun, hands-on counting game to help children learn numbers.

 ✓

 ✓

What You Need

 ✓

- *10 pieces of cardboard about 12 cm (4½ ins) square*
- *Felt pens*
- *Paper clips or clothes pegs*

What To Do

Number each of the pieces of cardboard from 1 to 10. Put the corresponding number of dots on each piece of cardboard so your children can count the dots if they cannot yet recognize numerals.

See if your children can slide the correct number of paper clips onto each piece of cardboard. When they are finished check to see if they are right. Older children could play this game with numbers to 20 or higher.

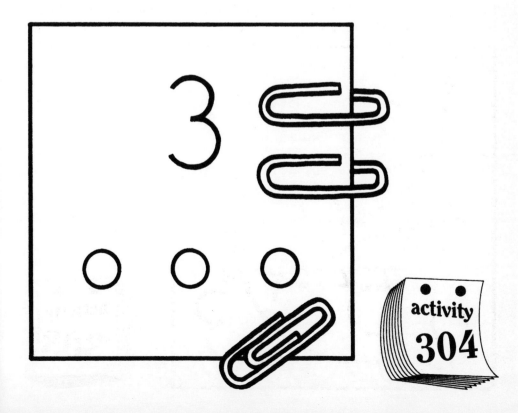

activity
304

PATTERNING

4+ ✓
 ✓
 ✓
 ✓
 ✓
 ✓

Children need many opportunities to explore patterns and relationships in their environment. Go for a walk through the garden or a local park with your children and collect some natural materials to use for making patterns.

What You Need

- *Container or bucket*
- *Cardboard*
- *Wood glue*
- *Materials to collect such as:*
  - ** leaves of different shape, colour, and texture*
  - ** grasses*
  - ** flowers*
  - ** pebbles*
  - ** small twigs*
  - ** bark and so on*

What To Do

Spread out the materials on a table outdoors and see if the children can use them for making patterns. If they are having difficulty with this concept, model some simple patterns for them such as:

leaf-flower-leaf-flower-leaf, and then ask what would come next.
Or, stone-bark-leaf-stone-bark - and again ask what would come next.

When the children understand, see if they can make some patterns of their own with the materials.

They may like to glue some of their patterns onto some cardboard with the strong glue to keep and look at later.

See if they can spot patterns in the environment, your home or in furnishings.

activity
305

SAND NUMBERS AND LETTERS

4+ ✓

 ✓

We all know how quickly young children learn. Make some letters and numbers out of sand to help them learn easily.

 ✓

What You Need

- *Cardboard*
- *Wood glue*
- *Fine beach sand*
- *Food colouring*

✓

✓

What To Do

This is a messy activity and is best done outdoors.

With your children, cut out 36 pieces of cardboard of the same size. Write a letter of the alphabet and the numerals 1 to 10 on each piece of card. Make them nice and large.

The children will enjoy helping trace over the letters and numbers carefully with glue on a brush. Then apply fine beach sand (this can be coloured if you wish by mixing it with different colours of food colouring and allowing it to dry).

Let the cards dry and then the children can learn their letters and numbers and how they are formed by running their fingers over them and feeling the sandy shapes.

activity

306

SHAPE MOBILES

4+

Help your children learn geometric shapes in a fun way with this balancing activity.

 ✓

 ✓

 ✓

✓

 ✓

What You Need

- *Stiff cardboard or polystyrene trays*
- *Sticky tape*
- *Scissors*
- *String*
- *Wire coat hangers*

What To Do

Help your children draw and cut out simple geometric shapes - circles, squares, rectangles and triangles. Cut two exactly the same of each shape.

At this stage, they may like to paint, collage or draw on the shapes to decorate them.

Next, cut a slit to the centre of each one and join them at right angles (use the sticky tape to hold them in place).

Your children will enjoy hanging up the shapes in their room on a wire coat hanger. A shape mobile - watch them move and spin in the breeze.

activity
307

WEIGHING

4+

Activities like this will help your children learn about weight and understand terms such as 'lighter than' or 'heavier than'.

 ✓

 ✓

What You Need

 ✓

- *Bathroom scales*
- *Kitchen scales*
- *Various items to measure*
- *Paper/pencil*

 ✓

 ✓

What To Do

Begin by measuring all the members of your family. Your children might like to draw a picture of each one and then help them write beside the pictures their weight in kilograms. Discuss who is the heaviest and who is the lightest.

Next, raid the pantry and find tins and packets of various shapes and weights. Let them weigh them and together work out which are the heaviest and which are the lighest. Try to find items that weigh the same but are different shapes or sizes, perhaps a tin of baked beans and a packet of flour.

activity
308

CALCULATOR FUN

6+

Teach your younger children to be familiar and comfortable with simple calculators with fun activities like these.

What You Need

- *A simple cheap calculator (if you are buying one, get one with number keys as large as possible)*
- *Pencils*
- *Papers*

What To Do

Show your children how to press the numbers and how to make them disappear. Show them what keys like + and - do.

Next, write some numbers on the paper for them to copy - 4792, 0876, 5398, or 6748. See if they can press the numbers from 1 - 10, or perhaps 1 - 20. Call out numbers and see if they can press them correctly on the calculator - 5, 8, 12, 17, and so on.

Let them also have lots of time to play with and explore their calculator in their own way. When you have things to work out with the calculator, involve them so they can see new ways to use it. Take it grocery shopping with you and show them how to work out the bargains too!

activity

309

FAMILY EYE-COLOUR GRAPHS 6+

Graphing is an important mathematical skill. Help your children make a graph of family eye colours and learn this skill in a fun way.

What You Need

• *Paper*
• *Coloured crayons, pencils or felt pens*

What To Do

Discuss together the colour of the eyes of members of your family and extended family. 'James and I have blue eyes like Nanny, and Amy has green eyes like Aunty Julie.'

Make a simple graph of eye colours - brown, hazel, green, blue, and so on, and help your children discover which are the most common eye colours in your family.

Encourage them to take their graphs to school to show their teachers or to use for a talk or Show and Tell.

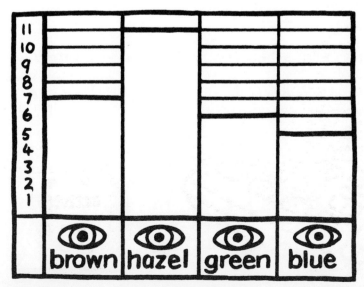

activity

310

MEASURING AND BALANCING 6+

Children love working out measurements, and this is a very important early numeracy skill. Turn it into a fun activity so they are learning through play.

What You Need

- *The sand pit, a large dish of sand, dried beans, rice, or some other grain (available cheaply from produce stores)*
- *Balance scales*
- *Measuring scales*

What To Do

If your kitchen scales are too expensive for use by the children, visit a second hand store and buy a set for them to play with.

Give them an assortment of containers and they will love measuring and pouring and comparing amounts.

Older children will enjoy recording their findings. Pose some questions for them to work out also.

If we add a cup of water to a cup of dry sand does that make it heavier?

Is a cup of rice heavier than a cup of corn?

Which sort of leaf in the garden is the heaviest. Is it necessarily the largest?

When they have had enough playing, send them into the kitchen to do some real measuring as they make a batch of pikelets (with some help from Mum or Dad) for everyone to enjoy!!!

activity

311

NAUGHTY THREES

6+

A simple dice game all the family will enjoy.

 ✓

 ✓

What You Need

 ✓

- *2 or more players*
- *Two dice*
- *Paper and pencil*

 ✓

What To Do

Elect someone to keep the scores first. The game is simple and the first player to reach fifty (or any other designated number) is the winner.

Players take it in turns to throw both dice and only score when two identical numbers are thrown (two 1s, two 2s and so on). All doubles score five points, except for a pair of 6s which scores 25, and a pair of 'Naughty' 3s, which wipes out the player's total score and they then have to start again.

activity
312

NUMBER HUNT

6+ ✓

A good game to play as you cook dinner to get the children out from under your feet.

 ✓

 ✓

What You Need

• *Time*

What To Do

Call out a number, then ask the children to find objects that represent that number from around the house. For example, a fork has four tines, so that is four; or a rolling pin has two handles - 2; or a chair has four legs - 4.

 ✓

You will be amazed at how inventive they become.

activity

313

ODDS AND EVENS

A fun, fast game to play with your children.

What You Need

- *2 players*
- *Paper for scoring*

What To Do

You and your children must clench your right fist. Together, count to three and on three each person extends either one or two fingers. As you extend your fingers, you must take it in turn to say 'odds' or 'evens'. If the players extend one finger it is 'evens'; if one extends one and others two, it is, of course, 'odds'.

If a player guesses correctly, they score a point and have another turn at calling. When they guess wrongly, it is the other player's turn to call again. Before you begin the game, decide when it will end - perhaps the first to 20, or maybe when the clock gets to the hour.

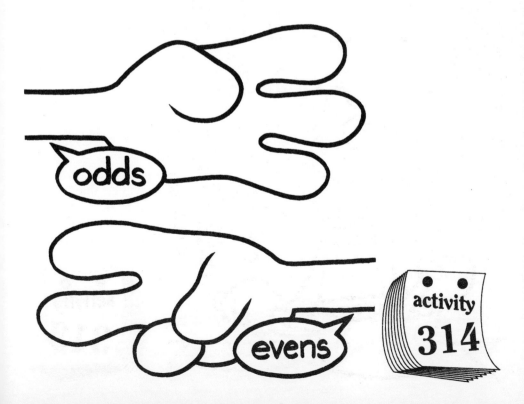

activity
314

POND FISHING

6+   ✓

Make some simple fishing nets with your children and take them pond fishing.

What You Need

- *Tights*
- *Strong wire (coathanger wire doubled for strength works well)*
- *A piece of dowel for a handle*
- *String or strong rubber bands*
- *Wire cutters*
- *Pliers*
- *A clear plastic jar or container*
- *Magnifying glass*

What To Do

Help the children make some nets to use for pond fishing. The tights will help you catch small water creatures that would pass through the holes in regular fishing nets.

Thread the wire through the top of the tights and cut off the legs about half way down. Attach the ends of the wire to the piece of dowel to form a handle and carefully twist the wire ends with the pliers so they are safe.

Attach the jar or container to the bottom of the tights net with the rubber bands or string.

Visit a local pond and see what you can catch. The children will be able to look at their catch in the jar at the bottom of the net. If they want to see it with the magnifying glass you may need to tip the water into another container to observe it carefully. Don't forget to return your 'catch' to the pond when you have finished with it. Always model care for the environment with your children.

activity

315

ADDING UP HOLES

8+ ✓

Improve your children's adding ability as well as their throwing skills with this activity.

 ✓
 ✓
✓

What You Need

- *Large cardboard box or piece of strong cardboard*
- *Stanley knife*
- *Blackboard or paper to score*
- *Felt pen*
- *Tennis ball*

What To Do

On one side of the box or on the cardboard draw five or six holes. Make the smallest one just large enough for the tennis ball to go through. Cut out the holes carefully. Above each hole write the score; the smaller the hole, the larger the score.

Prop up the cardboard or stand the box with the holes towards the players, who then take it in turn to try to throw the ball through the holes. If a ball goes through a hole, write that number beside the player's name.

Improve your children's adding abilities by making them keep a running total. The person with the highest score after a set number of throws is the winner.

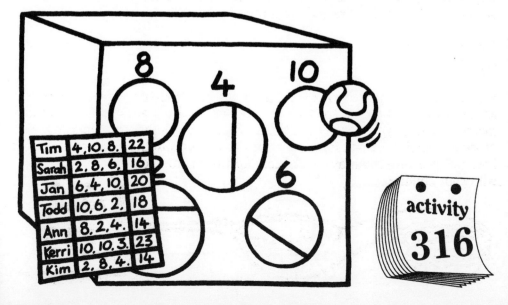

Tim	4, 10, 8,	22
Sarah	2, 8, 6,	16
Jan	6, 4, 10,	20
Todd	10, 6, 2,	18
Ann	8, 2, 4,	14
Kerri	10, 10, 3,	23
Kim	2, 8, 4,	14

activity
316

DROP DEAD

8+

A fun and exciting family dice game.

What You Need

- *2 or more players*
- *Five dice*
- *Paper and pencil to record the scores*

What To Do

The aim of 'Drop Dead' is to make the highest possible score at one turn.

The first player begins by throwing all five dice. Each time they make a throw that does not contain a 2 or 5, they add together the total number of that throw. They then have another throw. If they do throw a 2 or a 5, they score nothing for that throw and the dice that showed a 2 or a 5 is removed from their turn. A player's turn continues until the last dice shows a 2 or a 5 and they have to 'drop dead' and the next player has their turn.

See who can make the highest score from an individual turn or add up all the scores for the highest total score.

GUESS THE DISTANCE

8+ ✔

A good game to fill in those tedious times in the car on long trips.

 ✔

What You Need

• *To be travelling in the car*

What To Do

As you are driving in the car, have someone point out a distant landmark or object. Everyone else guesses how far away it is.

 ✔

The driver checks the kilometres (miles) on his speedometer and the person with the closest estimation is the winner.

activity
318

MATCH THE TIME

8+

Children have to learn to tell the time from analogue clocks, digital clocks and written time. Games like Match the Time will help them learn this in a fun way.

What You Need

• *Analogue clock (a clock or watch with a conventional round face)*
• *Digital clock*
• *Paper*
• *Pencil*

What To Do

Show your children how time is written - 4.20 - then show them what this looks like on an analogue and a digital clock.

Draw some circles on a piece of paper and put in the hours. These will represent the analogue clocks. Next, draw some rectangles. These will represent the digital clocks.

Next, write a list of times - 4.30, 7.20, 8.48, 1.10, 8.50 and so on.

Now your children have to show these times on both the analogue and digital drawings. When they can do it with no trouble, they can set some for you to work out.

activity
319

NUMBER WORDS

A fun family game to play with the children to help improve everyone's adding-up skills.

 ✓
 ✓

What You Need

- *Paper*
- *Pencils*
- *Hat or box*

 ✓
✓

What To Do

Cut up a piece of paper into 26 squares and write a letter of the alphabet on each square. Put them all into a hat or box and mix them well.

The children number their paper down the side from 1 to 26. As each letter is pulled from the hat, it is written beside the next number. Perhaps 'W' was pulled out first - if so, it will be '1'; T second - 2, M third - 3, and so on.

Now everyone makes up as many words as they can, trying to think of words with the highest possible numerical value. Set a time limit of 5 or 10 minutes, then add up everyone's scores and see who is the winner.

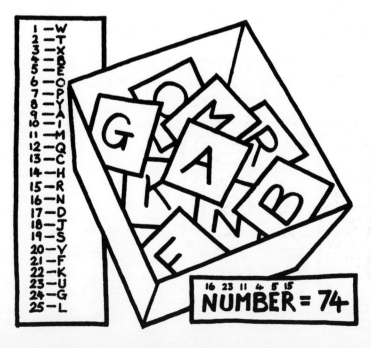

ROUND THE CLOCK

8+

A good family game to all play together.

 ✓

 ✓

What You Need

• *A few players*
• *Two dice*
• *Paper and pencil*

 ✓

What To Do

 ✓

One player has a piece of paper and a pencil to score. Down the left-hand side write the numbers 1 to 12 below each other. Across the top write the player's names. Draw a column for each player.

Players take it in turn to throw 1 to 12 in the correct sequence. The winner is the first to complete the sequence. The scorer ticks beside the number in each player's column as they throw the correct number.

Players throw both dice each turn. For numbers 1 to 6, a player can score with either or both dice - for instance, a 2 and a 4 could be a 2, 4 or 6. It is also possible at this stage to score twice on one turn - if a player throws a 2 and a 3, they could count both numbers.

From 7 to 12, however, a player will have to add together both dice. Good counting practice!

	Timmy	Sarah	Mum	Dad
1	✓	✓	✓	✓
2	✓	✓	✓	✓
3	✓	✓		✓
4	✓	✓		
5		✓		
6		✓		
7				

activity 321

CALENDAR CALCULATIONS 10+

Help your children learn more about using calendars with these simple problems. Buy a calendar for their room so they can write in important dates.

What You Need

- *Calendar*
- *Paper*
- *Pencils*

What To Do

Choose the last three calendar months to work from. Set some problems for your children to solve, such as:

What date was-

The second Friday in July?
The first Thursday in June?
The last day in August?
The last Wednesday in August?

- How many days from Thursday the 14th of June until Friday the 28th of July?
- How many school days are there in June?
  (Don't forget about public holidays and school holidays (if any).
- How many days are there from the second Saturday in June until the last Sunday in August?
- How many weeks altogether in June and July?
- How many Saturdays altogether in June, July and August?

Problems like these will help your children understand how to use a calendar and keeping one of their own will help them keep track of important events in their life.

activity
322

MAGIC NUMBER 9

10+

Teach your children some of the 'magic' properties of number 9.

What You Need

• *Paper*
• *Pencil*

What To Do

When your children are learning their nine times table, teach them some of the interesting properties of number 9.

Do they know that you can always tell whether a number is divisible by 9? Just add all the digits of the number together until you reduce it to one number. If that number is 9, the number you began with will be divisible by 9, no matter how big it is. Try 45 (4 + 5 = 9), then try 1214 (1 + 2 + 1 + 4 = 18; 1 + 8 = 9), or even 6,878,943 (6 + 8 + 7 + 8 + 9 + 4 + 3 = 45; 4 + 5 = 9). Let your children work out some of these for themselves.

Now try some number magic with the nine times table. To get the ten first results of the multiplication tables for 9, have them follow these simple steps.

Think of the number you want to multiply 9 by - say 7. Now, subtract 1 - which gives us 6. That number 6 is the first digit of your number.

Then take that number 6 from 9 and you will get the second digit of your answer - 3. The answer is 63.

(Of course, while all this is very interesting, remind your children that it will be a lot quicker to just learn their 9 times table off by heart).

activity

323

NINE MEN'S MORRIS

10+

An ancient game of skill to play with your older children.

 ✓
 ✓
 ✓
✓
✓

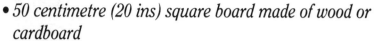

What You Need

- *50 centimetre (20 ins) square board made of wood or cardboard*
- *Ruler*
- *Marking pen*
- *Counters - 9 each of a different colour, e.g. 9 reds and 9 whites*

What To Do

First, mark out the board as shown below, then give each player 9 counters of the same colour. The youngest player begins and players then take it in turns to put their counters on the board one at a time. They must be placed on one of the 24 circles forming the corners and line intersections on the board.

The players try to get three of their counters in a line (called 'a mill') while stopping their opponents doing the same thing. When a player gets three counters in a line, they can take off one of their opponent's counters, but not one already from a line of three. That counter is then out of the game.

When all the counters are on the board, the players then take it in turn to move one counter at a time along the lines to the next unoccupied point. At this stage in the game mills can be made, broken and remade. The counters must move along straight lines, however. Each time a player makes or remakes a mill, they can remove an opponent's counter.

By the end of the game, if a player has only three counters left and they are in a mill, they must break the mill on their turn. At this stage that player is no longer restricted to the paths but can 'hop' to any point on the board.

The object of the game is to capture 7 counters from the other person or create a situation where the other person cannot move.

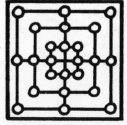

activity

324

SPEND THE MONEY GAME   10+

A good budgeting game to play with older children.

 ✓
 ✓

What You Need

• *Shop catalogues*

What To Do

 ✓

Here is a quick mathematics activity that will help your children learn how to budget money.

Pretend with your children that you are going to totally make over their room. Give them a budget - perhaps $1000 (£1000) - and a few shop catalogues.

They have to buy the furniture, bedding, etc. from the catalogues and come in under the budget.

You could also play this game at Christmas time and give them a budget for the family Christmas shopping!

activity

325

SQUARE NUMBERS

10+

 ✓

When your children have learnt all their multiplication tables, teach them this easy way to work out square roots of two digit numbers that end in 5.

 ✓

 ✓

What You Need

 ✓

- *Paper*
- *Pencil*
- *A calculator to check the answers*

 ✓

What To Do

The first step is to multiply the first digit of the number by the same digit plus one, for example 35 squared would be $3 \times 4 = 12$ - then simply add the number 25. The answer would be $35^2 = 1225$. Have your children check with their calculator to see if you are correct.

activity
326

OUR ENVIRONMENT/
SCIENCE EXPERIMENTS

OUR ENVIRONMENT/ SCIENCE EXPERIMENTS

BUBBLES

2+

Great fun to make on a windy day. Your children can work out which direction the wind is coming from.

What You Need

- *Detergent*
- *Cooking oil or glycerine*
- *Pipe cleaners or fine wire*
- *Plastic drinking straws*
- *Water*
- *Container*
- *Commercial bubble pipes*

What To Do

Make up a strong solution of bubble mixture with washing-up detergent and water. A teaspoon of cooking oil or glycerine added to the mixture makes the bubbles stronger.

Help your children make some bubble blowers out of pipe cleaners, fine wire, or just use drinking straws. Perhaps you already have some bubble blowers - large ones to make gigantic bubbles can often be bought at flea markets and provide hours of fun.

Make bubbles together and watch them float. See whose bubbles go the highest and drift the furthest. Young children love chasing the bubbles you make too!

activity
327

FOOTPRINT SPOTTING

2+ ✓

 ✓

 ✓

Play detectives in the sand and spot footprints with the children at the beach.

What You Need

- *The beach*
- *Children*

What To Do

When you go for walks on the beach with the children it is fun to look for and even track different footprints in the sand. Discover if the children can see different types of shoes, bird prints, dog prints, and different sized footprints.

When you turn round, see if you can follow your own family's prints back to where you began. If the sea has come in and covered them, explain tides to the children.

activity

328

INSECT HUNT

2+ ✓

 ✓

 ✓

✓

Keeping insects will help your children find out more about them and foster an interest in nature.

What You Need

- *Any small box, but a shoe box is ideal*
- *Piece of net and large rubber band or piece of elastic to hold it on*

What To Do

Go with your children on a 'bug' hunt. Take a bottle, a fine net or a bug catcher to trap them. Make sure you collect some of the leaves you trap your bug on to put in the bug box with it.

Make sure your children understand that we only keep insects and other creatures for a short stay, after which they must be returned to their 'families'.

activity

329

MAGNET FISHING GAME

2+

A fun game to teach your children some of the properties of magnets.

What You Need

- *Piece of dowel or long stick*
- *String or thin cord*
- *Horseshoe magnet*
- *Plastic ice cream lids or polystyrene meat trays*

What To Do

Cut lots of fish or other sea creature shapes out of the ice cream lids. You could make an octopus, some sea horses, squid, sharks, starfish, and even rays, as well as fish shapes.

Place a large paper clip on the 'mouth' of each sea creature and make a fishing line by attaching the magnet with a length of cord to the pole. You could turn a large cardboard box, or even just a pile of pillows, into a 'fishing boat'.

On hot days, take the fishing game outside and fill up the children's wading pool with water. Add a few drops of blue food colouring to the water and the kids will love fishing in the blue 'sea'.

activity

330

WATER PLAY

2+

Young children never tire of playing with water. Give your children lots of things to play with and they will be happily occupied for hours on a hot day. Remember, however, that young children must always be supervised near water.

What You Need

- *Large container for water*
- *A variety of plastic containers, measuring cups, plastic toys, large and small buckets, funnels, colanders, egg beater, plastic tubing, corks, tins with holes punched in them, sponges, plastic piping and anything else you can think of!*

What To Do

Place your children's wading pool, baby bath or a large dish in a shady part of the garden on a hot day. Turn on the hose and let them fill the container (best if they are wearing their swim suits!).

Provide lots of the above water play toys and they will have a great time.

For a change, add some food colouring to the water. This way they can see the water clearly as they pour and measure.

activity
331

BALLOON MYSTERIES

4+

Do your children ask you lots of difficult-to-answer questions such as 'Why does the moon stay up in the sky?', or 'Why do balloons bounce?'

Try this simple experiment together to discover why balloons do bounce.

What You Need

• *Balloons*

What To Do

Blow up a balloon for your children and tie it so the air will not escape. Tell your children to push it down as hard as they can and bounce it against different surfaces.

What happens when they push it down hard? Explain that when you blow air into balloons the air molecules are very tightly packed together. By pushing down on the balloon you are making the molecules resist. Because the balloon and the molecules inside it are elastic, they will bounce back.

Now help your children fill a balloon with sand and another with water and see what happens. Does the balloon bounce now?

Explain that the special elastic properties of air makes it bounce, which is why tyres and sports balls are filled with air.

activity
332

COMMUNICATION PICTURES 4+

Many thanks to my friend Lynne for this idea. She uses it in her work as a School Guidance Officer.

What You Need

- *2 children*
- *Paper*
- *Coloured pencils, crayons or felt pens*

What To Do

The children will need a hard book or a clip-board on which to balance their paper. They sit back to back with each other or in different parts of the garden, but close enough to communicate.

One child is chosen to be the speaker, the other is the listener. The first child begins to draw a picture, telling the other child exactly what he is doing. 'I am drawing a sun with a yellow pen in the top left hand corner of the page.' The other child has to listen carefully and draw exactly the same thing on his paper. The game continues - 'I am drawing a house in the middle of the paper. It has a steep roof with a chimney. The roof is red and the chimney is black.'

The game continues until the pictures are complete and then the children compare pictures and see how well they have communicated.

This game is very, very good for developing communication and listening skills. Play it with your children and see how well you do. I found it very difficult!

activity
333

FLOATING AND SINKING

4+ ✓

Children learn best by doing things themselves, and they will really understand these concepts if they are allowed to try them out with real objects.

 ✓

 ✓

What You Need

- *A variety of household objects that float and sink - plastic, paper, toys, corks, feathers, pegs, foam, ping pong balls, a golf ball, wood, containers with holes and so on*
- *A large washing up dish of water in the garden*

 ✓

 ✓

What To Do

This is a great activity outside on a warm, sunny day. The children will love seeing which items float and which sink and sorting them into the two categories. (Sorting is also an important numeracy skill.)

See if they can make some changes to some of the items that float to make them sink and vice versa. Encourage them to talk about what they are seeing.

Older children who can write may like to write about this activity to take to school for a class talk.

activity
334

FRAGRANT SHOE BOX

4+

See how well your children can distinguish different smells with this fun activity.

What You Need

- *Aromatic substances - perhaps an onion, vanilla essence, perfume, lemon peel, orange peel, soap, peanut butter, lavender, chocolate, etc.*
- *Shoe box*
- *Drinking straws*
- *Plastic bags*
- *Rubber bands*
- *Paper*
- *Coloured felt pens*

What To Do

Punch six holes just big enough to fit the drinking straws at intervals in the lid of the box. Put six smelling substances in plastic bags and attach the straws to the bags with rubber bands. Place them in the box and put the straws through the holes. Colour some small pieces of paper the colour of the substances, e.g. light brown for peanut butter, yellow for lemon peel, to give clues and help discussion about the scents.

Let your children smell the different scents and then talk together about what they think they are, or what they remind them of.

Happy sniffing!

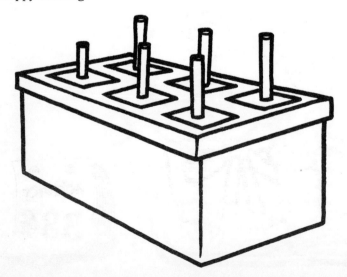

activity

335

GRASS HEADS

4+

While these can be bought from many craft markets, they are simple and fun to make with your children.

 ✓

 ✓

 ✓

 ✓

 ✓

What You Need

- *Old tights*
- *Plastic container, e.g. margarine, yoghurt*
- *Grass seeds*
- *Potting mix*
- *Stickers or felt pens*

What To Do

Cut off one leg of the tights and hold it open while your children measure in at least three tablespoons of grass seeds. Then add three to four cups of potting mix. Tie the stocking securely above the potting mix and form into a round 'head', and balance in the container.

Your children will enjoy making a face on the grass head and perhaps adding a bow or bow-tie and buttons to the container.

Keep the grass head damp and in a few days it will begin to grow a head of lovely bright green hair.

activity
336

HEART BEAT

4+ ✓

 ✓

 ✓

Children are always fascinated by a doctor's stethoscope. Make a simple home-made version with your children and they can listen to their heart beat and play 'doctors'.

What You Need

 ✓

- *2 plastic funnels*
- *1 metre (3 feet) of plastic tubing to fit the funnels*

 ✓

What To Do

The children can help you push a funnel into each end of the plastic tubing. Push it in as hard as possible so the funnels don't come out. Place a funnel over your heart and listen to the heart beat with the other funnel over your ear. (Jumping up and down a few times increases your heart beat and makes it easier to hear.)

Explain to your children that the heart is a large pump and the stethoscope is just a device to hear it better. It works by channelling the sound waves so you can hear them more clearly.

activity

337

INVESTIGATING ROCK POOLS   4+

Next time you visit a beach which has a rocky headland, spend some time with the kids investigating the fascinating world of rock pools.

What You Need

• *Time*

What To Do

Take the children to the beach and spend some time investigating the amazing life in rock pools. Many rocks which are covered by high tides are very slippery, so make sure everyone wears shoes that have good flexible soles. Warn the children not to walk on rocks that are green or look slimy.

Find some rock pools that are covered at high tide. See if the children can spot small fish, crabs, sea anemones, mussels and other living things amidst the rock and sea weed. Last year on holidays we even found many starfish in beautiful clear rock pools.

Sometimes you may have to help the children carefully lift up a few rocks to see what is hidden under them.

My son loves to place his finger carefully into anemones to feel them pull shut and try to suck in the finger. This helps him understand how the anemone catches its prey.

See if you and the children can count how many different animals you can find in the rock pools.

Rock pools are fascinating places for children to visit and observe. We must all make sure our beaches are kept clean and beautiful for many future generations of children.

activity
338

LEAF HUNT

4+ ✓

A fun matching game to play in your own garden that will encourage your children's interest in plants and trees.

 ✓

 ✓

What You Need

 ✓

• *Leaves from plants in your garden*

What To Do

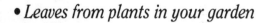

Collect a variety of leaves from different plants in the garden and show them to your children.

Then go for a walk around the garden with your children and see if they can match the leaves to the plant they come from. (If you don't have a garden, do it in a local park.)

(Later your children can try leaf rubbings. Place the leaf with the vein side up on a piece of paper. Put a piece of paper over the leaf and holding it very still, rub over the pages with the side of a pencil or crayon. You will see the shape emerge and all the veins and stem clearly on the rubbing.)

activity
339

MAGNET FUN

4+

Young children enjoy using magnets and finding out how they work. Explain to your children that magnets were made from a special sort of rock named magnetite or lodestone and they attract iron and steel. Show them that magnets have two poles, a north and a south, and how magnets can repel and attract each other. Buy a pair of similar strength magnets so your children will have the opportunity to discover the qualities of magnets for themselves.

What You Need

- *Collection of small items made from different materials, such as coins, safety pins, hair clips, small toys, stones, sticks, nails, buttons, pegs, cutlery*

What To Do

Let your children try each item with the magnet to see which ones are attracted by the magnet and which are not.

Try to help your children understand the concept of objects being pulled or attracted to the magnet rather than 'stick' like glue sticks.

Go around the house finding which other items and appliances are 'magnetic'.

Later they might enjoy a magnet 'treasure hunt'. Hide some small metal items in a dish of sand and they can use their magnet to hunt for the 'treasures' in the sand.

activity

340

MOBILE PHONES!

4+ ✓

Make a simple 'phone' with your children and whisper secrets.

 ✓

 ✓

What You Need

- *Two funnels*
- *Length of plastic tubing that fits the funnel ends*

 ✓

What To Do

Connect this simple 'phone' by pushing the funnel ends into the tubing. If you buy a really big length you can be in different rooms and still tell secrets.

Your children will love being able to talk to each other from different rooms - somehow they fight less that way!

If you don't have funnels, tins work well also connected to the tubing or just to string.

When they lose interest in the phones, cut the tubing into shorter lengths and they'll have lots of fun in the bath with the funnels and tubing.

activity
341

NEIGHBOURHOOD PLAY MAT 4+

Make a play mat of your own neighbourhood for your children to use with their little cars and trucks. A great way to teach simple mapping skills to young children.

What You Need

- *A sheet of heavy duty white vinyl*
- *Permanent marking pens in a variety of colours*

What To Do

Discuss with your children the features of your neighbourhood - where the roads go, the houses, parks, local shops and any other familiar landmarks. Then carefully mark them on the vinyl (you might like to do it in pencil or coloured chalk first and then draw over in permanent pen when you are happy with the result).

Mark your home, your neighbours' homes, the local streets, the school, the parks, shops and anything else your children are familiar with. Go for walks together and talk about the landmarks you could put on their map. When it is made, they will have great fun playing with it and learning about how maps are made as they play.

activity
342

OPPOSITES

4+ ✓

Go for a walk through the garden or a park with your children and play the 'opposites' game.

 ✓

What You Need

• *Time*

What To Do

Children need help to develop their language skills and to learn new words in their vocabulary. Go for a walk with your children and see if they can find something in the garden or park that feels bumpy. When they have found it, see if they can find another object that feels the opposite to bumpy.

Talk together about the words that would best describe the second object.

Next, ask them to find something that feels soft. Again, after feeling it, see if they can find something that feels the opposite to soft.

Try again with rough and spikey. The children will have experienced many different textures and will have learnt some new words in a fun way.

Keep the collected items and when you get home or when they go inside they may like to draw some of the things they found, and you can help the children to label them.

activity
343

OUTSIDE LISTENING GAME

4+

Listening well is an important aspect of good communication. We need to provide many opportunities to help build good listening skills in our young children before they begin school.

What You Need

- *Tape recorder with batteries*
- *Blank tape*

What To Do

When your child is not around, tape some of the sounds you hear outside. You might tape:
- vehicles
- the lawn mower or other garden tools
- the dog barking, howling or scratching
- birds in the garden
- children playing next door
- the sound of the sprinkler
- someone swimming in the pool
- a wind chime
- any others you can think of

Play the tape to your child and see how many sounds he can identify. If he is having difficulty go outside with him and see if this helps. Play this game in other environments - inside the house, at preschool and so on, to help him develop better listening skills.

activity

344

PLANT A TREE

4+ ✓

 ✓

Help your children develop a love of gardening and care for the environment with this long term project.

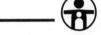 ✓

 ✓

What You Need

 ✓

- *A small tree to plant*
- *Gardening books or magazines*
- *Your camera*
- *A notebook for a tree diary*

 ✓

 ✓

What To Do

Planting a tree in spring was a tradition in schools when I was growing up. Revive this old idea with your children in your own garden.

Look through gardening magazines and books (borrow some from your local library if you do not have them at home) to find a tree suitable for your local climate and for the size of your garden.

Take your children to the nursery with you. Help them plant the tree at home and make them responsible for its care.

Don't forget to take photos of them planting and caring for their tree and yearly photos to add to their diary, recording both their growth.

Also for their diary, they could -

Do rubbings of the tree's bark
Press the flowers
Learn to use a tape measure to measure its height and girth
Do leaf rubbings of the leaves.

If you don't have room to plant a tree, your children could 'adopt' a tree in a local park and do the same activities there.

activity

345

PULSE BEAT

4+ ✓

Show your children a simple way of finding out if their heart is beating with this easy experiment.

 ✓

 ✓

What You Need

• *Toothpicks*
• *Playdough or plasticine*

✓

What To Do

✓

Form a small ball of playdough and stick a toothpick into it.
Have your children hold out their arm straight and keep it totally still. Place the ball of playdough on their wrist where the pulse is. (You may need to move it around to find the strongest beat.) Watch what happens to the toothpick.

Have your children run around for a little while or jump up and down a few times, and let them observe their pulse after exercise. Put the playdough ball on your own arm and they can see your pulse also.

Explain to your children that they saw the toothpick move because they are seeing the blood flow through their blood vessels to their heart. Doctors measure pulse rates to find out if a person's heart is beating at a normal rate.

They might enjoy counting the pulse rates of various members of the family and see who has the fastest heart beat.

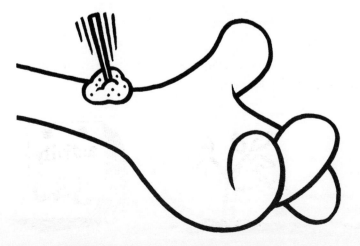

activity
346

RIVERS IN THE SANDPIT

4+

On hot days the hose in the sandpit is most children's idea of heaven. Turn a blind eye to the mess and the wet clothes and help turn it into a great geography lesson.

What You Need

• _The sandpit_ • _Hose_

What To Do

Join your children in the sandpit and bring the hose. Suggest you could make a little creek together. Dig out the creek and let the hose run into it - soon there will be pools, waterfalls, lakes and, eventually, a big river. Explain and name these features and compare them to real ones you have seen together. When it becomes too wet, turn off the hose, have a morning tea picnic, and then watch as the 'drought' dries up all the water.

Next time you go for a drive in the country together, look for the geographical features in real life that you made together in the sandpit.

activity
347

SNAIL MYSTERIES

4+   ✓

Do you have lots of snails in your garden? Children are fascinated by snails and they will love finding out how old the snails are.

What You Need

• *Snails*
• *A magnifying glass (most newsagents sell these)*

What To Do

Carefully look at the snails under the magnifying glass. Can you see the rings on their shells? Count the rings on each snail's shell and see which has the most. That snail is the oldest.

Explain to your children that, as the snail grows inside its shell, the shell must grow from the edge and so more and more rings are added. Each ring means a growth spurt.

Trees have rings too. Next time you see a log, see if you can count the growth rings and see how old the tree was.

activity
348

SPRING FLOWER PICTURES

4+ ✓

A beautiful way to preserve some of the spring flowers from your garden.

 ✓

 ✓

What You Need

- *Iron*
- *Small flowers and leaves*
- *Waxed or grease proof paper*

✓

What To Do

Go for a walk in your garden with your children and pick some flowers and leaves to make spring flower pictures. Small flat flowers work best for this project.

On a piece of waxed paper help your children arrange the flowers as artistically as they can. Then place another sheet of waxed paper on the top and iron carefully with a cool iron. The wax in the paper will bind together and seal the flowers inside.

Draw around the outside of the flowers with a thick marking pen - perhaps a heart or flower shape and your children can cut it out.

They look great *Blu-Tacked* on windows or use to decorate the front of their own gift cards.

activity
349

SPROUTING SEEDS

4+

 ✓

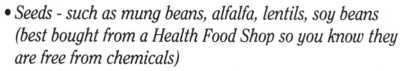 ✓

Your children can help add some variety to the family salads and sandwiches by growing their own sprouts.

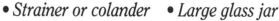

What You Need

 ✓

 ✓

- *Seeds - such as mung beans, alfalfa, lentils, soy beans (best bought from a Health Food Shop so you know they are free from chemicals)*
- *Strainer or colander* • *Large glass jar*
- *Piece of thin cloth such as muslin, cheese cloth or net*

What To Do

Help your children measure half a cup of seeds into a strainer. (For larger seeds use a colander.) Rinse well under running water. Pick out any damaged seeds and then place in the large jar. Pour in three cups of tepid water and leave to soak overnight. Next morning rinse again in the strainer then return the seeds to the jar and cover with the fine cloth. Secure around the top with a strong rubber band or piece of elastic. At least three times a day rinse the seeds well by filling the jar with tap water and draining through the cloth. Keep the seeds in a cool dark place - the kitchen pantry is ideal.

In a few days the seeds will be ready to eat and you and your children can concoct some lovely salads for the family.

activity
350

STORY TAPES

4+

We all have great intentions as parents but, unfortunately, time and other commitments tend to get in the way. When you have a little spare time make some Story Tapes for your children to listen to.

What You Need

- *A cassette player*
- *Blank tapes*
- *Favourite books or your imagination*

What To Do

One of the best presents we have ever given our son is a cassette player that runs on batteries that he can play in his room or take out into the garden.

When your children are starting to give up their afternoon nap but still need a quiet time (and so do you), spread out a rug under a tree in the garden, add some pillows and let them listen to story tapes.

These can simply be favourite books read on tape which they follow or, if you are imaginative, make up some stories to listen to. Include your children in the stories and they will really listen well. My son loves stories about himself being the hero! He also loves stories about his favourite toys doing amazing things.

Children need to learn to listen well without visual clues for school. As well as developing their listening skills they will also be developing their imaginations. Perhaps you could help them dictate some of their own stories onto the tape to listen to as well.

activity
351

TEXTURE RUBBINGS

4+

Develop your children's interest in their environment by showing them how to do texture rubbings.

What You Need

- *Paper*
- *Crayons or pencils*
- *Textures around your house and garden*

What To Do

Go on a 'texture hunt' together. Place the paper over car tyres, bark, leaves, carpet, coins, tiles, flowers, bricks and any other interesting textures you can think of. Your children then rub with their crayons or pencils. Label the texture rubbings for them so they can show them to the rest of the family.

Later you may like to play 'mystery rubbings' together. Rub some new things and then they go on a 'mystery rubbings' hunt to track them down and do matching rubbings.

activity
352

TORCH GAMES

4+

A torch makes a great gift for young children. Having their own torch close at hand can make them more secure in a dark bedroom.

What You Need

• *A torch*

What To Do

Your children can help you go on a 'treasure hunt' to collect lots of items made of different materials. Collect some made of wood, plastic, paper, metal, china and fabric.

Go outside when it's really dark, or turn off all the lights and darken a room completely.

Your children then turn on their torches and work out which objects are shiny and which are dull. They will enjoy finding out which objects the torch light will shine through and which are opaque.

Torches are great for shadow games also. Perhaps one warm night you could go for a walk together and look for 'spooky' shapes and then find out what they really are!

activity

353

WALKIE TALKIES

4+ ✓

Walkie talkies make a great birthday or Christmas present for your children.

 ✓

 ✓

What You Need

 ✓

• *A set of Walkie Talkies*

What To Do

Consider buying a set of Walkie Talkies for the children because it will give them hours of fun as they play in the garden.

 ✓

The Walkie Talkies will also help develop the children's language and communication skills as they play and send each other messages.

Talk to them about the other ways of sending messages across distances such as letters in bottles, carrier pigeons, telegraphs, telephones, faxes, E-mails, and so on.

They might like to try sending a message in a bottle or a message attached to a helium filled balloon.

Their Walkie Talkies will give them a great deal of fun and also provide a starting point for learning more about how we communicate.

activity
354

WATCHING DRAGONFLIES

4+ ✓

Visit a pond or other swampy area and watch some fascinating dragonflies with your children.

 ✓

What You Need

- *Time*
- *An insect net*

✓

What To Do

 ✓

Dragonflies are among the oldest insects on earth. We know this because scientists have found their fossilised remains and have discovered they lived more than 300 million years ago, long before the dinosaurs roamed the earth.

There are thousands of different dragonfly species in the world. They live near water, usually slow moving water such as dams, ponds, marshes or stagnant creeks.

Visit an area like this with your children and introduce them to the dainty, beautiful dragonfly.

Take an insect or butterfly net with you and see if you can catch one for the children to have a closer look. Carefully put it into a glass jar or an observation jar with a magnified lid. Take care not to damage its very delicate wings.

See if the children can see the enormous compound eyes which cover almost all of the dragonfly's head and give it an incredible wide vision.

Explain to the children that when dragonflies first hatch out of their eggs they are nymphs which live in the water, and even have gills to breath like fish and tadpoles. They can remain in the nymph form for a long time, sometimes years, but the actual dragonfly life is very short - in most species only a few weeks. When they are ready to change into a dragonfly they climb out of the water and find somewhere to change, and then dry themselves in the sun like a butterfly before flying away.

Make sure you return your dragonfly to its environment before you leave so it can enjoy the rest of its very short life.

Encourage your children to draw and write a story about the dragonfly when you get home.

activity

355

WEATHER CHARTS

4+

Since time immemorial children have had weather charts at school. Help them build their knowledge of weather and weather patterns by keeping their own weather charts at home.

What You Need

- *Paper*
- *Calendar*
- *Symbols*

What To Do

With your children draw up a large calendar of the next month on a piece of paper or cardboard and hang it in a place your children can easily access. At the end of each day, discuss with them what the weather has been like and they can take it in turn to draw the symbol or symbols for the weather in that day's square.

Think of simple symbols for storms, rain, clouds, wind, sun, and so on.

Look back at the end of the month and see what the weather pattern has been. The children will really be enthralled by this activity and will show much more interest in the weather report on the news and in unusual weather phenomena occurring in other parts of the world also.

activity
356

WINDMILLS

4+

On a windy day coloured windmills are lots of fun to make and watch spin in the wind.

What You Need

- *Paper*
- *Pins*
- *Drinking straws or small sticks*

What To Do

Draw up some squares on some coloured paper for the children to cut out. Talk about what makes a square different from a rectangle while they are cutting. Next, help them draw four lines with a ruler from each corner to near the middle of each square (see the illustration below).

Bring the outside of each triangle into the middle and secure with a pin or drawing pin poked into the drinking straw.

Take them outside and hold them in the wind and watch how fast they fly.

activity
357

WRITING STORIES

4+

Children need to develop knowledge of the 'language of language' before they can begin to read.

What You Need

• *Paper or a scrap book*
• *Colour pencils, felt pens or crayons for drawing*

What To Do

When you have family excursions or special occasions encourage your children to draw pictures about them. It is a nice idea to have a special scrap book they can keep exclusively for these special pictures.

To help them understand the 'language of language' ask them to tell you the sentence they would like you to write about their drawing. Talk to them as you write, pointing to the individual words and what they say. Talk about any punctuation marks you use and show them what a sentence is. 'It begins with a capital letter and ends with a full stop and makes sense.'

They need to understand the difference between a sentence and a story and this will take time. Drawing about a special family outing also helps develop children's recalling skills as they remember the things they enjoyed most.

By linking these early literacy experiences to fun family events, children will enjoy drawing and learning about words and language, and these early phonological skills are the stepping stones to learning to read.

activity
358

ANT FARMS

6+   ✓

  ✓

Children are fascinated by small creatures like ants and spiders. Help your children learn more about ants by building an Ant Farm together.

   ✓

What You Need

- *Large plastic soft drink bottle*
- *Drinking glass*
- *Garden soil*

✓

✓

What To Do

Cut the soft drink bottle in half with a *Stanley* or sharp knife. Discard the top section. Find a drinking glass that will fit inside, leaving a space about 4 cm (1½ ins) wide between the glass and the plastic bottle (it should not be any wider or you will not be able to see the ants and their tunnels).

Carefully spoon in garden soil to fill the spaces. Add some ants from the garden and cover the top with some flyscreen so they cannot escape. Add a very small amount of cake, sugar or honey-soaked bread every few days.

Your children will be enthralled by the ants' busy lives and by their tunneling skills.

Although you may consider ants in the garden to be pests (we do when they dig up the sand between the pavers!), it is best to teach your children to have respect for animal life by returning the ants to their natural habitat after a few days.

activity
359

ART AT THE BEACH

6+

When the children are tired of swimming, or need something to do at the beach in winter when it's too cold to swim, do some beach art with them.

What You Need

• *Buckets for collecting bits and pieces*

What To Do

Go for a long walk on the beach with the children (don't forget the sunscreen!) and collect bits and pieces such as shells, seaweed, driftwood, stones, and so on.

The children will have great fun making pictures in the sand and using their beach materials for collage.

Take some photos before you leave and before the waves wash it all away!

activity

360

CATERPILLAR COLLECTIONS 6+

During the year many different types of caterpillars live in our gardens. Your children will enjoy observing and watching them change during their life cycle.

What You Need

- *An ice cream container*
- *Fine flyscreen mesh*
- *Caterpillars and some of the leaves on which they were found*

What To Do

When the children find a caterpillar in the garden, an icecream container with fine mesh across the top makes an ideal home. Place some of the leaves on which they found the caterpillar in there and add fresh ones daily. Sprinkle a few drops of water on the leaves each morning.

We have lots of Balsam or Busy Lizzy plants in our garden and we often find very large caterpillars on them.

When the caterpillar is in its cocoon put it in a safe place where the children can see it but not touch. A chrysalis in a cocoon doesn't like being bumped. If they are lucky they will be able to see the butterfly or moth emerge from the cocoon. Release the butterfly to live its brief life in your garden.

Different caterpillars live in your garden during the year; perhaps the children might like to keep a diary of which ones they see. They could draw the caterpillars and butterflies and see if they can identify them in books from your local library.

Go to your local nursery to find out which butterfly attracting plants grow well in your area and the children will enjoy helping you plant some in your garden and encouraging a variety of butterflies to visit you.

activity
361

FINGERPRINTS

6+

Explain to your children that everyone has different fingerprints. They can then fingerprint the whole family!

 ✓

 ✓

 ✓

What You Need

 ✓

- *Stamp pad*
- *Small soft paintbrush*
- *Corn flour*
- *Magnifying glass*

✓

✓

What To Do

Help your children fingerprint all the family by putting their index finger on the stamp pad and rolling it backwards and forwards. Then place the finger on a piece of paper and again roll it backwards and forwards. Help them write the person's name beside each fingerprint.

Now they can play the detective and look for fingerprints in the house and see if they can identify them. When they find one, show them how to lightly dust it with cornflour using a little paintbrush. Then they carefully blow away the excess cornflour and they'll be able to clearly see the fingerprint. They may need to use a magnifying glass to clearly identify the print. Sherlock Holmes!

Now you'll be able to find out who's been raiding the 'fridge and biscuit jar!

Mum   Dad

activity

362

FISHING

6+

Encouraging your children to fish is introducing them to a great, relaxing sport.

What You Need

• *Bait*
• *Fishing lines and tackle*

What To Do

Fishing need not be an expensive sport. Fishing rods and reels make great birthday and Christmas presents, but a hand line or fishing line strung on a bottle works just as well.

Visit your local bait and tackle shop and ask for some advice. They will be happy to help and let you know about local conditions and the best bait to use. (It is in their best interest to encourage children to take up fishing, isn't it!)

Remember that fishing takes patience and if your children are not endowed with that virtue, maybe fishing is not for them. Also, remember that fish bite best at sunrise and dusk so you may have to rise a little earlier than usual. However, the best reward of all is the excitement when the children really catch a fish and have the pleasure of eating their own cooked fish for dinner!

activity
363

FISHING NET FUN

6+

A simple home-made fishing net will provide hours of fun and sport for your children.

What You Need

- *A wire coathanger*
- *A pair of wire cutters*
- *Some fine but strong mosquito netting or tulle*
- *Needle and thread*
- *Thin rope or strong cord*
- *Bait such as fish or meat*

What To Do

Bend out the coathanger to make a circle and clip off the handle section with the wire cutters. Cut out a large circle from the netting. If it is not very thick, use two layers for extra strength. Stitch the netting onto the circle of wire.

Across the top join two pieces of rope to form a cross and tie them onto the circle of wire. Attach a long piece of rope to the middle of the cross with which to pull the net up.

Place some bait in the net and the children carefully lower it into the water and wait until some small fish have entered the net and are nibbling on the bait.

Then they slowly pull up the net and catch some little fish for a fish tank or to use for bait.

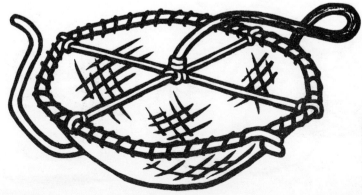

activity
364

LAVENDER SACHETS

6+

Most gardens have a bush of one of the many lovely lavender varieties. When your lavender is flowering profusely, pick the flowers to make delightful scented lavender sachets together.

What You Need

- *Lavender flowers*
- *Muslin or other thin cloth*
- *Narrow lavender ribbon*
- *Large bottle*
- *Marking pen*
- *Pinking shears*

What To Do

Together, pick flower heads that are nearly all open and spread them in the sun for a few days to dry. The flowers are easily detached by running your fingers along the stem to strip off the dried flowers.

Make the muslin sachets by tracing around a bottle with chalk and then cutting out the circles with pinking shears. Your children can put a few spoonfuls of the lavender flowers in the middle of each muslin circle and then tie securely with the lavender ribbon.

Put some lavender sachets on coathangers in your wardrobes, in drawers with clothes and in the linen cupboard. The crisp, strong srnell helps repel insects.

They also make great gifts.

activity
365

LEAF GRAPHS

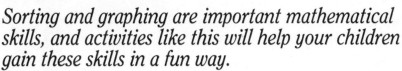

6+ ✓
 ✓
 ✓
 ✓
 ✓
 ✓

Sorting and graphing are important mathematical skills, and activities like this will help your children gain these skills in a fun way.

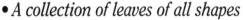

What You Need

- *A collection of leaves of all shapes*
- *Paper*
- *Pencils*
- *Cardboard*
- *Wood glue*

What To Do

Go for a walk in a park or the bush with your children and collect a large bag of leaves of all shapes and sizes.

Help your children sort the leaves into various categories - smooth, rough, pointed, rounded, eaten by insects, whole, etc.

Help them make a simple graph by drawing the shapes of leaves they have collected and see which is the most common shape.

When they have finished, give them some cardboard and wood glue and they will enjoy making an interesting leaf collage with their collection of leaves.

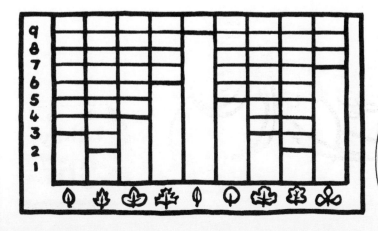

activity

366

LET'S FIND OUT

6+

 ✓
 ✓
 ✓

Help your children develop their inquiring minds by posing these questions about the insects they find in the garden.

What You Need

• *Insects*
• *See 'Insect Hunt' - activity 329*

What To Do

After you have gone on an 'Insect Hunt' with your children and they have caught something to investigate, pose some of these questions.

What does it eat? - leaves, other insects, grains, nectar, wood or sap?

What does it look like? - Is it multi or one colour?
Is it dull or shiny?
Can it be camouflaged?

Where does it live? - In flowers, on leaves or stems, in plants or water?

How does it move? - Does it fly, crawl, burrow?
Does it fly quickly, slowly, straight or in zig zags?

Does it have - Wings and how many?
Legs and how many?
Feelers and how many?

What happens if you go near it or even touch it?

Older children may like to start a 'bug book'. Photograph or help your children draw the insect, see if you can identify it and then list all characteristics you have discovered.

Have your children show their teacher at school.

All this may lead on to an interesting project for the whole class.

activity

367

NIGHT SKIES

6+ ✓

 ✓

 ✓

Spend some time at night looking at the sky with your children and help them understand more about the universe.

What You Need

• *Clear warm nights*

What To Do

Go outside with your children at night in summer and observe the sky together. Over a period of weeks, watch the changes in the moon. Look at the stars and, using a star guide, see if you can find some star patterns.

See what other things you can observe at night - shooting stars, birds, clouds and planes.

Borrow some books from your local library and help your children learn more about our galaxy. Toy shops and newsagents sell luminous stars and moons. Make a 'night sky' on the ceiling of your children's room.

activity

368

ONION POWER

6+

My children are always amused when Mummy cries when chopping up onions. They are not so amused when I put one near them! Ask your children to chop up an onion and explain what is happening to their eyes.

 ✓
 ✓

 ✓
 ✓

What You Need

- *An onion*
- *Chopping board*
- *Knife*

What To Do

When your children peel the onion and chop it, their eyes will begin to water. Why is it so?

Explain that onions contain a highly irritating oil that combines with the air when we are chopping them. This becomes a vapour that affects nerve glands that are actually in our noses, but connect to our eyes. This is how a strong smell or even a sneeze can make our eyes water.

Try some ways with your children to see if you can stop onions making eyes water. Some people say to keep them in the refrigerator, or peel them under running water, or even peel them with sunglasses on! See what other creative solutions your children can come up with.

Other substances can have the same effect - try (carefully) with some spices and chilli.

activity
369

OVAL EGGS

6+

 ✓

 ✓

 ✓

 ✓

 ✓

Have your children ever wondered why eggs aren't round? This is one of the eternal questions children ask poor parents. Try this simple experiment together to discover why.

What You Need

- *A hard-boiled egg*
- *A tennis ball or other small round ball*

What To Do

Put both the egg and the ball on the floor and roll them. Which is easier to roll? Can your children work out why?

Explain to them that if eggs were round they would roll so easily they could roll out of the nest. The oval shape is also stronger and less likely to break.

activity
370

ROCKETS

6+

Help your children understand about propulsion and what happens to air under pressure with this interesting experiment.

 ✓

 ✓

 ✓

 ✓

What You Need

- *2 chairs*
- *Drinking straw*
- *Masking tape*
- *Pieces of string about 2 to 2.5 metres long (6½ ft to 8 ft)*
- *Balloon (as large and as long as you can find)*

What To Do

Thread the string through the straw and tie the chairs together about two metres apart. Move the chairs apart until the string is stretched tight. Next, blow up the balloon and hold it firmly tight as you tape it to the straw. Then release the balloon! Your children will be fascinated by the result.

Explain that when you blew up the balloon, the air molecules were forced into it and, although we could not see them, they were tightly packed. When the balloon was released, the air escaped with so much force that the balloon was propelled along the string.

Explain that rockets use similar force, but not with air. Rockets use rocket fuel. Sky rockets that we see at fireworks displays use gunpowder as force, as do firearms.

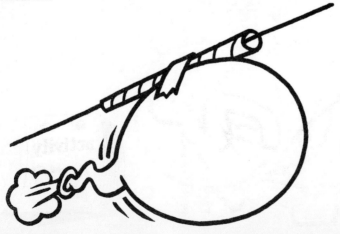

activity

371

SHAPE SPOTTING

6+

Take up shape spotting with the children when you go for a walk and improve their geometry skills.

What You Need

• *Time*

What To Do

Shape spotting certainly livens up walks and stops children getting 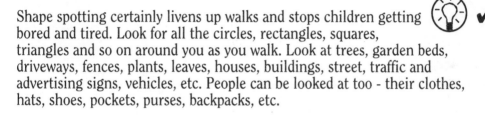 bored and tired. Look for all the circles, rectangles, squares, triangles and so on around you as you walk. Look at trees, garden beds, driveways, fences, plants, leaves, houses, buildings, street, traffic and advertising signs, vehicles, etc. People can be looked at too - their clothes, hats, shoes, pockets, purses, backpacks, etc.

Finally, look up at the sky and see how the power lines and clouds form their own interesting shapes.

This game is a lot of fun and really encourages the children to look at their world in a new way. Just be warned, it is quite addictive and once you start it is really hard to stop!

activity

372

SILK WORMS

6+

As children, most of us were fascinated by the life cycle of these amazing little creatures; watching them change from an egg to a larva (the 'silk worm'), spinning their beautiful silken cocoon, then turning into a moth.

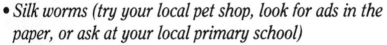

What You Need

• *Silk worms (try your local pet shop, look for ads in the paper, or ask at your local primary school)*
• *A shoe box*
• *Mulberry leaves*

What To Do

If you are lucky enough to be given eggs, your children can watch the changes in the eggs. Mostly, you will be given the small silk worms. As they grow, the silk worms increase their weight thousands of times. Older children will be able to measure and weigh (use a very tiny set of kitchen scales) and graph the results.

Isolate one silk worm and keep a count of how many mulberry leaves it can eat in a day. Older children will be able to record changes weekly. Also your children will be able to observe the caterpillars moulting, when the silk worms become very inactive as their skin is stretched and while they are getting ready to shed it. Look at the changes in the new skin; it will be darker and wrinkly to allow room for more growth.

The next most fascinating event is when the silk worms begin to spin their cocoons. Explain to your children that at this stage they are no longer silk worms, but pupas. The cocoons must not be bumped or handled, but just watched for the next three weeks.

Finally, the adult moth will emerge from the hard cocoon but, in doing so, it destroys the cocoon. Use some of the cocoons for spinning (see Silk Works - Spinning the Cocoon, activity 374), but keep the rest so you will have a supply of eggs for next year's silk worms.

activity
373

Put all the moths in a clean, dry shoe box in a cool place. Now the moths will mate and lay eggs. The male moth then dies and the female dies also after laying approximately 500 eggs. Keep the eggs in a cool cupboard until next year, when the cycle will begin again.

Some other actvities to try together:

- take photos of the stages
- your children can draw pictures of each stage - older children can write the story also
- do rubbings of the mulberry leaves
- look for other sorts of caterpillars to keep and observe.

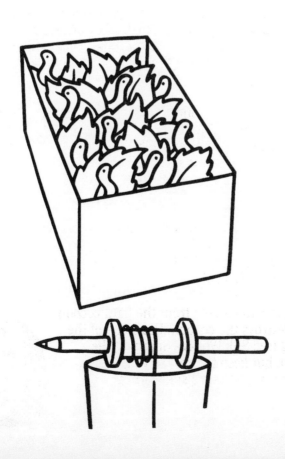

SILK WORMS - SPINNING THE COCOON

6+

As well as watching the life cycle of the silk worm, your children will enjoy spinning the silk from some of the cocoons. Make a simple spinner with directions below.

What You Need

- *Lead pencil*
- *Old cotton reel*
- *Drinking glass*
- *Wood glue*

What To Do

When I was a child my father made me a silk spinner from four pieces of dowel, but this simpler version works just as well.

Push the pencil through the hole in the cotton reel and glue in place.

Put the cocoon into a glass that is half filled with warm water. You will then be able to easily peel off the loose outside layer of the cocoon. Next, find the end of the thread and wind it around the cotton reel. Put the cocoon back in the glass and begin winding.

Keep some of the silk in each cocoon to protect the eggs, but it is also a good idea to keep a few cocoons unwound to be sure to hatch out some moths.

Take the silk off carefully and tie together to form a narrow piece about 30 cm (12 ins) long. It makes a great book mark.

Show your children some real silk; perhaps look in a haberdashery for some silk fabrics.

Go to the library together to find some books about the silk industry in China. You will all learn something new!

activity
374

SIPHONS

6+

Show the children a quick way to drain the wading pool or take some excess water out of the swimming pool by making a simple siphon.

What You Need

- *Length of plastic tubing or some garden hose*
- *Funnel*
- *Jug of water*
- *Container of water*

What To Do

To make a siphon you simply take a length of hose and push the spout of a funnel into it.

Hold the funnel up while your child pours some water into it until a steady stream of water is coming out the other end. Then quickly take the funnel off and cover both ends of the hose with your thumbs - don't let any air in. Immerse one end of the hose in the pool, put the other end at a slightly lower level and the water will begin to drain out, as you have made a siphon.

Explain to the children how a siphon works. The air is pressing on the surface of the water in the pool and, with the hose full of water, there's no counter air pressure in the hose, hence the water will flow out from the hose.

activity
375

SKIN DEEP

6+

As we age, our skin loses its elasticity and becomes older and lined. With a magnifying glass your children will enjoy seeing the differences in skin as it ages.

 ✓

 ✓

What You Need

 ✓

- *A magnifying glass*
- *Children and adults of different ages*

 ✓

What To Do

Take a magnifying glass along to a family gathering and your children will be astonished by the differences between older and younger hands.

Explain to them that skin is actually an organ of the body and expands and contracts as you grow and lose weight. Unfortunately, as we age, our skin becomes less elastic and will not so easily contract to its original shape. Let them examine their own hands, then yours, then Grandma's and Grandpa's. Apply some hand lotion to your hands and let them see if this makes any difference.

Don't forget to remind them that the sun can damage skin and, to keep it looking young longer, they must always remember to apply sunscreen lotion when going out in the sun.

activity

376

SMELLING TRAILS

6+ ✓

Set up a smelling trail in the garden for your children and let them test how accurate their sense of smell really is.

 ✓

What You Need

- *A blindfold*
- *Foods with distinctive smells such as onions, mint, cheese, apple, etc.*
- *Flowers, a tissue dipped in perfume, a cake of soap, garlic, and so on*

 ✓

What To Do

Take it in turn to blindfold the children and give them each a turn at trying to identify a selection of the 'smelly' things.

See who has the best sense of smell in the family!

activity
377

SOLAR SYSTEM MOBILE

6+

When your children really become fascinated by outer space and our solar system, help them make a solar system mobile to hang above their bed.

What You Need

- *An old umbrella*
- *Cardboard*
- *Polystyrene balls (available in different sizes from craft shops)*

- *Yellow paint*
- *Fishing line*
- *Silver spray paint or silver foil)*

What To Do

Together, remove all the fabric from an old umbrella, then make the 'solar system'. Paint the largest polystyrene ball yellow and cover the others with silver foil or spray paint silver. Cut some cardboard stars and moons.

Borrow some books about space from your local library to get the exact positioning of all the planets, then attach them all with fishing line to the umbrella.

Buy a pack of 'glow in the dark' stars from a toyshop and stick these to the ceiling, too. Your children will want to spend a lot of time lying on their bed!

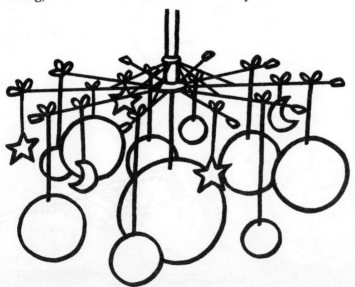

activity

378

SPIDERS

6+

Help your child learn more about spiders and their importance in our environment.

What You Need

• *A spider and its web to observe*

What To Do

Find a spider's web in the garden and watch it together for a few days. See what the spider does in the daytime and go out with a torch at night and observe its activity. Watch the small insects it has caught in the web and see how long the spider takes to eat them.

If you can find an old uninhabited web, you can make a 'web picture' by lightly spraying the spider's web with white spray paint. Hold a piece of black paper behind the web and at the anchoring points of the web. The wet paint will stick the web onto the paper. Your children will be amazed by the spider's line work.

It's fun to go into the garden early in the morning also and watch any spider's web glistening with dew. Look at the shapes in the web and see how many squares, triangles, rectangles and even hexagons and pentagons you can find.

Talk about safety and spiders also. See if you can find a book at the library about spiders and read it together.

activity
379

SUNSHINE FACTS

6+

We all know how important the sun is for life on earth. Help your children discover this for themselves with this simple experiment.

What You Need

- *Birdseed*
- *Small pots*
- *Potting mix*
- *Shoe box*

What To Do

Help your children fill the pots with some potting mix and sow the soil liberally with the birdseed. Place outside in a sunny spot in the garden or on a balcony and water regularly. When the little plants are strong and green it is time to begin the experiment.

Put a couple of the pots into a dark cupboard - remember to keep watering them regularly, though.

Place another pot into a shoe box with the lid on and make a small hole in one end so this is the only light source for that plant. Again, remember to water regularly so the plant doesn't die.

Return the other pots to the sunny spot in the garden again.

In a week or so check all the pots to see what has happened. The plants in the dark cupboard will have grown tall and spindly and probably turned yellow without sunlight. The plants in the box will have grown towards the light but the ones in the sunny garden should be lush and healthy.

This shows the children that an adequate supply of sunlight is necessary for healthy plant growth.

activity

380

TERRARIUM GARDEN

6+

A simple and inexpensive way to make a little garden with your children - ideal for apartment dwellers.

What You Need

- *Large plastic soft drink bottle with a black base*
- *Potting mix*
- *Small plants or seeds*

What To Do

Cut the soft drink bottle in half with a *Stanley* knife and then soak the bottom half in warm water until the clear plastic comes out of the black base. When this section is inverted and pushed into the black base, you have a simple but most effective terrarium to make a little garden in, with your children.

Fill the base with some good quality potting mix and plant together with small plants or seeds. Water it and then seal. Terrariums are best kept in a warm spot away from direct sunlight. They will only need watering every ten days as it is a sealed environment like a hot house, so be careful not to over water.

Terrariums make ideal places to raise seeds in cooler climates, and to grow cuttings. Happy gardening!

activity
381

USING THE STREET DIRECTORY 6+ ✓

Use your local street directory to help your children learn about maps.

 ✓

✓

What You Need

• *Street directory or map of your local area*

What To Do

Before you go for walks with your children, or short drives in the car together, look up where you are going in your street directory. Work out a route together and take it with you. Check it as you turn corners and change directions. Look for local landmarks such as schools, churches, shopping centres and parks on the map.

As your children gain mapping skills, make them the 'navigator' for longer trips to places you have not been before. Keep your cool! You will probably get lost a few times, but many adults go through their whole lives without ever developing a good sense of direction. Help your children gain mastery over this important life skill in a fun and relaxing way. Besides, all the walks will be great for your own fitness level!

activity

382

WORM HOUSE

6+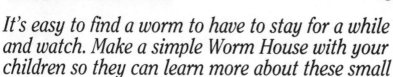

It's easy to find a worm to have to stay for a while and watch. Make a simple Worm House with your children so they can learn more about these small animals.

What You Need

- *Worms*
- *Tall, thin jar*
- *Sand, earth, peat moss or compost*

What To Do

Take your children and the tall, thin jar into the garden and fill the jar with layers of different coloured things like peat, sand, compost and, most importantly, earth containing lots of leaf mould, because this is what the worms will eat. Make sure the bottle is kept cool and moist, but not wet.

Dig in the garden together until you find a worm. Put it on the top of the bottle so your children have a good chance to observe it.

As the worm tunnels down through the layers it feeds on the earth, and what it exudes is called the worm-cast. Your children will be able to watch the patterns the worm makes as it moves through the layers of dirt.

When your children have learnt all they can about worms, make sure you dig a hole together and place the worm back in the garden.

Find out more about worms from your local library or even invest in a Worm Farm to make great compost for the garden.

activity
383

CRYSTAL MAKING

8+

Help your children understand more about how rocks are formed by making some easy crystals from sugar.

 ✓

 ✓

What You Need

- *2 cups of sugar*
- *1 cup of boiling water*
- *Wooden kebab sticks or pieces of string*
- *Food colouring*
- *Shallow bowl*

 ✓

 ✓

What To Do

Carefully stir the sugar into the boiling water, add a few drops of food colouring and let it cool to room temperature.

Your children will enjoy arranging the kebab sticks or pieces of string in the bowl. Then they slowly and carefully pour on the sugar solution. Cover and let it stand for a few days. More and more crystals will form as the mixture stands.

Instead of adding the food colouring at the start, your children could add drops of different food colouring with an eye dropper to the crystals to make a garden-like effect.

activity

384

GENE POWER

8+

Genetics are big news in today's world, with new genetic breakthroughs being discovered almost daily. Help your children understand what genes are and how they affect us all.

 ✓

 ✓

 ✓

What You Need

 ✓

• *Pencil*
• *Paper*

 ✓

What To Do

Help your children list all the members of your immediate family on the top of a large piece of paper. Under each family member help them think of physical characteristics of that person - their eye colour, hair colour, hair type (curly, wavy or straight), ear shape (detached or undetached lobes), and perhaps even whether they can curl their tongue. Remind your children that all of these characteristics are inherited and that we have dominant and recessive genes. Work out how individual family members are similar and yet different.

Remind your children that Genetics is the science of why living things behave and look the way they do. Inside each cell are tiny chromosomes which carry different genetic messages and help make us what we are. Explain to your children that they receive a mixture of genes from both parents and they can see sometimes which parent provided which characteristic. 'Thanks, Dad, for the big nose!'

Mum	Dad	Timmy	Sarah
brown hair	red hair	brown hair	red hair
blue eyes	brown eyes	brown eyes	blue eyes
wavy hair	straight hair	straight hair	wavy hair
small nose	big nose	small nose	small nose
mole on neck	scar on cheek	birthmark on arm	scar on knee

activity

385

NATURE SCAVENGER HUNT

8+

A good game to play in the backyard, at the beach or in a park.

What You Need

- *Paper*
- *Pencils*
- *Paper or plastic bags*

What To Do

Make a list of 10 to 20 things you may be able to find in a particular area. Protect the environment by making sure living plants or animals are not on the list. You will have to check out the area first to see just what sort of things you can put on the list.

At the beach you could list items such as a broken shell, a perfect shell, a stone, some seaweed, driftwood and so on. In a park the list could include a pine cone, a white stone, a brown leaf, etc.

Each child has a copy of the list and a bag for the 'treasures'. Set a time limit and, at the end, the person who has found the most items is the winner.

activity
386

POT POURRI

8+

Help your children store the flower scents of spring and summer blossoms by turning them into beautiful, fragrant pot pourri.

What You Need

* *Lots of scented flowers - roses, carnations, annuals, freesias, lavender and so on*
* *Orris powder (available from chemists)*
* *Mixed spice or allspice*   * *Brown sugar*
* *Large storage bottle with a lid*   * *Salt*

What To Do

Early one warm morning, gather all the flowers you will need together (at least enough for about three cupfuls of petals). Stand the flowers in a bucket of water for a day. Then the children will love stripping off all the petals. Put them in a shady place on newspaper for a few days and turn them at least once a day. When the petals are dry and stiff, you can make the pot pourri.

Mix together: 1 tablespoon orris powder
5 tablespoons of spices
1 tablespoon of sugar

Put a layer of petals in a large jar and sprinkle on lots of salt. Then sprinkle over a small handful of spices. Do this in layers until the petals are all used up.

Stir every couple of days for about three weeks. By then the oils and scents will have mingled. Pot Pourri is great in bowls in the house as room fresheners, or your children might like to give it away for gifts. When it begins to lose its fragrance, add a few drops of an essential oil like Boronia or Lavender to refresh it.

activity
387

PRESSED FLOWER CARDS

8+

Preserve the beauty of your garden by making pressed flower cards with your children. A special gift to give to grandparents, other relatives and friends.

What You Need

- *Flowers*
- *Absorbent paper - kitchen paper or blotting paper*
- *Cardboard*
- *Telephone books*

What To Do

Gather small flowers from the garden - preferably using ones the size of a five cent or ten cent piece. Some flowers press better than others, so you will have to experiment together.

There are many flower presses on the market and if your children really become interested in this hobby, one of them would make a lovely gift. However, old telephone books work just as well. Press the flowers between the kitchen paper and help the children place them between the pages. Leave at least 20 pages between each set of flowers. Stack some heavy books or even bricks on top of the telephone books and leave for a couple of weeks.

Help your children cut out the card, draw oval or round shapes on the front and creatively arrange the pressed flowers, glueing in place with dots of craft glue. Leaves, a little lace and ribbon and some grasses can all be glued with the flowers for a pretty effect.

Perhaps you could frame one of their creations to hang also!

activity
388

RAINDROP SPOTS

8+ ✓

Help your children learn more about rain with this simple experiment.

 ✓

 ✓

What You Need

 ✓

- *Blotting paper (available from newsagents)*
- *Pens*
- *Rain*

  ✓

What To Do

Next time it begins to rain, take some sheets of blotting paper out into the garden and hold them out in the rain. Bring them in and help the children draw around the outlines of the rain drops.

Ask them questions like:

Are they all the same shape and size?
Do they change when the rain is heavier or lighter?
How long does it take for a whole sheet of blotting paper to be soaked?
Does light rain sound different from heavy rain falling on a sheet of blotting paper?

Collect some rain in a see-through container and observe how clear the water is.

Add some soap to it and compare it to tap water. Which one lathers the most? Which one is the softest?

Children will be really interested in rain after doing these simple experiments.

activity
389

SCAVENGER HUNTS

8+

Go for a bush walk or a beach walk with the children and send them on a Scavenger Hunt.

What You Need

• *Lists written before you leave*

What To Do

Go for a walk through a park, beach or forest and ask the children to use their eyes or to think creatively. Give them a list each and a bag to collect their items in.

Remind them to only collect things they can return safely and without damage.

Things on the list may include:

    2 different types of seeds
    a flower
    a chewed leaf (not by them)
    something prickly
    something soft
    something smooth
    something that is a covering
    a camouflaged animal or insect
    something that reminds them of themselves
    something that is dead
    something from an animal
    and so on ...

Sit down on a log or patch of grass and let them be the scavengers. The first child to complete the Scavenger Hunt List correctly is the winner.

Share the contents of everyone's bags together and discuss the interesting items they have found. Remind the children to return them before you leave.

activity

390

SHELL MOBILE

8+ ✓

Keep holiday memories alive by collecting shells and driftwood at the beach and make a shell mobile together.

 ✓

 ✓

What You Need

✓

• *Pieces of driftwood*
• *Shells with small holes in them*
• *Fishing line*

✓

What To Do

Next time you are at the beach, collect as many shells as you can find that have small holes in them. These are quite easy to find. Also see if you can find some interesting pieces of driftwood.

When you come home help your children thread the shells with the fishing lines. (You won't be able to use a bodkin or tapestry needle as the holes in the shells are usually too tiny.)

Attach the threading to the driftwood and hang outside in the breeze.

The delightful tinkling will bring back lots of holiday memories.

activity
391

SNAILS

8

Help your children learn more about these fascinating creatures.

What You Need

• *Snails from the garden*
• *Aquarium or very large glass jar*

What To Do

When snails invade your garden, before you reach for the snail bait, collect a few for your children to observe and study for a few days. It's fun to go on a snail hunt together at night with a torch - you'll find lots more that way.

Put the snails you have collected in the aquarium and give them some food - lettuce is ideal, in fact that is what they are given to cleanse them before eating.

Your children will enjoy seeing the snail's large foot as it travels across the glass using its wave-like contractions. Observe the mucous trail that is left, which protects the snail from sharp surfaces. Did you know snails can crawl over very sharp objects without being hurt? Put a razor blade or sharp knife in the aquarium and watch.

Snail races are fun too! Mark the snails with different coloured stickers on their shells and put them on a marked path. Time the snails to see how far they can move in a minute.

Your children will be fascinated to learn that snails are considered to be gourmet fare in France and Japan. If they are adventurous eaters, buy a jar of snails from a good deli and cook them gently in butter and garlic. Yummy!

Make your children's snails the focus of a school project or talk to the class. Go to the local library together and find out more interesting facts about snails. Their classmates and teachers will be fascinated too!

activity

392

MESSAGE ON THE BEACH

10+

Next time you are at the beach help the children leave a message behind.

What You Need

• *Sticks or natural materials*

What To Do

Brainstorm with the kids to decide what they want to write and how. They could use large pieces of driftwood to write giant letters on the beach or use natural materials such as shells, pebbles, seaweed, driftwood and so on to make the words with.

Perhaps they could make them large enough to be seen by planes or, if they use their imaginations, by alien spacecraft. Well, you never know!

activity
393

NATURE DIARIES

10+ ✓

Encourage your children's interest in and knowledge of the environment by helping them keep a Nature Diary. ✓

 ✓

What You Need

 ✓

- *Notebook*
- *Pencil*
- *Coloured felt pens or pencils*

 ✓

What To Do

Every time you visit a park, National Park, Botanical Gardens or so on with your children encourage them to take along their Nature Diaries.

Help them make a list of the different types of animals and plants that they see there. Later you may be able to help them discover to which species those flora and fauna belonged by referring to books at home or in the library. It is important to use correct terminology with children.

Encourage them to note down which animals and plants were associated together and what the animals were eating.

If you visit the same places at different times of the year encourage them to consult their Nature Diaries and note down any changes they can observe. If you have had a very wet season or are in a drought visit the areas again and observe any changes.

Sometimes they will see something very special and unusual such as a tree covered with fungi. Take along your camera and photograph anything really special for them to add to their diaries. Encourage them also to develop their drawing skills by drawing animals or birds they see. If you can't identify the animal or bird look it up in reference books later.

Activities like this will encourage a love of and care for their environment in your children.

activity

394

SOLAR POWER

10+ ✓

 ✓

Kids today are really environmentally conscious and are truly concerned about saving fossil fuel and conserving our natural resources. Try this simple experiment to find out which materials absorb heat best and see if you can make some changes with your kids to the way your household uses heating fuels.

 ✓

 ✓

What You Need

 ✓

- *Pencil and paper*
- *A variety of objects such as a dark house-brick, white vinyl, curtain lining, carpet square, a ceramic tile, some silver foil and white paper*

What To Do

This activity is best done on a hot, sunny day. Put all the objects chosen for the experiment out in the full sun. Come back in a couple of hours and see which objects are the hottest and which are the coolest. The children can order the heat-absorbing properties of each material from the most effective to the least effective.

Talk together about ideas they have to make your home cooler in summer and warmer in winter. Go for a walk together and see how many houses in your area have solar heaters on their roof. You may even see some homes with solar heating for swimming pools on their roofs. Think of ways your family can save power - always wash clothes on sunny days so you don't use the clothes dryer, or turn off your electric blanket when you get into bed instead of leaving it on all night!

activity
395

TAKE IT APART

10+

Develop your children's interest in how things work by letting them take things apart.

 ✓

 ✓

 ✓

 ✓

What You Need

• *Screwdriver*
• *A pair of pliers*
• *Old appliances*

What To Do

If your kids are interested in how things work (and there are very few who aren't!), develop their inquiring minds by letting them take apart simple broken appliances instead of just throwing them out.

Always keep safety a high priority. Cut off any power cords first and, of course, appliances that must remain sealed such as TV's, refrigerators, microwaves and freezers are not to be touched.

However, items such as bike parts, broken toys, clocks, watches, phones, old radios (not with tubes), small appliances such as toasters and hairdryers, torches and old record players can all be taken apart and examined. Make sure there is always an adult around to supervise and to help if necessary.

Components also make great art. Maybe when they've finished checking out why the clock no longer works they might like to make a robot or a super machine artwork out of all the bits.

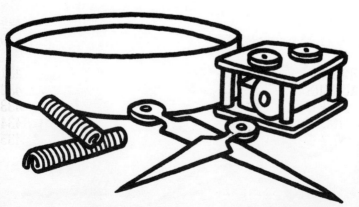

activity

396

OUTDOOR PLAY

OUTDOOR PLAY

BACKYARD MAZES

2+

Most young children love to wiggle and squirm through small places and if this applies to your children, try this activity with them in the backyard.

What You Need

- *Garden furniture*
- *Cardboard boxes*
- *Buckets*
- *String or thin rope*

What To Do

Set up a backyard maze by using some of your outdoor furniture. The children have to crawl underneath the furniture and reach the end of the maze in an allotted amount of time.

Increase the difficulty by placing some obstacles in their way such as rope tied across two chairs that they have to wriggle under or climb over and not touch. Or you might place a bucket full of water on one of the chairs so they have to wriggle under it and not touch the bucket which could move and spill.

Give older children a handicap by making them complete the maze in a much shorter time or make them carry a plastic cup of water. If they spill some of the water they have to fill up the cup and start again.

See if the children can come up with some new ideas to add to the maze!

activity
397

CARDBOARD TUNNELS

2+

Cardboard boxes are great because they are free and are also terrific for children's creative play. Fill up your car with boxes from your local fruit shop or electrical store and let the children make a great tunnel maze in your backyard.

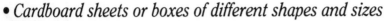

What You Need

- *Cardboard sheets or boxes of different shapes and sizes*
- *Strong masking or insulating tape*

What To Do

Help the children open out different sides of boxes and join them together to make tunnels. Long boxes can have a hole cut in the side so another box can be fitted into it. Use the masking or insulating tape to hold the boxes firmly together. Use a variety of boxes of different shapes and sizes to make the tunnel maze a real challenge.

When the tunnels are finished the children might enjoy decorating them with some acrylic paints.

They could even make a textured tunnel with different surfaces to crawl along bubble wrap, towels, carpet, hessian mats or just the grass.

If they want a spooky tunnel they could hang things from the roof of the tunnels such as wet plastic gloves, lengths of cellophane, crepe paper, or partly blown-up balloons.

Let them keep up their tunnels for a few days. By then their interest will probably have waned and you can take the whole lot to the tip and let the grass grow again!!!

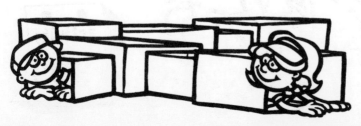

activity
398

FOLLOW THE LEADER

2+

Play a game of follow the leader with your little ones.

What You Need

- *Time*
- *Room to play*

What To Do

Line the children up and show them how to play the old favourite 'follow the leader'. Try to move in lots of different ways such as skipping (they will have trouble with this one but it's hilarious watching them try), jumping, walking sideways, walking backwards, taking little fairy steps or big giant's steps, running, crawling and so on.

When you run out of ideas one of the children can be the leader and think of things for the others to follow!

activity 399

JUMPSCOTCH

2+ ✓

Younger children find traditional hopscotch too difficult. Develop their balance and co-ordination with simpler 'Jumpscotch'. (see Hopscotch - activity 414)

 ✓

What You Need

- *Chalk to draw on pavement tiles or concrete*
- *Stone or bean bag for throwing*

 ✓

What To Do

Draw a pattern on the concrete, making sure the spaces are large enough for your children to jump in.

Show your children how to jump with their feet together from space to space until they reach the end of the jumpscotch. Show them how to turn around at the end and then jump back. When they have mastered this, play the game together using a stone or bean bag to throw.

You can vary the game by drawing different shapes (ovals, semi-circles, circles, squares, triangles and rectangles) and using their names. You could also draw the rectangles with just one foot shape in each so your children have to jump with their feet apart. Happy jumping!

activity

400

PAINTING THE HOUSE

2+

Young children want to be involved in whatever you are doing. However, letting them help when you are painting with 'real paint' is not usually possible. This activity will let them pretend they are really 'painting the house'.

What You Need

- *A real paint brush*
- *String, thin rope or cord*
- *A small well-washed paint tin with a handle or a small bucket*
- *Food colouring*

What To Do

Attach the brush to the tin or bucket with the cord so it doesn't get lost in the garden.

Half fill the tin or bucket with water and add some drops of food colouring. If the children want a non-primary colour such as purple this is a great time to see how colours mix together and change.

Now they can paint the house, the drive, paths, garden edging, the pavers or whatever they like outside and it can all be hosed off later. Best of all, you can do some painting knowing they are happy playing.

activity

401

SOAPY WATER

2+

Kids love playing in water and they love bubbles. Use up your old, hard, soap pieces and your children will have a ball.

What You Need

- *A large washing-up dish*
- *Old pieces of soap*
- *Graters, whisks, egg beaters, jugs, plastic cups, bowls*

What To Do

On a nice sunny day let the children have fun with all those little bits of left-over soap we all keep. Fill up a dish with water and place the pieces of soap into it. Put it out on the lawn and they will have a great time making wonderful soapy bubbles with whisks and egg beaters.

If they have some plastic dolls they will enjoy bathing them in the bubbles, too, or simply enjoy measuring and pouring with some plastic containers.

DON'T FORGET!
Any activity involving water and young children must be carefully supervised at all times.

activity
402

SPONGE TARGETS

2+

Lots of fun for the whole family on hot days.

What You Need

- *Sponge offcuts*
- *Chalks*
- *Bucket*

What To Do

Draw a clown's face or some other target on the brick walls of the house. Fill a bucket with water, dip the sponge pieces in the water and take it in turns to throw them at the target and 'wipe' it out. Great for a hot day as everyone gets nice and wet while you do it.

activity
403

SUN SENSE

2+

Even young children need to understand the importance of protecting ourselves from the sun.

 ✓

What You Need

- *Paper*
- *Coloured pencils or crayons*
- *Collection of items*

 ✓

 ✓

What To Do

Collect some items we need to protect ourselves from the sun such as sun glasses, hats, sun protective clothing, water bottle, sun screen, beach umbrella, and so on. Next, collect some items that wouldn't be of use.

Sit down with the children and talk to them about which items we need if we go out in the sun and why. Children need to learn from an early age about the dangers of too much sun exposure without protection.

After you have discussed this thoroughly with the children and sorted out the items we need if we go out in the sun, they could draw them or list them if they wish.

activity
404

TEDDY BEARS' PICNIC

2+ ✓

 ✓

Next time you and your young children are having a bad day, arrange a Teddy Bears' Picnic with their favourite soft toys. They will be enchanted and you will be good friends again!

 ✓

 ✓

What You Need

- *Picnic food and drink*
- *Soft toys and, of course, your children's Teddy*

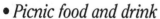 ✓

What To Do

Begin by making some simple invitations together. Decide with your children which 'toy friends' they would like to invite. They can decorate the invitations while you do the actual writing. Then they can be the 'postman' and deliver them.

Together, decide on the picnic fare - fruit, chunks of cheese, sausage and savoury biscuits, fairy bread make a simple but appealing picnic lunch. Don't forget cool drinks too!

Arrange it all on a rug or tablecloth in a cool part of the garden. A tea set adds to the fun also - your children will enjoy 'pouring' all their guests a drink.

Sing the 'Teddy Bears Picnic' song and read any books you have about bears together.

After the picnic is cleared away, pop your children into bed with all their cuddly friends for a nap and put your feet up. You deserve it!

activity
405

ZOOS

2+

Young children are fascinated with zoos. Help your children make a toy animal zoo in the sand pit.

What You Need

- *Toy zoo animals*
- *Boxes*
- *Polystyrene cups*
- *Scissors*
- *Poster or acrylic paints*
- *Drinking straws*
- *Sticky tape*
- *Small pieces of plants*

What To Do

If your children haven't visited a zoo take them along.

After the visit help them make a zoo in the sandpit. Help them cut holes in the boxes and cups to make animal homes and they will enjoy painting them. Next, sticky tape the straws together to make fences for the zoo.

Use a piece of card to smooth down paths for the visitors to walk on and add the plants and flowers to make gardens. Help the children fill the lids with water and bury in the sand to make ponds and drinking pools for the animals.

Arrange the animals in the zoo and leave the children to have a great time playing with their sandpit zoo.

activity
406

BEAN BAG BALANCING

4+

Fun games to help develop your children's body co-ordination, balance and control.

What You Need

- *Bean bag for balancing*
- *Simple obstacle course using a tyre or hoop, cardboard boxes, beach towels or hessian bags, and a broom*

What To Do

Make an easy bean bag by filling a sock with lima beans, split peas or rice. Tuck the sock inside its mate so no filling can spill out.

Your children can help you mark out the obstacle course.

Think of lots of different ways together that they can carry the bean bag without using their hands - on their head, under their arm, jumping with it between their legs, under their chin, between their elbows and between their wrists.

They then choose a way to carry the bean bag from the start to the first object, then choose a different method, and so on until they have gone through the whole course. If they drop the bean bag at any stage, they go back to the start of that section and try again.

Have a turn yourself - it is not as easy as it sounds!

activity
407

BIRD'S NEST GAME

4+ ✓

A fast and lively game to play with three or more children.

 ✓

What You Need

- *3 plastic hoops*
- *5 bean bags (fill old socks with sand, rice or dried beans to make quick and easy bean bags)*

 ✓

 ✓

What To Do

Explain to the children that the hoops are pretend birds' nests and that the bean bags are the eggs. Put the bean bags outside on the grass and put the three hoops equidistant from them.

Choose three children to have the first turn. They each stand in their 'nest' or hoop and, when you say 'go', the children run in, pick up a bean bag and run back and place it in their nest. They then run back for another one. When the bean bags have gone from the middle they can 'steal' them from each others nests. When a child has three 'eggs' in their nest, they sit down on them and yell 'bird's nest' and win the game. Remind the players that only one bean bag at a time can be placed in the nest and that they must be put in, not thrown from a distance.

This game is fast and furious and is just as funny for the onlookers as for the players. It moves so fast I often think it should be called 'perpetual motion'!

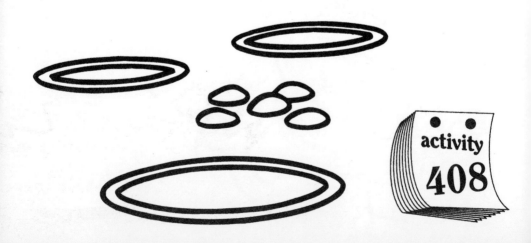

activity
408

DIFFERENT BUBBLES

4+

Children love blowing bubbles and, on a windy day, they are even more fun as everyone tries to catch them. However, many common household items can also be used to make bubbles. See below for ideas.

What You Need

- *Detergent*
- *Water*
- *A little glycerine or cooking oil to make the bubbles stronger*
- *A variety of potential bubble makers such as straws, funnels, plastic spools, wire and pipecleaners*
- *Clear plastic*

What To Do

It's fun to make bubbles with commercial bubble makers, but it is even more interesting to make them with a variety of things we all have around the house.

Let the children help you make up the bubble mixture and enjoy some time playing with any commercial bubble makers you may have.

Now give them a variety of materials as listed above and challenge them to use these items to make great bubbles.

Don't forget to have the camera handy to record some of the beautiful bubbles they will make.

activity
409

DOGGY, WHERE'S YOUR BONE? 4+

A game that children of all ages love to play. All you need as a prop is a simple 'bone' cut out of a plastic ice cream lid or from cardboard.

What You Need

- *Children*
- *'Bone'*
- *Blindfold*

What To Do

The children join hands to make a circle and then sit down. Choose a child to have the first turn. This child sits in the middle of the circle, wearing the blindfold, and with the 'bone' behind their back.

Choose another child from the circle to creep out and steal the doggie's bone, hiding it behind their back.

Everyone then chants:

DOGGIE, DOGGIE, WHERE'S YOUR BONE?
SOMEBODY STOLE IT FROM YOUR HOME.
WHO STOLE THE BONE?
The child who stole the 'bone' replies:

'I STOLE THE BONE.'

The blindfolded child then has to guess who has the bone. If the children don't know each other well enough to name, they can point at who they think has the bone. The game is harder if you encourage the children not to tell who has the bone, not to giggle if they have it, and everyone puts their hands behind their back - not just the person with the bone.

activity

410

FREEZE

Another good outdoor game to play with a group of children.

What You Need

- *Space*
- *A few players*

What To Do

One person is 'in' and stands, with their back to the other children, a fair distance away. The other children advance in a line towards the person who is 'in', who, every now and then turns around, and all the others have to instantly freeze. If any of these children are spotted moving, they are named by the person who is 'in' and must leave the game.

The first player to reach and touch the 'in' player is the winner and is 'in' for the next round.

activity
411

GARDEN OBSTACLE COURSES 4+ ✓

Make an obstacle course in the garden to help develop your childrens balance and muscle control.

What You Need

- *Rope or the garden hose*
- *Old mattress*
- *Cardboard boxes*
- *Strong smooth boards*

- *Ladder*
- *Tyres*
- *Hoops*
- *Broom*

✓

✓

What To Do

With your children, set up obstacle courses in the garden. Incorporate any structures you may have such as a slide or swings. Try to use as many different ways of moving as possible. Your children could try to:

Crawl under some garden chairs
Jump ten times on the mattress
Jump through three or four tyres or hoops
Jump over the broom
Walk along the curvy rope or hose
Run around a tree
Crawl up a plank balanced on a strong box
Hop through the rungs of a ladder laid flat on the ground
Walk sideways back to the start

This game is as endless as your imaginations.

activity
412

HANDKERCHIEF TUGS

4+ ✓

A new way to play tug-of-war.

 ✓

What You Need

- *Three players*
- *A rope tied together to make a circle*
- *Three handkerchiefs*

 ✓

What To Do

 ✓

The three players hold the rope at equal distances. They then pull
the rope tight. Place the handkerchiefs at equal distances from each child.
When you say 'Go', they must pull as hard as they can on the rope with one
hand to try to reach their handkerchief. The first person to pick up their
handkerchief is the winner.

activity
413

HOPSCOTCH

4+ ✓

After your children have mastered Jumpscotch, playing Hopscotch will further develop their co-ordination and balance, and also help them learn numbers in a fun way. (see Jumpscotch - activity 400)

What You Need

 ✓

- *Chalk to draw on pavement tiles or concrete*
- *Stones or small bean bag to throw*

✓

What To Do

Mark out a traditional hopscotch pattern or the one shown below on some concrete or pavement tiles. Perhaps you and your children can come up with some new patterns of your own, maybe a rocketship hopscotch game?

Explain the rules of hopscotch to them. Throw the stone into section 1, jump over it and then hop in all sections up to 10. Do a jump-turn on 10, hop back again and then, while balancing on one leg in section 2, retrieve the stone. Next time, throw into section 2, then hop over that and so on. If one child throws a stone into the wrong section, it is the next player's turn.

Each player must remember which number they are up to for their next turn. Younger children can play by jumping rather than hopping on one leg.

activity

414

JUMPING ROPES

4+

Activities like these will help improve your children's co-ordination and balance.

What You Need

- *A length of rope*
- *Small cushion, bean bag or half a sock filled with dried beans*

What To Do

Tie a cushion or the bean bag/sock to the end of the rope. Swing the rope around just above the ground (not too fast at first!). Your children jump over the rope as it comes around.

This is fun to do with a few kids or other family members. When the rope hits someone they are out and the winner is the last one left in.

activity
415

KNOCK 'EMS

4+

Develop your children's throwing skills with a game of home-made 'Knock 'ems'.

What You Need

- *6 tins with lids (powdered milk or baby formula tins are ideal)*
- *Paint or collage materials for decorating the tins*
- *Sand or dirt*
- *Balls or bean bags*

What To Do

Put some sand or dirt in the tins so they don't topple over too easily and replace the lids and tape closed.

Paint or decorate the tins with your children. Show them how to arrange the tins in a pyramid.

Throw the bean bags and count how many they knock down. Keeping the scores will be good counting practice too!

activity

416

NAILING FUN

An activity that encourages the development of excellent eye-hand coordination.

 ✓

 ✓

 ✓

✓

What You Need

- *Small nails* • *Small tack hammer*
- *Piece of pine board about 25 cm square*
- *Threading material*

What To Do

If you are buying a piece of pine for this activity the above size is ideal but really any shape will be fine as long as it is large enough to work on. Timber furniture makers are always happy to let you have their pine off-cuts. Pine is ideal for hammering with young children because it is a soft timber.

Mark dots about 1-2 cms apart around the outside of the board and your children can hammer a nail part of the way into each dot.

Then give them a selection of wool, string, elastic, raffia or perhaps even coloured wire to wind from nail to nail to make interesting patterns and shapes.

Another time you might like to mark the dots in the shape of a circle or perhaps a star to make a different pattern for your children to try.

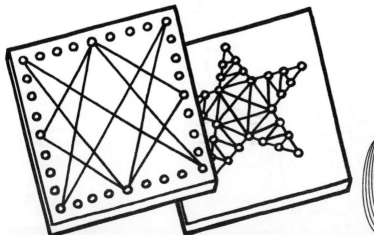

activity

417

ORANGES AND LEMONS

4+ ✓

 ✓

An oldie but a goldie! A game most of us have played at birthday parties when we were young. Teach it to your children at their parties and it will be just as popular today as it was then.

What You Need

• *Children*

What To Do

Choose two taller children to form an archway with their hands. Then they decide, with an adult, which one is going to be the Orange and which the Lemon. The other children make a line behind a leader and walk through the archway chanting:

ORANGES AND LEMONS SAY THE BELLS OF ST. CLEMENTS
YOU OWE ME FIVE FARTHINGS SAY THE BELLS OF ST. MARTINS
WHEN WILL YOU PAY ME SAY THE BELLS OF OLD BAILEY?
WHEN I GROW RICH SAY THE BELLS OF SHOREDITCH
HERE COMES A CANDLE TO LIGHT YOU TO BED
HERE COMES A CHOPPER TO CHOP OFF YOUR - YOUR - YOUR - YOUR - YOUR - YOUR HEAD!

On the final words 'your head', the archway is lowered and a child is caught. The archway children then take the 'caught' child away and ask him if he wants to be an Orange or a Lemon (keep it a secret which child is which). After making a choice, the 'caught' child lines up behind the Orange or Lemon. When all the children have been caught in the archway and have chosen to be an Orange or a Lemon, they form two teams and have a tug-of-war!

activity
418

PULLEYS

4+

Make a simple pulley with your children for lifting loads and playing rescue games with their teddies or dolls.

What You Need

- *Fishing line reel or large cotton reel*
- *Strong cord or string*
- *Two wire coat hangers or length of wire*
- *Pliers and wire cutters*

What To Do

Cut the wire coat hanger and, with the pliers, bend the wire through the reel (see the illustration) into the correct shape. Put the cord over the reel and tie a hook made from the second coat hanger hook onto the bottom.

Your children can use the pulley over the branch of a tree, from a cubby house, or even from the verandah.

They can use it for all sorts of games such as lifting lunch up into their cubby, lifting sand tools, or even playing 'Police Rescue' and lifting injured dolls or teddies.

To add to their interest, visit a building site together and watch cranes lifting their loads.

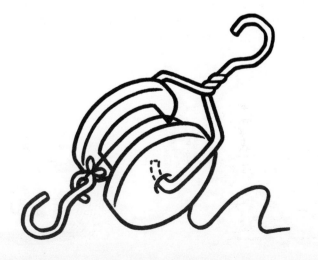

activity

419

ROPE FUN

4+

Use a length of rope to help your children develop their body control and co-ordination.

What You Need

• *A long piece of rope*

What To Do

Stretch out a long length of rope on the grass.
See if your children can think of lots of different ways to move along it (your children should be barefooted).

They could try:

Walking along the rope
Walking backwards
Jumping from side to side along the rope
Doing bunny hops over the rope
Walking with one foot on either side of the rope without touching it
Hopping along the rope on one foot
Crawling along the rope
Moving along the rope using one hand and one foot

See if you can think of other ways of moving with your children. After they have tried them with a straight rope, try them on a rope that is laid in a wiggly line.

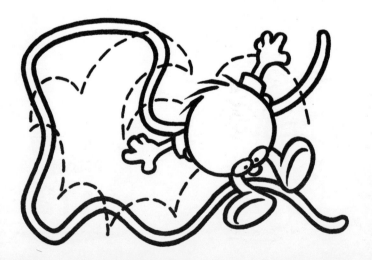

activity
420

SACK RACES

4+

I remember sack races from school sports days and Sunday School picnics when I was a child, and they were always lots of fun and very popular. Try it when the children are bored or when you have a birthday party.

What You Need

• *Sacks - today these are usually polystyrene and available from Fruit shops or produce agencies*
• *Pillowcases can be used, too*

What To Do

Make starting and finishing lines. The players each have a sack. They get into it feet first and line up. The aim of the game is to jump, holding onto the sides of the sack up to the finishing line.

Of course it is much harder than it sounds and there will be many tumbles and lots of laughter.

activity

421

SAND COOKING

4+

Children love to pretend; play is often their way of acting out the social situations they encounter in their world. Give them the opportunity to play cooking in the sand pit.

What You Need

- *Cake tins*
- *Muffin or patty cake trays*
- *Old frying pans and saucepans*
- *Jelly moulds*
- *Plastic containers*
- *Plastic bowls*
- *Sieves*
- *Ice cube trays*
- *Wooden, plastic or metal spoons*

What To Do

Give the children a basket of cooking implements for the sand pit. If you don't have old things to donate to the sand pit, a visit to a charity shop will give you a terrific assortment for a very small cash outlay and your small children will be enchanted.

Turn an old box into a stove by drawing some hot plates on the top and putting in a couple of 'trays'. They will mix with sand and water and make the most delicious dinners ever.

Make sure you leave some time in your busy day to visit and be waited on!!!

activity
422

SHIP TO SHORE

4+

Another great group game to play with the children.

What You Need

• *Space to run*
• *Children*

What To Do

Designate areas in the play space to be the 'ship' and the 'shore'. The command '4' means to stand in the middle and 'z' means to sit down wherever you are. Someone is chosen to call the commands - to be the Captain. The players have to run as fast as they can to the area when the Captain calls. The last to react to the command each time steps out and joins the Captain, The last player in is the winner and becomes the next 'Captain'.

activity
423

TARGET PRACTICE

4+

Make some targets in the garden with your children and help improve their throwing skills.

What You Need

- *Wire coathanger or a child's plastic hoop*
- *String*
- *Balls or bean bags*

What To Do

Pull the coathanger into a round shape or use a hoop and lash it to a tree or the clothes line to make a stable target.

Your children will have lots of fun throwing balls or bean bags through the target.

To make it more interesting, tie balloons on strings or junk threadings to the target so they move when the children score a 'hit'.

As their aim improves, make them stand further away to increase the challenge.

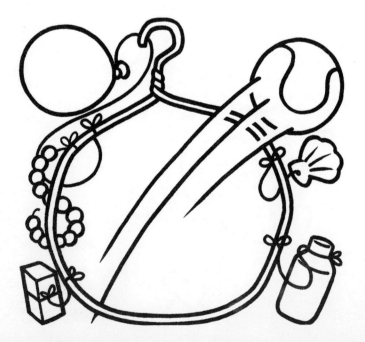

activity
424

THE BEANSTALK GIANT'S TREASURE

4+

A great chasing game to play when you have a group of children together.

If they don't know the story of Jack and the Beanstalk, tell it before the game begins.

What You Need

• *Lots of space to run*
• *Lots of children*
• *A bean bag or sock filled with rice or beans*

What To Do

One child is the Giant and sits down with his treasure behind him. The other children are all Jack and have to try to steal the Giant's treasure.

Designate an area that is safe and home. The other children start there and try to sneak up behind the Giant.

If the Giant hears them they have to freeze or return to the start - home. When someone succeeds in stealing the treasure the Giant has to try to catch them before they reach home.

If the Giant doesn't catch them, a new Giant is chosen. If he does, anyone who is caught joins the Giant's team and becomes an assistant Giant and tries to catch the Jacks.

activity

425

THE FARMER IN THE DELL 4+

A traditional game that children always love to play at a party or a group gathering.

What You Need

• *Lots of children*

What To Do

Begin by standing the children in a circle and choose a 'farmer' to stand in the middle, then the song begins. As each new character is introduced, choose a child to play that role in the middle of the circle.

THE FARMER IN THE DELL, THE FARMER IN THE DELL
HI HO THE DAIRY-O THE FARMER IN THE DELL.
THE FARMER TAKES A WIFE, THE FARMER TAKES A WIFE,
HI HO THE DAIRY-O THE FARMER TAKES A WIFE.
The song continues:

THE WIFE TAKES A CHILD etc.
THE CHILD TAKES A NURSE etc.
THE NURSE TAKES A DOG etc.
THE DOG TAKES A CAT etc.
THE CAT TAKES A MOUSE etc.
THE MOUSE TAKES SOME CHEESE etc.
WE ALL EAT THE CHEESE etc.

Don't choose a timid child for the cheese or they may not enjoy being eaten!

activity
426

THREE-LEGGED RACES

4+ ✓

An old Sunday School picnic favourite from my childhood.

What You Need

 ✓

• *Old tights or scarves*
• *At least four children*

What To Do

 ✓

Mark out a starting and finishing line first.

The children divide into pairs. Make sure they remove their shoes, and then tie each pair of children firmly together around their ankles with a scarf or old tights. They then hold each other around the waist.

Line up all the contestants and begin the race. If the children are having difficulties, remind them to start walking by moving their joined legs together first. Speed is not essential at first - it's more important to get a rhythm going.

Give them lots of practice until everyone gets the hang of it!

activity
427

WACKO

A fun variation on a game of skittles.

4+

What You Need

- *Empty plastic soft drink bottles*
- *Chalk*
- *Sand*
- *Large ball*

What To Do

Your children can help by pouring about a cup of sand into the bottom of each soft drink bottle so they don't topple easily.

Draw a large circle on the concrete or pavement tiles with the chalk, or make a circle on the lawn with the hose.

Place all the bottles inside and take it in turns to roll a ball along the ground and see how many bottles you can each knock out of the circle.

Use this activity as a counting game as well and your children can keep the scores on paper or their blackboard.

activity
428

WASHING THE CAR

4+

There's nothing like having a nice shiny clean car - and the kids love helping to wash it!

What You Need

- *Buckets*
- *Sponges, rags, or chamois*
- *Car washing liquid*
- *The hose*

What To Do

Most children love helping to wash the car - specially if they do it on warm sunny days when they can wear their swimming outfit and get wet. If the children are trying to avoid this task, however, turn it into a game that's fun for everyone.

Assign each child to a specific part of the car to wash - the number plates, hub caps, bonnet, doors and so on.

Give them all a bucket and cloth and when you say 'go' they clean their section/sections as fast as they can. Of course, Mum or Dad has to inspect the job to make sure that fast doesn't mean dirty!

activity

429

WHAT'S THE TIME, MR WOLF? 4+

A great party game.

What You Need

- *Lots of space*
- *Lots of players*

What To Do

One child is 'Mr Wolf' and stands a fair distance away with their back to the other children. The other children hold hands and advance in a line, step by step, as they chant, 'What's the time, Mr Wolf?' Then they stop walking. After each question Mr Wolf turns around and says a time, e.g. '7 o'clock'. Finally, when they are very close, Mr Wolf turns and says 'Dinner Time!'

The children turn and run away as fast as they can with 'Mr Wolf' chasing them. When someone is caught, they are the next 'Mr Wolf'.

activity

430

APPLE BOBBING

6+

My son played this game recently at his friend Billy's sixth birthday party.

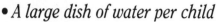

What You Need

• *A large dish of water per child*
• *An apple per child*

What To Do

The children each kneel in front of their dish containing the apple floating in the water. An adult says 'go' and the children have to try to catch the apple in their teeth and eat it without using their hands.

A fun party game but best played on a nice warm day because all the kids get rather wet!!

WARNING!
Any activities that involve children and water must always be carefully supervised by an adult.

activity

431

FLYING SAUCERS

6+ ✓

 ✓

Make some exciting Flying Saucers to fly in the garden with the children. See whose Flying Saucer will fly the greatest distance.

 ✓

 ✓

 ✓

What You Need

- *Paper plates*
- *Paper cups*
- *Scissors*
- *Sticky tape or masking tape*
- *Felt pens*

What To Do

Begin by helping the children cut the paper cups in half. Keep the bottom part and cut small slits along the top edge, and then bend them out to make flaps. Put the cup with the flaps down onto the paper plate and fasten with pieces of sticky tape or masking tape. Finally, help the children cut flaps around the outside of the plate. Fold each flap alternately forwards or backwards. These flaps will help the flying saucer fly.

Your children will enjoy using felt pens to draw windows and doors on their flying saucers, or buy a can of silver spray paint and spray them silver to look really hi-tech.

Go out at night sky-watching and see if you can really spot some alien visitors!

activity
432

FRENCH CRICKET

6+ ✓

 ✓

A great family game that helps younger children learn some of the skills needed for playing conventional cricket later.

What You Need

 ✓

- *A large soft plastic ball*
- *A small cricket bat, old tennis racquet or piece of wood shaped like a bat*

What To Do

Gather the family together to play a fast and furious game of French Cricket. One player holds the bat in front of their legs and the other players space themselves out in a large circle around that player. The object of the game is to try to hit the batsman's legs with the ball.

The batsman has to try to hit the ball away and is not allowed to move except when the ball has been hit and a player is running to fetch it. The batsman can then jump to another position. However, if the player fetching the ball sees this move, the batsman is out.

A fun family game!

activity
433

HOME-MADE QUOITS

6+

We always played quoits at Nanna's house when we were children. Help your own children make a set and improve their throwing skills.

What You Need

- *Empty plastic soft drink bottle*
- *Stones*
- *Metal coat hangers*

What To Do

Put the stones into the soft drink bottle to stop it falling over and securely tape on the lid. To make the hoops, untwist the handle section of the coat hanger and retwist the wire to form circles. (If this is too hard on the fingers, cut off the handle with wire cutters and just use the rest).

Place the bottle on the ground and mark a spot for the children to throw from. (Older children will need a handicap!) Each player has ten throws at a time. Keep the scores and the person who hoops the most quoits over the bottle is the winner.

Quoits is a good game to play on a picnic or family gathering - even the older members of the family will love to have a go.

activity
434

PAPER PLANES

6+ ✓

Make some simple paper planes and have a competition with your children to see how far they can fly. If you have a house set on high ground have them fly their planes from the verandah top and watch which way the wind takes them.

 ✓

 ✓

What you Need

 ✓

• *A4 paper*

 ✓

What To Do

Fold a piece of A4 paper in half lengthways. Fold the top corner of the paper into the middle to form an arrow shape. Then fold it in again. Next, fold the 'wings' down on the sides to form the plane.

The wings can be closer in to make it like a high speed fighter jet, or sit further out to increase the aerobatics potential. You can staple along the body of the plane to make it stay in shape better. A paper clip attached to the nose will make it fly even faster!

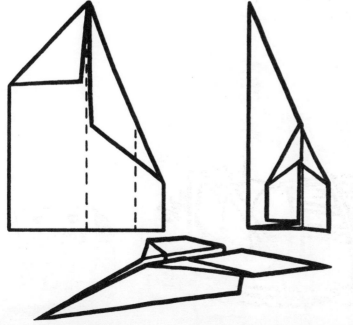

activity
435

PIGGY IN THE MIDDLE

6+ ✓

A game most of us have played in our youth!

What You Need

• *Three players*
• *A ball*

 ✓

 ✓

What To Do

 ✓

Stand two of the children about ten metre (11 yards or 33 ft) apart. The third child is 'Piggy' and, of course, stands in the middle.

'Piggy' has to try to catch the ball as the other two players throw it to each other. If the ball is dropped, any of the three can try to retrieve it. When 'Piggy' has managed to catch the ball, the person who was last to throw it becomes the new 'Piggy'.

activity
436

POCKET MONEY

6+

Children need to earn pocket money and to understand that we work to receive pay. There are many outdoor jobs they can do around the house to help earn pocket money.

What You Need

• *List of jobs*

What To Do

Discuss with your children some of the jobs that you need to do regularly around your home. They can help list them for writing practice.

They might include weeding or digging the garden, emptying the kitchen compost container daily into the compost bin, turning the compost in the bin, raking the lawn after mowing, hosing, sweeping paths, and so on.

Decide who would like to do which jobs and make a roster. Children will gain confidence and a sense of responsibility if they have their own special chores, and will learn that everyone in a family has to help - not just Mum and Dad.

Make some lists for the 'fridge door or noticeboard and the children can tick off when they have completed their allocated chores. This is good for their memories and also a literacy experience.

activity

437

PUNCH BAG

6+

Next time your children are squabbling, make a punching bag with them so they can punch that instead of each other.

What You Need

- *Sugar bag (or sew a calico bag)*
- *Rope*
- *Filling such as newspaper old rags, foam, dried grass*

What To Do

Your children can fill the bag with the selected filling. Tie a rope securely around the top of the bag and hang it from a beam or the branch of a tree.

A pair of boxing gloves would make a good birthday or Christmas gift to go with the punching bag.

Have a go yourself next time the children have stressed you out! It's better to punch the bag instead of yelling at them.

activity
438

SIMON SAYS

An oldie, but a goldie!

What You Need

- *Players*
- *Space to play*

What To Do

Explain the rules to the children. You will give them instructions, but they can only do them if they hear 'Simon says'. So, if you say 'Run on the spot', they must remain still until the command 'Simon says, run on the spot!'

Players are eliminated if they do the wrong thing. The last player in is the winner and can give the commands next time.

activity
439

THE CHICKEN AND HAWK GAME 6+

Another old playground favourite that is great for birthday parties or whenever you have a group of children together.

What You Need

- *Children*
- *Space to run safely*

What To Do

Mark out the boundaries for the game by drawing two lines about three metres (10 ft) apart. Choose two of the children to be the hawks and they stand in the middle of the two lines while the rest of the players - the chickens - stand behind one of the lines. When you say go the chickens must run across to the other line, trying to avoid being caught by one of the hawks. Any players who are caught join the hawks until all the children have been caught.

The last child to be caught becomes the next hawk and chooses a friend to help him.

activity
440

TUG OF WAR

6+

A Tug of War at family picnics or birthday parties is always great fun.

What You Need

• *A long, strong rope*
• *Willing participants*

What To Do

Arrange the participants evenly on either side of the rope. Put the smallest pullers closest to the middle and the larger children and adults at the ends of the rope.

Mark a spot on the ground in the middle. The aim of the game is for one team to pull the other over the mark on the ground.

Someone yells 'go' and everyone starts pulling as hard as they can. Lots of fun and you will probably all have sore muscles the next day!!

activity
441

WHEELBARROW RACES

6+

Lots of fun to do and even more fun to watch.

What You Need

• *At least four children*

What To Do

Mark out a starting and finishing line for the wheelbarrow race.
Divide the children into pairs. Each pair has to decide who is going
to be the wheelbarrow first and who will be the pusher.

The 'wheelbarrow' gets down on his hands and his partner lifts him around the
knees. Line them all up and begin the race.

Next time, swap over, so everyone has a turn at both roles.

Loads of laughs, but make sure you play it on soft grass.

activity
442

COIN TOSSING

8+   ✓

 ✓

Another good game that not only improves your children's throwing skills, but also gives them counting practice.

What You Need

 ✓

• *Muffin tin*   • *Pencil*
• *Paper*   • *Coins*

 ✓

What To Do

✓

Cut out circles of paper to fit in the holes in the muffin tin. Give each hole a different number. Stand the tin against some books so it stands on an angle.

Mark a spot for the players to throw from and take it in turn to try to toss a coin into one of the holes in the muffin tin. Coins that land in a hole score that number of points.

Players must add up their own scores and keep a running total. The first player to reach a designated score (perhaps 100!) is the winner.

activity
443

DONKEY

8+

Most adults will remember this game from their own childhood. Play it again with your children and their friends.

What You Need

- *Children*
- *Tennis ball*

What To Do

This was one of my favourite playground games at primary school, and the children of today will enjoy it too.

The children line up facing a wall - about two metres (6 feet) from it - except for the person who is 'it'. This person is the ball thrower - all the players will have a turn at this. The player with the ball throws the ball at the wall and, as it rebounds, everyone must jump over it. If a player is hit or touched by the ball they gain a letter, eventually spelling D O N K E Y!!
The player is out when they get the whole word.

The winner of each game is the person who has the least number of letters when the game ends. (Time each game so everyone can have a turn at throwing). Keep a score sheet to see who is the overall winner.

activity
444

FIND THE BELL

8+

Listening games like this help children develop good listening habits in a fun play way.

What You Need

- *Blindfolds (if you know a frequent traveller, ask them to collect some sleep-masks for you)*
- *A bell*
- *Plenty of open space to play the game*

What To Do

Blindfold all the players except one. That person is 'it' and carries the bell. This must be rung all the time while the others try to catch the player with the bell, who must work very hard to stay out of the way of the other players.

Whoever tags that player has the next turn at ringing the bell.

activity

445

YO-YO FUN

8+ ✓

Yo-yos are one of those perennial toys that surface every few years. When I was a child they were really big! My six year old son considers them 'cool' so they must be back in popularity again!

 ✓

 ✓

 ✓

What You Need

• *A yo-yo*

✓

What To Do

✓

If you think you are a bit of a yo-yo champ from way back it might be a good idea to practise some of these tricks while the kids are at school or otherwise occupied, or you may end up with egg on your face as I did!!

One basic trick is called the Sleeper. Toss the yo-yo out of the back of your hand with a flick of your wrist. When the yo-yo drops to the bottom of the string try to stop it slightly and the yo-yo will spin. Jerk your hand upwards slightly and the yo-yo will come back up the string very quickly. This is a really basic trick but, like all yo-yo tricks, it takes practice and in time you will be able to let your yo-yo rest for a few seconds at the bottom before it comes back up the string.

Another famous trick is called 'Walking the Dog'.

First you do a 'sleeper' as hard as you can so the yo-yo really spins at the bottom of the throw. As it is spinning, place it gently on the floor. Tiles, wood or other hard floors work much better than carpet. Walk a few steps as your yo-yo spins and you'll be walking the dog. Again this takes a lot of practice even though it sounds simple!

Another trick the kids will have to master before doing more complicated moves is the 'forward pass'. Begin by holding the yo-yo by your side just above your waist with the palm of your hand facing down and the string coming off the top of the yo-yo. Flip the yo-yo straight out in front of you with a backhand throw and when it comes back catch it in the palm of your hand.

You and the kids will have lots of fun revisiting yo-yos and learning all the tricks together!

activity

446

STONE SKIPPING

Teach your children this age old pastime.

What You Need

• *Flat stones*
• *Still water*

What To Do

My father taught me to skip stones across water just as his father probably taught him.

The first thing to do is to pick out stones that will skip well. The best skipping stones are thin and flat as they really can bounce across the water.

Next, show them the correct technique, as this is where the art of successful stone skipping comes from. Demonstrate to them how to hold their throwing hand in front of them so that their thumb and forefinger forms a letter 'c'. The stone should be sitting in the grip with the flat side parallel to the ground.

Throwing should be done with a sidearm movement, away from the body, similar to the action needed to throw a frisbee or quoit. At the last second before releasing the stone show them how to give a flick of a wrist so the stone takes off spinning.

When they have perfected the technique, have competitions to see who can make their stone do the most skips or who can skip a stone right across the watercourse!

activity
447

WEATHER INFORMATION

10+

Encourage your older children's interest in the environment by helping them set up a weather station and recording and measuring each day's weather.

What You Need

- *Strong cardboard*
- *Thermometer*
- *2 broom handles*
- *Large tin*

What To Do

The weather station will need a rain gauge, a wind vane and a thermometer.

Attach the tin with suitable glue to the side or top of a broom handle and bury in the ground in an open part of the garden. Make sure it is firm enough not to be knocked over by strong winds. Your children will need a ruler to place in the tin to measure rainfall - a simple rain gauge.

To make the wind vane, you need a piece of strong cardboard about 15 cm (6 ins) square. Mark each corner with the initials for the compass directions of North, South, East and West. Make a hole in the centre of the card so a broom handle fits in snugly and cut an arrow out of strong cardboard to attach to the top of the wind vane. Attach it so it will swing freely and point to the positions on the card. Bury it in the garden and use the early morning sun or a compass to make sure you have the correct positions.

Your children are then ready to begin measuring things like the amount of rainfall each month, the daily temperature, cloud formations, wind directions, and the amount of daylight hours.

Help them graph their findings. Their teacher will be most interested in this project also!

activity
448

PARTY, FAMILY & GROUP GAMES

FAMILY PICNICS

2+

Everyone loves a picnic, and they provide great opportunities to spend happy, relaxed times with the kids. I have many wonderful memories of picnics when I was a child and I hope my child will have lots also, so spend lots of time out-of-doors with your family having happy family picnics.

What You Need

- *Picnic baskets*
- *Lots of food and drinks*
- *Rug, pillows*
- *Balls, cricket bat, etc.*
- *Damp face washers or pre-moistened towelettes for sticky fingers*

What To Do

I keep a large picnic basket already packed with plastic plates, cups, thermos, sugar, salt and pepper, tablecloth, serviettes, and tea towels, so packing a quick picnic becomes much easier.

Take food which travels well and pack it in an esky with lots of freezer blocks; no one wants upset tummies after picnics. Take lots more food and drinks than you think you will need as everyone always gets hungry in the open air.

We love marinated chicken wings or drumsticks for picnics, lots of fruit and something tasty for dessert. Call in to your local hot-bread shop on the way and stock up with delicious breads or rolls.

Take a container with easy, already prepared salad vegetables such as celery and carrot sticks, radishes and baby tomatoes, and bring along some mayonnaise with a little curry added for dipping, or a commercially bought dip.

activity

449

LET'S GO OUT

2+

 ✓

So often outings with children involve spending lots of money but there are many, many places you can take young children for free. For them the most important aspect is that they are with their parent or parents and you are spending time with them.

What You Need

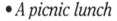

- *A picnic lunch*
- *A rug*

What To Do

The excursion venue will depend on your child's age and experience. For many young children the local park is a great outing. Pack a ball and a book for when they tire of playing on the playground equipment and don't forget sunscreen and a hat.

Older children might enjoy an outing to a beach, river, dam or a local swimming hole. Pack swimming togs in summer and a ball to kick and throw in winter. If you all enjoy fishing take some fishing gear.

The main thing is that a picnic is a great way for the family to enjoy each other's company without spending a great deal of money.

activity
450

RING A ROSY

2+

Younger children love this falling-down fun game.

What You Need

- *Children*
- *Room to play safely*
  - *a good outside game on the grass*

What To Do

All the children and adults hold hands and dance around singing:

RING A RING A ROSY
A POCKET FULL OF POSY
AH TISHOO AH TISHOO
WE ALL FALL DOWN

Then, sitting on the ground they can sing:

PICKING ALL THE DAISIES, THE DAISIES, THE DAISIES
PICKING ALL THE DAISIES
WE ALL JUMP UP!

Repeat a few times until everyone is exhausted!

activity
451

SINGING IN THE CAR

2+ ✓

Use trips in the car as an opportunity to sing together and to teach the children new songs. Even if you can't sing in tune the kids will still love singing with you.

 ✓

What You Need

• *Time in the car*

What To Do

 ✓

So often, time in the car with children turns into squabble time on the back seat. When we were children we loved singing in the car with Mum and Dad and I still sing many of those old songs with my son.

Singing is great for language development, for developing children's sense of rhythm and for developing their memories. Begin with simple nursery rhymes with your younger children and then sing some of the songs they are learning at kindergarten, preschool or school. If you don't know the words, why not ask their teachers to write them down for you. They will be happy to do this because teachers always value parental interest and support.

If you still need more songs to sing, have a look at the great selection of tapes or CDs in your local shops. They have a wide range of songs for children which would be great to sing along with in the car.

activity
452

BIRTHDAY PINATA

4+

Make a Mexican pinata with your children to use at their next birthday party.

What You Need

- *A balloon*
- *Newspaper and coloured paper*
- *Paint*
- *Wallpaper paste*
- *Streamers*
- *Sweets (candies)*

What To Do

Blow up the balloon if your children can't manage this, and then begin the papier mache process. Your children can help cut or tear the newspaper into strips. Next, dip them in the glue and paste them over the balloon. Papier mache is best done over a few days to allow the layers to dry. Hang the balloon from the clothes line to dry really well.

When the papier mache is thick enough, burst the balloon and carefully cut a hole in the top. Decorate it with colourful paints and bright patterns and hang streamers from the bottom. Fill with sweets (candies).

At the party, hang up the pinata and the children take it in turns to hit it with a stick (blindfolds add an extra challenge) to break it so the sweets (candies) fall out. Lots of fun!

activity
453

CAR BINGO

4+ ✓

 ✓

Prepare some simple bingo cards for the children before undertaking a long trip in the car. They will have great fun spotting various items and places, and the trip will be a pleasure for everyone.

 ✓

What You Need

- *Cardboard*
- *Coloured pencils, crayons, or felt pens*

What To Do

Before the trip talk to the children about some of the things they may spot on your trip. These may include animals, different types of vehicles, various buildings, landscape features and so on.

Prepare some cards with the words and simple pictures such as

1. cow   2. dog   3. mountain   4. police car   5. oak tree

6. pink flowers   7. truck   8. river   9. bridge   10. stop sign

When they are getting restless hand out the cards and a pencil each. When a child spots an item he calls it out and 'crosses it off his card. Only the first child to spot the item and call out its name can cross it off. The first child to cross off all the items yells BINGO and is the winner.

To make preparation of the cards easier, just draw one, take it to your local photocopying shop and have it copied and the cards laminated. Then the children simply mark their cards with a non-permanent pen and later the cards can be wiped off and used again and again.

activity

454

HEY, MR. CROCODILE!

4+ ✓

A good game to play at a children's party or any time a group of kids is together.

 ✓

What You Need

• *Children*

What To Do

Choose one child to be Mr. Crocodile or play it yourself for a while if the children are not familiar with the game. The rest of the children line up on the other side of an imaginary river. They then begin asking Mr. Crocodile if they can cross the river. Mr. Crocodile replies 'Yes', but with a condition.

HEY, MR. CROCODILE, CAN WE CROSS THE WATER
TO SEE YOUR LOVELY DAUGHTER
FLOATING IN THE WATER
LIKE A CUP AND SAUCER.

Mr. Crocodile replies:

YES, IF YOU'RE WEARING RED! (or shoes, buttons, hair ribbons, etc.).

A fun game that helps young children discriminate and use language well.

activity
455

RHYMING IN THE CAR

4+ ✓

Children need to be able to hear rhyming words before they can begin to read. Knowledge of rhyme needs young children to first recognise and then be able to produce words that end with the same sounds. This is an important stage in phonological awareness and essential for literacy development.

 ✓

What You Need

• *Car trips*

 ✓

What To Do

We all need to have activities to fill in long, boring car trips and your children will love playing rhyming games.

Begin by saying four or five words in a row. All of them will rhyme except for one. See who is first to call out the one that doesn't rhyme.

Dog, log, frog, stone, bog.   Answer is stone.
Cat, car, mat, fat, chat.   Answer is car.
Ball, hall, small, tall, foot.   Answer is foot. And so on.

Another game is to say a few words and the children have to tell you if they rhyme or not.

Door, floor, store.   Answer is yes.
Cat, do, elephant.   Answer is no.
Horse, course, source.   Answer is yes.
Fish, dish, wish.   Answer is yes.
Ship, boat, canoe.   Answer is no.

The children will enjoy making up their own lists of rhyming words to try and trick each other and Mum and Dad!

activity

456

SARDINES

4+ ✓

A very funny game that is just right to play at family gatherings or with a large group of children.

 ✓

 ✓

What You Need

• *A house with lots of hiding places*

What To Do

One person is chosen to be the 'SARDINE', and then goes to hide while the rest of the players close their eyes and count to 100. They then go and look for the 'SARDINE'.

When the 'SARDINE' is found by someone, that person must squeeze into the 'SARDINE'S' hiding place with the 'SARDINE'. (Don't forget to remind the players before they start to keep as quiet as possible while they are hiding - giggling is a real give-away!) As each player finds the 'SARDINE', they must squeeze into the same hiding place. Finally, everyone is there - squeezed in like a tin of sardines!

The person who found the 'SARDINE' first, becomes the next 'SARDINE'.

activity
457

SHOPPING

4+

Although it is tempting to leave young children at home when you shop for the groceries, it can really be made into a learning experience for them.

What You Need

- *Supermarket catalogues*
- *Paper*
- *Pencil*

What To Do

Before you go to do the weekly grocery shopping, sit down with the children and do some brainstorming about what you need. I find my son is much better than I at remembering what we have run out of - especially if it is something he likes! Write the items down for younger children - older children can write the shopping list for you.

If you have any advertising from your local supermarket look at the specials with the children and decide if you are going to buy any.

Talk about budgets and the amount you have to spend. Children need to understand that we plan what we buy and why.

Planning shopping trips also provides opportunities to talk about balanced diets and why you buy certain items.

Perhaps older children could assist in planning some meals they would like to help prepare, and you can add what you would need to the shopping list. Small children will enjoy finding items as you shop and putting them into the trolley for you.

The children can also help to sort out the groceries when you come home and, for instance, put away the cold items in the 'fridge.

Shopping together offers many opportunities for writing, counting, comparing, choosing and sorting. All of these are important literacy and numeracy skills.

activity

458

TEN PIN BOWLING

4+ ✓

An evening at your local ten pin bowling alley is a great family night out that children and adults can all enjoy.

 ✓

 ✓

What You Need

- *Time*
- *Money*

✓

✓

What To Do

✓

Ten pin bowling is a great game for the whole family to enjoy together and is quite inexpensive. We all enjoy bowling and it is a great family outing, either at night or in the school holidays.

You can hire the special shoes at the bowling alley and the balls are provided. We like to go with at least one other family so we can have a kids' lane with buffers working and a lane for the adults.

Smaller children can simply roll their bowling balls down a stand so they don't have to pick up the heavy balls. By using a lane with the gutters covered they enjoy it much more.

Try it and you, too, will find ten pin bowling is one of those simple activities the whole family can enjoy together that helps build good family relationships.

activity
459

WHO STOLE THE COOKIE?

4+

A fun party game to play with a group of children.

What You Need

• *A group of children*

What To Do

Sit the children in a circle for this game so everyone can see each other. Start the rhythm of the game by doing one clap of hands and then a knee tap. CLAP TAP CLAP TAP. When the children are all following the rhythm, teach them the chant:

WHO STOLE THE COOKIE FROM THE COOKIE JAR?
TOM STOLE THE COOKIE FROM THE COOKIE JAR.
Tom then says,
WHO ME?
The group responds with:
YES YOU!
Tom then says:
COULDN'T BE!
The group then says:
THEN WHO?
Tom then chooses the next player:
ANDREW!
The game continues:
WHO STOLE THE COOKIE FROM THE COOKIE JAR?
ANDREW STOLE THE COOKIE FROM THE COOKIE JAR.

A great game, which also develops children's memory and verbal skills.

activity
460

ALLITERATIVE FUN

6+ ✓

 ✓

Next time you have a long car trip, long wait for an appointment, or time to fill in, play a game with the children that's fun but will also teach them those important phonological awareness skills so necessary for good readers.

 ✓

 ✓

What You Need

 ✓

• *Time to play together*

 ✓

What To Do

Make up your own alliterative sentences - alliteration is the ability to hear the first sound in words.

Freddy Fryer freaks out at football.

Billy Bloggs booted the ball.

Samantha Sly skated on Saturday.

See how many the children can think up. Encourage them to think of silly ones if possible. Soon they will all be 'enjoying' the game and having lots of fun.

activity
461

I WENT TO THE PARK GAME   6+

Next time the children have had enough of running around and playing in the park, sit down on a rug and play a great memory game with them.

What You Need

• *A group of children*

What To Do

Sit the children on the rug in a circle and begin the game by saying:

'*I went to the park and I climbed a tree.*'

The next player says-

'*I went to the park and I played football and I climbed a tree.*'

The third player says-

'*I went to the park and I had a swing, and I played football and I climbed a tree.*'

The game continues around the circle with everyone trying to remember all the activities.

NEIGHBOURHOOD BOARD GAME 6+

Make a Neighbourhood Board Game to play with your children.

What You Need

- *Cardboard*
- *Coloured felt pens, pencils or crayons*
- *Coloured counters*
- *Dice*

What To Do

Next time you go for a neighbourhood walk with your children encourage them to look at street signs, how streets intersect, parks and other unusual features of your neighbourhood. You may even like to take a small notebook with you to jot down any ideas they have on the walk.

When you have time at home, make a Neighbourhood Board Game together on a large piece of white cardboard. Use your home as the start and another feature - perhaps a park or a corner store, or a friend's home - for the finish. Mark the route out in squares and the children will enjoy marking in features they remember from walks.
The children will have many ideas such as:

a local shop
miss a turn while you eat your iceblock or
move ahead 2 squares for picking up a paper
post box
throw a 5 to move after you post your letter
move ahead two squares because you crossed at the crossing
move ahead 5 squares for taking the dog for a walk or miss a turn while you have a swing at the park

The whole family will enjoy playing a board game that is about your own neighbourhood.

activity

463

NOISY ANIMAL PAIRS

A noisy, funny game to play at a party or with a group of children.

6+

What You Need

- *An even number of players*
- *Pieces of paper*
- *A cardboard box or container*

What To Do

Divide the number of children by two and think of that many animals. They must be animals that all the players are familiar with, and know what sounds they make. Write the name of each animal on two pieces of paper. Place all the animal names in a box and the children take it in turn to draw out a name. (They must keep this a secret.)

Now the game begins. The children pretend to be the animal they have drawn out and they must make the noise that animal makes. At the same time, however, they must also listen to the others to find the child who is making the same noise as themselves. The first animal pair to find each other are the winners, but the game continues until everyone has found their pair

activity
464

NURSERY RHYMES IN THE CAR   6+

It is still important for young children to learn their Nursery Rhymes as it helps develop their memories, as well as being important for developing phonological awareness skills so necessary for reading success.
Older children, however, will love changing nursery rhymes and making up their own variations.

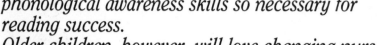

What You Need

• *Long car trips*

What To Do

Say an old Nursery Rhyme with your children as you drive along. Then make a change in the first line and see if they can make up the second rhyming line.

Little Miss Tool sat on her ....,
Eating her curds and whey,
Along came a spider and sat down beside her,
And frightened Miss Tool away.

Old Mother Lantry, went to the ...., etc.

Humpty Dumpty sat on a chair ....,

Neigh, neigh, black horse, have you any ....,

The children will soon enjoy this game and everyone will have lots of fun thinking of unusual Nursery Rhyme variations.

activity
465

NUMBER PLATE BINGO

6+

A great game to play in the car on long trips that needs just a little preparation before you start.

What You Need

- *Paper*
- *Pencils or pens*
- *Hard books or clip boards*

What To Do

You need a piece of paper per child for this game. Before your leave home write the letters of the alphabet from A-Z in capital letters on a piece of paper or have the children do it.

When they start to become restless on a long car trip, hand them out. The children have to cross off the letters of the alphabet as they spot them on the number plates of other vehicles. When they spot a letter they yell it out so Mum or Dad or the other players can verify it. The letters do not have to be crossed off in alphabetical order, so the game is fairly fast.

activity
466

RHYMES IN THE CAR

6+ ✓

 ✓

 ✓

Another rhyming activity to fill in time on long car trips while helping to develop the children's phonological awareness skills that are so essential for them to become good readers.

What You Need

• *Car trips*

What To Do

 ✓

Children love rhymes and enjoy making up their own, particularly if they are silly. Start them off and not only will they have lots of fun, but the trip will be over in no time. Perhaps they could make up rhymes about things they see from the windows.

I see a car riding on a star.

There goes a dog dancing with a hog.

I see a horse eating tomato sauce.

Once there was a train and it fell in a drain.

I see a bloke driving in a moke.

Once they get the idea, the children will be fascinated and will love making up their own silly rhymes all the time!!

activity

467

SANDHILL SLIDING

6+

If you live near the beach your children will love sliding down high sandhills on cardboard shapes. If you don't live near the beach, find a grassy slope and they will enjoy sliding down that.

What You Need

- *A steep slope to slide down safely*
- *Cardboard shapes to slide on*

What To Do

Many parks are built with high grassy mounds for children to slide down or to ride bikes or skateboards down safely. If you live near the beach, high sand dunes are great to slide down also.

Visit your local electrical store, who usually have a supply of large cardboard boxes. Flatten a couple out and take them home and the children can help you cut the cardboard into small shapes for sliding on.

Take them to a park with grassy mounds or to the beach with sandhills and let them enjoy themselves having races down the slopes. Why don't you let your hair down and have a go too!!!

activity

468

STATUES

6+

A good game for a party or play it any time you have a group of children to keep occupied.

 ✓

 ✓

What You Need

• *Music - a cassette or C.D. player or the radio*

 ✓

What To Do

The players spread out. When the music starts they begin dancing around the room. Suddenly stop the music and everyone has to 'freeze' in whatever position they were in. Watch the children carefully and the first person to move is out.

The game continues until only one person is left, who is the winner.

activity
469

AUTOGRAPH BOOKS

8+

When I was at school Autograph Books were treasures, and we all loved writing in our friends' books and reading our own. Guess what! They are back in the shops again. Buy some for your own children to help their reading and writing skills.

What You Need

• *Autograph books - available from toy stores, stationers, etc.*

What To Do

Your children will enjoy taking their autograph books to school, parties, and other social occasions to collect autographs from family and friends.

Tell them that one of the rules of autograph etiquette is that you wait to read what someone has written until later; the autograph writer has to be able to get away. Of course, if they have written something rude you can always write something equally rude in their autograph book.

Some autographs I remember from my school days are:-

When you see a monkey sitting in a tree,
Pull his tail and think of me!

Roses are red, violets are blue,
Honey is sweet and so are you.

I'll see you in the ocean,
I'll see you in the sea,
I'll see you in the bathtub,
Oops! Pardon me!

When you get old and cannot see,
Put on your specs and think of me!

By hook or by crook,
I'll be last (or first) in this little book.

activity

470

KITES

8+   ✓

All children love flying kites. If your children don't have a kite why don't you try making one with them.

 ✓

 ✓

What You Need

 ✓

• *Plastic or a plastic bin liner* • *2 thin bamboo canes*
• *Ruler* • *Acrylic paints or permanent pens* • *Ball of string*
• *A ruler or short piece of dowel for the handle* • *Scissors*
• *Paint brushes* • *Insulating tape* • *Hole punch*

What To Do

Start with a piece of plastic 50 cm (20 inches) by 50 cm (20 inches). Help the children measure and cut out a kite shape from this. Fold each corner of the kite over and punch a hole through the double thickness. Stick strips of the insulating tape in the centre of the kite - 11 cm (4$\frac{1}{4}$ inches) from the top and 7 cm (2$\frac{3}{4}$ inches) from the bottom. Use a *Stanley* knife to help the children cut very small slits through these reinforced sections.

The children can now paint or use permanent pens to decorate their kite. When it's dry they can cut some more strips of plastic to attach to the bottom for a tail.

Push one of the thin bamboo stakes through the hole in the top of the kite. Tape the stick in place with insulating tape and then do the same at the bottom. Stick on the extra plastic strips for the tail. Push the second bamboo stick through the side holes of the kite and again stick in place with the insulating tape. Make sure the plastic is as taut as possible.

To attach the string, thread a metre long piece through the slits you cut earlier in the kite and turn the kite over and tie a small loop in the string. Pull it tight and the loop should be over the top slit.

Tie one of the ends of the large ball of string onto this loop and then carefully wrap the rest of the string around a short ruler, a short length of dowel or piece of strong cardboard. Now the kite is ready to try on a windy day.

activity
471

NATURE COLLAGE

8+   ✓

 ✓

 ✓

Next time you take the children for a bush walk or a picnic they might enjoy collecting some materials for a nature collage. (Remember not to take anything home from a National Park though!)

 ✓

 ✓

What You Need

- *Natural items such as mosses, leaves, twigs, bark, flowers, grasses and seeds*
- *A piece of strong cardboard, polystyrene tray or piece of wood*
- *PVA glue or a glue gun*

What To Do

Art framers will often let you have offcuts of cardboard that they use for framing and these are perfect for making nature collages. Otherwise a washed meat tray or a piece of thin wood is fine also.

Your children will enjoy making the picture - encourage them to make it look as close to nature as possible. If they are using glue they can apply it with a small brush or cotton bud, but if they use a glue gun it needs close adult supervision.

When the collage is finished let it dry in a safe place for a few days. It can be hung or displayed standing in a plate stand and makes a lovely reminder of a family day out.

activity
472

PARTNERS

8+

An excellent ice-breaker to play at a party, or fun to play with the family.

What You Need

- *An even number of players*
- *Pieces of card*
- *A pencil or pen*

What To Do

Put on your thinking cap and try to think of as many things that go together as you can. Here are some to get you going:

- Adam and Eve
- Knife and fork
- Bacon and eggs
- Hide and seek
- Bat and ball
- Night and day
- Batman and Robin

- Spaghetti and meatballs
- Bread and butter
- Soap and water
- Cup and saucer
- Jack and Jill
- Cats and dogs
- Hansel and Gretel

I am sure you will be able to think of lots more. Write down half of each pair on one piece of card and its pair on the other. Shuffle up the cards and deal them out. Each player receives a card. The players then go round the room trying to find their partners (and meeting everyone else as they go).

The first pair to find their mate are the winners, but the game continues until everyone is matched.

Then do some brainstorming to think of other things that go together.

activity
473

THE ANATOMY OF A FLOWER 8+

Older children will be interested in the names and functions of different parts of a flower.

What You Need

- *Different sorts of flowers to observe*
- *A magnifying glass*

What To Do

Children need to learn that although flowers look beautiful they are also an essential stage in a plant's growth. When pollen from one flower reaches another of the same species the plant can produce seeds. They need to learn that, although pollen can be spread by wind or water, it is most often spread by animals and insects. Insects and birds all help in spreading the pollen of flowering plants. With your children see if you can observe some bees flying from flower to flower and gathering pollen and nectar. As the bee gathers pollen it is also spreading it, helping fertilisation to take place.

Your children will enjoy looking at different flowers under the magnifying glass or a microscope (if you have one) and identifying the parts.

- Petal - attracts insects
- Sepal - the green petals that protects the bud at the base of the flower
- Pistil - the female part of the flower. The pistil has three parts:
  1. the sticky top stigma that traps pollen from other plants
  2. the stalk or the style that holds the stigma
  3. the ovary which contains the plant's eggs which develop into seeds when fertilised.
- Stamen - the male part of the flower that is made up of two parts. One is the anther which produces the pollen and the other is the filament which basically holds up the anther.

Some plants have separate male and female flowers and some plants such as pawpaw trees have separate male and female plants.

You children will be fascinated by plants. Encourage their interest and you may one day have a botanist in the family.

activity
474

WHO IS IT?

A good game to play at a party.

8+ ✓

 ✓

What You Need

 ✓

- *A baby photo of each child coming to the party (obtain them secretly from the children's parents beforehand)*
- *Pencils and sheets of paper*

 ✓

What To Do

✓

Pin or *Blu-Tack* up the baby photos and number each one. Give each child a piece of paper with a list of all the children who are at the party on each one.

The children then wander around looking at the photos (and probably at each other) until they have written a number beside each name.

Have a time limit on the game and then see who has the most right. Have an appropriately funny prize for this game - perhaps a big tin of baby powder or a big baby's dummy!

activity
475

A DAY IN THE LIFE OF YOUR FAMILY VIDEO

If you don't own or can't borrow one, hire a video camera for a day and capture some shots of your family to look at in the future.

What You Need

- *A video camera*
- *A family day together*

What To Do

Video cameras are very user-friendly today and, like most technology, our kids are better with them than us. Your older children will love making a video of a day in the life of your family.

Begin with normal family shots of everyone having breakfast and so on. Perhaps you could go for a picnic or somewhere special so the day is really different. Videoing special occasions such as a birthday is always a good idea, too.

However, you may prefer to simply video everyone doing their normal weekend activities such as gardening, cleaning the car, washing the dog, having a roast for Saturday night dinner or a barbecue with friends. Make sure everyone is on the video; sometimes the person holding the camera gets left out!

In the years to come, family videos will provide lots of laughs and great opportunities for reminiscing.

activity
476

GUESS WHO?

10+

A family game to play together or use it as a game at a child's birthday party.

What You Need

- *Pieces of paper*
- *Sticky or masking tape or safety pins*

What To Do

Before you begin the game, write the names of several famous people on the slips of paper. Choose one person to have the first turn and pin a famous name on their back. They then have to try to discover who they are by asking questions like - 'Am I a female?' 'Do I star in movies?' 'Am I Australian?' 'Was I born in England?' and so on.

They can only receive YES or NO answers and they can only ask each person one question before they ask someone else.

At the end of the game, the player who discovered the identity of the famous person with the least number of questions is the winner.

activity 477

NEIGHBOURHOOD WATCH

10+

Go for a walk with the children and see if they can spot all the items in this neighbourhood watch game.

What You Need

- *Paper*
- *Pencils*

What To Do

Before you go for your walk do some brainstorming with the children about things they may be able to spot in the neighbourhood. They may see:

a dog
a cat
a pet bird in a cage
a house number whose digits add up to 13
a house numbered 5
a flag pole
a white gate
a brick fence
a metal letter box
a blue roof
a basketball hoop in a driveway
a house with two garage doors
a house with double front doors
a truck or van parked at a house
a caravan in someone's yard
a set of swings in a yard
a swimming pool
a sprinkler working

The children can write out their own copy of the list and, as you walk, the first person to spot an item on the list crosses it off. The first child to cross off all the items on the list is the winner and gets to choose their favourite meal for dinner one night soon!

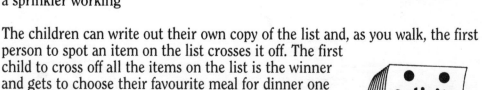

activity
478

ORIENTEERING

10+

Orienteering is a very popular sport world wide and is great for teaching children how to use a compass, as well as for fitness.

What You Need

- *Compass*
- *Maps*
- *Paper*
- *Pen*
- *Space to run a course*

What To Do

Work out a track that you could take the children on to try some simple orienteering. Parks and forests are ideal. Buy a map of the area to study with the children.

Set out on the day before and work out a route; leave some markers under logs, stones, on bushes and so on. Of course, you must disturb the natural environment as little as possible. Mark the compass reading of each station and mark that for the children to follow.

They begin with the first clue giving them the compass readings. With your help, they look it up on the map and set out. When they reach the next clue, they look it up and so forth.

If all this sounds too complicated, it could be an idea to enquire if there is an Orienteering Club in your area and take the children along to participate. A fun, healthy family activity to try together.

activity
479

SPECIAL OCCASIONS

SAINT VALENTINE'S DAY

4+

February 14th is traditionally the day for lovers. Make a Valentine's card with your children for them to give to someone special.

 ✓

 ✓

 ✓

What You Need

 ✓

- *Cardboard - pink or red look great*
- *Strong glue*
- *Decorations such as ribbon, lace, pretty stickers*
- *Flowers from the garden*

 ✓

What To Do

Draw some hearts on the cardboard and your children can cut them out. Let them use their own imagination to decorate them. Help younger children write on the back of their heart, older children can do their own.

Your children may like to write their name, but traditionally Valentine cards are anonymous! Deliver the Valentines together!

activity
480

SHROVE TUESDAY PANCAKES   6+

Shrove Tuesday is the Tuesday just before Lent begins. Lent is the period of forty days before Easter and is a time of fasting. Make some pancakes together with your children for breakfast or dessert on Shrove Tuesday (Pancake Tuesday).

What You Need

Ingredients:
- *1 cup sifted plain flour*
- *l egg*
- *1 Cup milk*
- *Pinch salt*
- *Butter for cooking*

Utensils:
- *Whisk*
- *Mixing bowl or jug*
- *Measuring cup*
- *Crepe pan*
- *Spatula*

What To Do

Your children can help you collect the ingredients. Beat the egg and stir in the flour and salt. Gradually add the milk to the mixture and stir until it is smooth.

I prefer to make pancakes in a jug as it is easier to pour the mixture into a pan. Melt a small amount of butter in the crepe pan and pour in enough mixture to cover the base of the pan.

Turn once. We love pancakes with lemon juice and castor sugar or strawberries in our family. You will probably have your own favourite topping.

activity
481

HUNT THE EASTER BUNNY

2+

Childhood is so short but so very precious. Your littlies will love hunting the Easter Bunny on Easter morning.

What You Need

- *A small basket of Easter eggs*
- *Flour*

What To Do

Wake up very early before the children and, using the knuckles of your index and middle fingers, dip them in some flour and make 'bunny footprints' through the house and out into the garden. Give them quite a trail to follow and at the end - wow! - a basket of eggs.

The amazing part about this activity is that someone always spots the Easter Bunny while you are following his trail!

activity
482

EASTER EGG HUNTS

2+

Make it a little harder for the children to find what the Easter Bunny has left with an egg hunt on Easter morning.

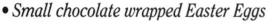

What You Need

- *Small chocolate wrapped Easter Eggs*
- *A basket or plastic dish for each child*

What To Do

Rise early before the children and lock up your dog so he can't eat the eggs before the children find them!!

Hide the eggs in the garden but in fairly obvious places so the children can find them. Make sure you know how many you have hidden.

Make it a rule that the children can only eat a couple now and save the rest for later to avoid upset tummies!

activity

483

COLOURFUL EASTER EGGS

4+

Make some brightly coloured Easter eggs with the children to decorate the house for Easter.

What You Need

- *Hard boiled or blown white eggs*
- *Masking tape*
- *Birthday candles*
- *Food colouring or powder paints*
- *Plastic containers*
- *Spoons*
- *Paper towels*

What To Do

This is a fairly messy activity so it is best done out of doors. Make sure the children are wearing old clothes or put a painting smock or old shirt of Dad's over their clothes.

Make up some strong solutions of water and food colouring in the containers. Have a spoon for each container.

The children carefully draw interesting patterns with the birthday candles on their eggs. If you are using blown eggs remind them to be gentle as the egg shells are fairly delicate.

If they would like to have multi-coloured eggs, wrap some masking tape around sections of each egg.

Now dip an egg into a colour and then take it out carefully and wipe dry. Remove some of the masking tape and dip into a second colour. Repeat the procedure until the egg is multi-coloured with interesting designs.

The eggs will look beautiful on the table for Easter lunch.

HINT!
If you are using hard-boiled eggs, boil them for at least
20 minutes and store in the 'fridge until you want to
use them for display. Do not eat them?

activity
484

EASTER EGG CLUES

6+

Make it harder for your children to find their Easter eggs when they begin to read by leaving some written clues for them to follow.

What You Need

- *Paper*
- *Pen*
- *Easter eggs*

What To Do

Begin the clues at the bottom of their bed, in the basket they've left out for their eggs or wherever else the Easter Bunny usually leaves the eggs at your place. Be as creative as you can in thinking of clues such as:

Look in the place where the dirty socks go (the dirty washing basket)

Under the tree where the lemons grow

Look beside where you like to swing, and so on

Make the clues simple enough for emergent readers to sound out, or use words they already know.

Eventually they will find the treasure trove of eggs but hopefully they will have used up a little energy and practised their reading before they get there.

activity
485

EASTER CANDLE CARVING 10+

A simple, but most effective decoration for your older children to make for Easter.

 ✓

 ✓

 ✓

 ✓

 ✓

What You Need

- *White wax candles*
- *Sharp pencil*
- *Small sharp knife*
- *Acrylic paint*
- *Rags*

What To Do

Your children warm a candle by rubbing it between their hands. Next, they carefully scratch a pattern onto the candle with the pencil and, using the knife, they carve out the pattern.

When that is finished, they polish the candle with a soft rag and then rub the candle surface with some acrylic paint, making sure the paint goes into the carved surface.

When the paint is dry they polish it again with a soft cloth.

Group the candles together for a decorative effect and light them for Easter lunch.

activity

486

LIVING CHRISTMAS TREES

2+

Instead of having an artificial Christmas tree, plant a living Christmas tree that you can bring indoors every year at Christmas time.

What You Need

- *A small Norfolk pine or other conifer*
- *Large pot*
- *Potting mix*

What To Do

Visit your local nursery or a nursery specialising in conifers. Do this some months before Christmas as there will be a much better selection, and they are usually cheaper then also.

Buy a large pot in which to plant your Christmas tree and some fresh potting mix.

The children will enjoy helping look after your family Christmas tree. Don't forget to find out any special requirements for your tree from the nursery and the best position in which to place the pot.

Look after it all year and the children will enjoy having a real living tree to decorate at Christmas time.

activity

487

CHRISTMAS CARDS

4+

Encourage your children's creativity and give them a holiday activity by making wonderful Christmas cards for friends, family and neighbours.

What You Need

- *White cardboard cut to size*
- *Red and green acrylic or poster paint*
- *Small brushes or potatoes for printing*
- *Ice block tray*
- *Take away plastic containers*
- *Kitchen sponges*
- *Glitter*
- *Hole punch*

What To Do

Begin by cutting the cardboard. If the cards are to be posted, make sure they will fit comfortably into white envelopes. If they are to go with gifts, cut small rectangles or squares to attach as gift tags. The children will enjoy helping you cut the cards and punching a hole in the corner of the gift tags.

Now comes the really fun part and, like all messy painting activities, it is best done outdoors.

If the children want to print, help them cut Christmas shapes from potatoes - stars, trees, bells etc. Put some red and green paint onto kitchen sponges in plastic take-away containers and they can carefully push the shape into the paint and then print with it. They'll love sprinkling on some glitter while the paint is still wet.

If they want to paint their own Christmas pictures, put some paint into iceblock trays and, with small brushes, they can paint the cards, again adding some glitter for a really Christmassy effect.

Much, much nicer than bought cards and a lot cheaper!

activity

488

CHRISTMAS PAPER CHAINS 4+

Decorate the house for Christmas or a special occasion with old-fashioned paper chains. They not only look festive, but they are a fun way for your children to improve their cutting skills and learn how to use a stapler.

What You Need

- *Scrap paper (old Christmas wrapping looks bright)*
- *Scissors*
- *Stapler*
- *Ruler*

What To Do

Help your children use their ruler to mark out lengths of paper about 5cm (2 inches) wide. Cut out the strips, and then they can cut each long strip into 20cm (8 inches) lengths.

Take the first piece and fold it over to form a loop and then staple.
Remind them to always use the stapler flat on a table and to press it down hard with both hands until they hear two clicks. Learning to staple needs quite a lot of hand strength, so help them practice and be patient!

Next, they put another piece of paper through the loop and staple, and so on until the chain is as long as you need or as long as their interest lasts!

Hang them up together and admire their hard work.

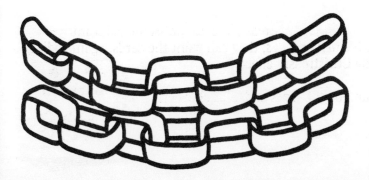

activity
489

CHRISTMAS HATS

4+

Set the children up outside with all the bits and pieces to make Christmas hats for Christmas Day for all the family.

What You Need

- *Crepe paper in Christmas colours*
- *Scissors*
- *Glue*
- *Old Christmas cards or Christmas wrapping paper*
- *Glitter*

What To Do

Show the children how to cut strips of crepe paper about 60 cm (23½ ins) long and 5-8 cm (2-3 ins) wide. They can cut lots of triangles out of one edge of each hat to make them look like crowns.

They will enjoy cutting out small motifs and Christmas pictures from the cards and wrapping paper to decorate the hats. Show them how to apply glue lightly and then sprinkle on the glitter while the glue is wet.

When the strips of decorated crepe paper are dry, measure the family's heads and glue the ends together to make them into lovely Christmas hats.

activity
490

LETTERS TO SANTA

4+

Help your children write a letter to Santa Claus and post it together. Write a reply and send it back to them so they have the excitement of receiving a letter also.

 ✓
 ✓
 ✓
 ✓

 ✓

What You Need

- *Paper*
- *Pencils and drawing pens*
- *Envelope*
- *Stamp*

What To Do

Talk about Santa with your young children. Tell them that Santa would love to hear all about them. They can draw pictures of themselves, the family and your home. Your children can tell you what to write.

Next, they might like to draw or cut out from toy catalogues the things they might like from Santa. I always stress to my son that Santa can only bring one large present and fill his stocking as he has lots of children to deliver to and we must share.

Finally, address the letter together. Your children can stick on the stamp, and then together you can go for a walk to the mail box to post it.

Make sure the reply comes in a few days as young children find it very difficult to wait for special things!

Dear Santa,
I hope you are well.
I have been a good
girl. Yesterday
I helped my mum
clean my room
I have written
a list of things I
want for Christmas
on the next page.
Love
xxx
Sarah

A bike
doll

activity

491

CHRISTMAS TREE ORNAMENTS 6+

Mix up a batch of baker's clay and make some
very individual decorations for your Christmas tree.

What You Need

- *3 cups of plain flour*
- *1 cup of salt*
- *1 teaspoon of glycerine (buy it from a pharmacy. It is also useful for adding to bubble mixture to make bubbles stronger)*
- *1 cup water*
- *Mixing bowl*
- *Christmas shaped biscuit or play dough cutters*
- *Thick nail, skewer, knitting needle*

What To Do

Mix the flour and salt and add the glycerine. Pour in the water, stirring as you add it. Mix until the mixture is fairly stiff and then the children will enjoy kneading it until it is smooth like bread. The children can roll out the dough or simply push it flat with their fingers until it is a centimetre (about ¾ of an inch) thick.

Set them up on a table outside with a plastic or vinyl cloth and cutters, and they will have great fun making shapes. Show them how to make a hole near the top of each shape with the nail so they can hang the decoration.

Put the shapes on a baking tray and bake slowly in a cool oven until they are hard.

When the dough is dried, the children will have fun painting their decorations with Christmas colours. Provide some glitter to sprinkle on while the paint is wet.

When they have dried the children can thread some thin Christmas ribbon or wrapping ribbon through the holes and hang them on the tree.

activity

492

CHRISTMAS SCENTED PINE CONES

6+

 ✓

 ✓

 ✓

 ✓

 ✓

Make some attractive scented pine cones together to decorate your home at Christmas, or give some away as special gifts.

What You Need

- *Pine cones*
- *Cloves*
- *Red or green crepe paper or fabric*
- *Scissors*
- *Red or green ribbon*
- *Thumb tacks or craft glue*

What To Do

Show your children how to wrap each clove in a tiny piece of the crepe paper or fabric and insert in the pine cones (do this part carefully because some pine cones are quite prickly!). When all the holes are filled, help them attach a length of red, green or 'Christmassy' ribbon to hang it by. The ribbon can be glued to the top of the pinecone with strong craft glue, or attached with a tack.

They look lovely hanging from the tree, or hang several with different length ribbons together from a curtain track.

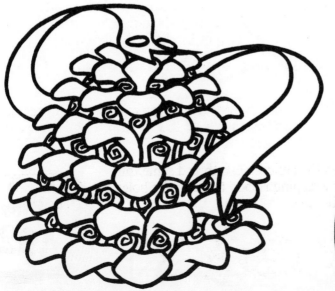

activity
493

CHRISTMAS SNOWFLAKES 6+

Use up scraps of gold, silver and Christmas paper by making pretty Christmas snowflakes with your children.

What You Need

• *Coloured paper*
• *Scissors*
• *Ribbon*
• *Blu-Tack*

What To Do

Help your children cut up the scraps of paper into different sized squares. Next, they fold the paper square into a triangle and then fold it again. They then cut out notches along the edges with their scissors. When they open out the paper they will have beautiful snowflakes.

Hang them with coloured wrapping ribbon and attach them to the ceiling with small blobs of *Blu-Tack*.

They will look pretty and festive hanging above your Christmas tree or twirling in front of an open window.

activity
494

CHRISTMAS WRAPPING PAPER 6+

Save money and have fun too by making your own individual Christmas wrapping paper with your children.

What You Need

- *Red and green paint (acrylic paint works best and is available from toy or art & craft shops)*
- *Two kitchen sponges*
- *Two plastic plates or polystyrene trays*
- *Potatoes*
- *Sharp knife*
- *Glitter*
- *Newsprint paper*

What To Do

Place the kitchen sponges on the plates and pour a little green paint on one and red on the other. Spread the paint thickly across the sponges.

Next, cut some large potatoes in half and carefully cut some simple Christmas shapes out of them with a sharp knife. The shapes must stick out at least 2cm (³/4 inch) above the rest of the potato half. Stars, bells, Christmas trees or a candy cane all look effective.

Your children press the potato onto the paint then print with it on the newsprint. While the paint is still wet, sprinkle a little gold or silver glitter on to add a festive touch.

Your Christmas gifts will look wonderful wrapped in your children's art work.

activity
495

CHRISTMAS STARS

8+

These biscuits make delightful gifts for friends and neighbours at Christmas time.

What You Need

- *1¼ cups of plain flour*
- *1 tablespoon of white vinegar*
- *Strawberry or raspberry jam*
- *90g (3 ozs) softened butter*
- *1 tablespoon of water*
- *Beaten egg for glazing*

What To Do

Using a large bowl, rub the butter into the flour with fingertips until it resembles fine crumbs. Mix the vinegar with the water and add to the mixture to form a firm dough.

Lightly knead on a floured board until it is smooth. Wrap it in some plastic food wrap and chill in the 'fridge for about an hour. On the lightly floured board roll out the dough until it is about 4-5mm (¼ inch) thick.

Cut it into 6cms (2½ inch) squares then, using a small knife, cut from the corner of each square to almost the centre. Next, carefully fold the right hand corner of each section in to meet at the centre. Press firmly so they stay down.

Put a little jam in the centre of each star and glaze the stars with lightly beaten egg white using a brush. Bake on an ungreased baking tray for 10 minutes in a moderate oven. Cool on biscuit racks and store in airtight containers until needed.

HINT!

Christmas stars look lovely wrapped in red or green cellophane bundles tied with red, gold and green curling ribbon.

activity
496

CHRISTMAS NEWSPAPER

8+

A great way to keep in touch with distant family and friends at Christmas time.

 ✓

 ✓

What You Need

 ✓

- *Family photos*
- *Family news*

 ✓

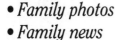 ✓

What To Do

 ✓

Suggest to your children a few weeks before Christmas that they could help you make a family newspaper to be sent to family and friends with the Christmas cards.

They can be the 'reporters' gathering news and interesting items from the rest of the family. They might like to try their hand at drawing some cartoons or pictures to include in it.

If you have a computer and printer, printing it out will be simple. If not, collate it and take it to your nearest photocopying shop.

Lots of fun and the folks you send it to will love receiving it.

activity
497

CHRISTMAS WREATH

10+

*Older children will love making a colourful
Christmas wreath to hang on the front door.*

What You Need

- *Glue gun*
- *Twig wreath base*
- *Selection of dried leaves, flowers, pine cones, wheat, gum
  nuts*
- *Tin of gold or silver spray paint*
- *Christmas tartan ribbon*
- *Wide red ribbon*

What To Do

Visit your local flower markets with the children and buy any of the bits and
pieces you need that you can't collect from your own garden or local parks.

Set the children up outdoors, with newspaper spread out to protect tables and
pavers. Decide which items they would like to spray and do this first on plenty
of paper away from furniture. Leave to dry.

You will have to help with the glueing as glue guns can give a nasty burn.
Attach a string loop to the top of the wreath for hanging. Next, help the
children tie lots of small bows with the tartan ribbon to be interspaced on the
wreath. They will enjoy deciding where to position all the other bits and pieces
and helping you glue them in place on the twig wreath.

Leave a space at the bottom for a large bow and attach this last of all. Hang it
on the front door for a lovely Christmassy entrance to your home.

activity
498

COLOURFUL PASTA WREATHS 10+

This idea came from Karen Bourne, another teacher. Thanks, Karen!

What You Need

- *Paper plates*
- *Dried pasta of various shapes and sizes*
- *Wood glue*
- *Gold or silver spray paint*
- *Christmas ribbon*
- *Hole punch*

What To Do

This is easy enough for older children to do on their own. It is best done outside - especially the painting.

They begin by cutting the middle out of the paper plates, leaving the crinkly edge. Use the hole punch to punch a hole in one spot; this will be the top of the wreath. Next, they use the strong glue to stick pasta all over the remaining plate until it is well covered.

When the glue is completely dry they will need to put down lots of newspaper before they spray their wreaths really well. (Don't spray on windy days and make sure they follow the directions on the spray can carefully.)

When the paint is completely dry the children can tie a lovely tartan or Christmas ribbon to the bottom of their unusual wreath.

Perhaps they could make some to sell to friends, family or the neighbours for Christmas funds or make some to give as gifts. These would also be great sellers at school fetes.

HOLIDAY SCRAPBOOK

4+

A great way to keep family holiday memories alive.

What You Need

- *Scrapbook*
- *Glue*
- *Photos and holiday mementos*
- *Drawing and writing materials*

What To Do

While you are on holidays, save all the memorabilia, such as train tickets, fun park entries, postcards and photos. (When you have your holiday snaps developed, have doubles made - one set for your children's holiday scrapbook and the other set for the family photo album).

Assemble all the mementos and photos (pick a rainy day to do this) and glue them in the scrapbook in chronological order - a good memory activity. Encourage your children also to draw some pictures about the holiday in the scrapbook. Your older children can write the sub-titles, younger children tell you and you do the writing.

Older children can write a story about the best thing they did on holidays, while younger children can dictate their story for you to write. You may be surprised - our child recently spent a night in a small country hospital on holidays after a fall and that still rates as the best part of the holiday!

activity
500

NEW YEAR RESOLUTIONS

6+

Teach your children some traditions to see in the New Year and encourage them to begin something new - maybe keep their room tidier or pick up their toys without being nagged by Mum or Dad!

What You Need

• *Time together*

What To Do

Do some reading about New Year traditions and discuss them with your children. The Scots celebrate New Year in a big way with their Hogmanay festival and the Chinese New Year (which occurs later in January to mid-February) is a great festival to be part of. If you have a Chinatown near where you live, there is usually a procession, or take your children to a Chinese restaurant for lunch to sample some delicious Yum Cha.

Together plan some New Year resolutions and make a list. Involve the rest of the family too! Check your lists again in March and see how everyone is going. Perhaps you could make some family resolutions too, like making Sundays a family day where you try to do something special together.

activity
501

ALPHABETICAL INDEX

ALPHABETICAL INDEX

ALPHABETICAL INDEX

ALPHABETICAL INDEX

ALPHABETICAL INDEX

ALPHABETICAL INDEX